PRAISE FOR PREVIOUS EDITIONS OF

Colorado
Off the Beaten Path®

Help Us Keep This Guide Up to Date

Every effort has been made by the author and editors to make this guide as accurate and useful as possible. However, many changes can occur after a guide is published—establishments close, phone numbers change, hiking trails are rerouted, facilities come under new management, etc.

We would love to hear from you concerning your experiences with this guide and how you feel it could be improved and be kept up to date. While we may not be able to respond to all comments and suggestions, we'll take them to heart, and we'll make certain to share them with the author. Please send your comments and suggestions to the following address:

The Globe Pequot Press
Reader Response/Editorial Department
P.O. Box 480
Guilford, CT 06437

Or you may e-mail us at: editorial@GlobePequot.com

Thanks for your input, and happy travels!

INSIDERS' GUIDE®

OFF THE BEATEN PATH® SERIES

Off the Beaten Path®

EIGHTH EDITION

colorado

A GUIDE TO UNIQUE PLACES

CURTIS CASEWIT

Revised and updated by

ALLI RAINEY

INSIDERS' GUIDE®

GUILFORD, CONNECTICUT
AN IMPRINT OF THE GLOBE PEQUOT PRESS

The prices, rates, and hours listed in this guidebook
were confirmed at press time. We recommend,
however, that you call establishments to obtain
current information before traveling.

INSIDERS' GUIDE®

Text design by Linda Loiewski
Maps created by Equator Graphics © The Globe Pequot Press
Illustrations on: page 4, rendered courtesy of Denver Metro Convention & Visitors Bureau;
page 86, based on a photograph by Carl Scofield.
All other illustrations by Carole Drong
Spot photography © J. A. Kraulis/Masterfile

ISSN 1539-6614
ISBN 0-7627-3518-X

Manufactured in the United States of America
Eighth Edition/First Printing

Acknowledgments

This book was written with the help of many people. The author thanks Richard Grant, Denver Metro Convention and Visitors Bureau; Deborah Powell, C.E.C.S. Wordprocessing; Bill Saul, National Western Stock Show; Leo Goto, Wellshire Inn; Lillian Wyles, Denver researcher; JoAnn Sims, Central City Opera House Association; Elena Valdez, Aspen Ritz Carlton Hotel; J. S. Munn, Vista Verde; Christy Metz, National Park Service; Kristine Meyer, Beaver Village, Winter Park; Robert Levine, Antlers Lionshead Vail; Barbara Jennings, Colorado Ski Country USA; Paula Sheridan, Winter Park Resort; Kristine L. Bittner, researcher, and Sarah Lawlor, assistant editor; and finally, Helen Evans, his special travel companion.

The editor would like to thank her family, Steve and Jan Babits, the Fremont County Library, Andy Skiba, and most of all, her husband, Matt Wendling.

Contents

Introduction

I first saw Colorado in 1948.

It was love at first sight. I have never been able to tear myself away, despite opportunities elsewhere. The state's beauty kept me here; indeed, there followed almost forty years of exploration. By automobile, train, plane. On foot and on horseback. On skis and on snowshoes.

From the tourist's viewpoint, Colorado has everything one could desire; travelers spend roughly $7 billion here each year. The state even holds surprises for natives or longtime inhabitants. Indeed, after all those years of roaming through Colorado, I still wrote this book in a constant state of amazement.

Denver itself is packed with the unexpected. And remarkably enough, you can drive a mere thirty minutes from the state capital to reach the swish and rush of mountain streams, view dramatic rocks, or wander among thick forests. Higher and higher mountains beckon to the west; to the east the placid plains offer new sights as well.

Colorado Off the Beaten Path® has assembled some of the state's most unique locales—some of which are rarely found in travel books. The selections cover a wide area but are purely personal choices. Some of the attractions may be readily recognized but were visited and reviewed with a fresh slant. Many of the descriptions will interest new settlers as well as those who have lived here for many decades.

Author's Note

I lived in the Austrian Alps before I settled in the United States, or more precisely, in the Colorado Rockies, first in Aspen and then in Denver. High mountains have attracted me most of my adult life. The beauty of Southern Colorado—"The Switzerland of America"— always leaves me spellbound. In my younger years, I skied almost every weekend. In summer, I rock-climbed or followed one of the myriad hiking trails to higher elevations (Colorado has 1,500 peaks more than 10,000 feet above sea level and fifty-four giants over 14,000 feet.) Flowers were everywhere. I breathed deeply and decided that I was very lucky. The mountains gave health and contributed to inner peace.

As I grew older, I shortened distances and switched from high-powered downhill skis to old-fashioned cross-country skis. I learned to pace myself and to put in rest stops. One afternoon not long ago, on the return from a summer hike, I paused at one of those Forest Service information posts with maps and the usual mountain do's and don'ts. Another Colorado outdoor worshiper, perhaps aging, too, and equally fatigued, had affixed one more message onto the post. "GO UP INTO THE MOUNTAINS," it read. "YOUR BODY NEEDS IT."

About the Book's Organization

Few people hereabouts know the names of counties. So each chapter deals with a region. In chapter 1, for instance, you visit the foothills and Front Range. In chapter 2 you explore the interesting sights of Colorado's Northwestern Mountains via U.S. Highway 40 and Trail Ridge Road through magnificent Rocky Mountain National Park. Chapter 3 takes you along one of Colorado's main arteries—Interstate 70—to famous Western Mountains, all the way from historic Georgetown to Glenwood Springs and beyond, with one or two side trips into nearby valleys. Chapter 4 deals with the state's southern region, including Colorado Springs. Lastly, chapter 5 covers Denver and the Plains. In every instance the focus was on the uniqueness of a destination.

Happy traveling!

Fast Facts about Colorado

COLORADO TOURISM OFFICE

1625 Broadway, Suite 1700
Denver, CO 80202
(800) COLORADO, (303) 892–3885
www.colorado.com

COLORADO'S MAJOR NEWSPAPERS

The Denver Post (daily), www.denverpost.com
The Rocky Mountain News (daily), www.rockymountainnews.com
Westword Newspaper (weekly), www.westword.com

TRANSPORTATION: REGIONAL TRANSPORTATION DISTRICT (RTD)

RTD has an extensive bus system in addition to light rail.
1600 Blake Street
Denver, CO 80202
(800) 366–7433
www.rtd-denver.com

CLIMATE OVERVIEW

Semiarid
Short springs
Dry summers
Mild winters, except in mountains

Average highs and lows in Denver (temperatures Fahrenheit)

Jan 43/16	Apr 61/34	July 88/58	Oct 66/36
Feb 46/20	May 70/43	Aug 85/56	Nov 52/25
Mar 52/25	June 81/52	Sept 76/47	Dec 44/17

FAMOUS COLORADANS

Clive Cussler (world-famous author)

Major Stephen Long (explorer)

Lieutenant Zebulon Pike (expedition leader)

Kit Carson (trapper)

H.A.W. Tabor (miner)

Marshall Sprague (historian)

BRIEF FUN FACTS ABOUT COLORADO

The weather—if you don't like it, wait an hour—is known to go from clear skies to thunderstorms, tornadoes, and flash floods and back before you've had time to complain about any of it. It also can drop thirty degrees overnight, and just when you thought it was Indian summer in October, a blizzard can dump 3 feet of snow in two days' time.

Colorado Foothills

Front Range

When you come upon the seventy-million-year-old **Red Rocks Park and Amphitheatre,** west of Denver, for the first time, the primeval scene takes your breath away: Huge reddish sandstone formations jut upward and outward. Each is higher than Niagara Falls. The view conjures up dinosaurs, sea serpents, and flying reptiles; indeed, tracks of those long-extinct creatures have been found here, along with valuable fossil fragments. The colors are those of the Grand Canyon; one can easily believe the geologists who speak of earth-shattering, monolith-building cataclysms, of retreating ancestral oceans, iron oxide color, and water erosion. Geographers once considered this site one of the Seven Wonders of the World.

The U.S. Geographical Survey showed up eager for surveys in 1868. By 1906 financier John Brisben Walker had acquired the land; the acoustics of these rocks would be perfect for an amphitheater. A visiting opera singer, Dame Nellie Melba, was quick to agree that it would make one of the world's greatest open-air stages. Walker eventually donated the land to the community, and in 1927 it was incorporated into the Denver Mountain Parks System.

Construction started a few years later; dedication of the tiered outdoor area followed in 1941. The local symphony soon brought its famed orchestra to the site. The latter not only produced perfect sound and aesthetic inspiration but also allowed a magnificent look at Denver far below.

For many years the outdoor theater experienced triumphant ballet performances, and audiences heard celebrated orchestras and even portions of Wagner operas. Singers such as Lily Pons, Jennie Tourel, Jessye Norman, and Helen Traubel all raved about Red Rocks. Even the difficult-to-please Leopold Stokowski was impressed by a setting that included a "Creation Rock."

In 1959 Denver's manager of parks flew to Germany at his own expense in the interests of still further improvements. He persuaded Wolfgang Wagner, grandson of the composer, to inspect Red Rocks. Wagner eventually remodeled the orchestra pit and made other design changes.

The cost of bringing large groups of classical musicians and opera companies proved to be financially difficult, however. What's more, performers sometimes fought with winds that would tear away the orchestra's notes or with sudden five-minute rains that would drench the singers to the depths of their costumes.

AUTHOR'S FAVORITES IN THE COLORADO FOOTHILLS

Beaver Brook Trail,
(303) 697–4545
www.co.jefferson.co.us/ext/dpt/
comm_res/openspac/windy.htm

Buffalo Bill Grave and Museum,
(303) 526–0747
www.buffalobill.org

Central City Opera House,
(800) 851–8175
new.centralcityopera.org

Eldorado Canyon,
(303) 494–3943
http://parks.state.co.us

Flagstaff Mountain,
(303) 441–3440
www.ci.boulder.co.us/openspace/

Glacier Homemade Ice Cream,
(303) 440–6542

**Lookout Mountain Nature Center
and Preserve,**
(303) 271–5925
www.co.jefferson.co.us/ext/dpt/
comm_res/openspac/natstart.htm

Matthews/Winters Park,
(303) 271–5925
www.co.jefferson.co.us/ext/dpt/
comm_res/openspac/maw.htm

Red Rocks Park and Amphitheatre,
(303) 295–4444
www.redrocksonline.com

Tiny Town,
(303) 697–6829
www.tinytownrailroad.com

Red Rocks Park and Amphitheatre

Since 1961 Red Rocks rarely heard any more classical music; instead, by the mid-1960s the Beatles made a full-throttle appearance here. Through the 1970s, 1980s, and 1990s, there followed assorted high-decibel rock, pop, blues, jazz, and country western stars—often with sellouts of the 9,000 seats. Tickets are expensive. However, the public gets free admission to Red Rocks facilities at all other times. Traditionally, too, a free Easter Sunrise Service has taken place here for several decades. (The stage has meanwhile been covered.)

Spring 2003 brought with it the completion of the 30,000-square-foot underground **Red Rocks Visitor Center** at the top of the Amphitheatre. Featuring high-tech telecommunications capabilities, fabulous views from terraces, elevators to provide access for people with disabilities, and new restrooms, the Visitor Center is open to the public free of charge year-round. Also included are a meeting center (call 303–697–6047 for details), a restaurant, and an interesting exhibit detailing Red Rocks' geology and the history of its role in the entertainment world.

Red Rocks, located at 16352 County Road 93 in Morrison, is easy to reach via numerous routes. From Denver you can take West Alameda Avenue west, drive U.S. Highway 285 west to County Road 470 to Morrison Road, or follow Interstate 70 west and watch for the marked exit. The total distance varies between 14 and 17 miles, depending on your route. Hours are 5:00 A.M. to 11:00 P.M. daily; admission is free. For more information call (303) 295–4444; www.redrocksonline.com.

You can see the stunning Red Rocks Amphitheatre from the hiking trails of **Mount Falcon Park,** for which we can thank the same John Brisben Walker, financier, entrepreneur, and visionary. Walker wanted to build a Summer White House in the park, and a marble plaque still indicates the spot. He had an eye for the best views: The Mount Falcon area is surrounded by blue mountains, and at a distance you can recognize Mt. Evans (elevation 14,264 feet) and the Continental Divide. Other vistas of the 2,130-acre Mount Falcon Park include the Colorado plains and, with a little imagination, Nebraska.

The park seems surprisingly serene; it is so vast that the walkers and the mountain bikers and the occasional horseback rider can spread over many a flowered hill and dale. No motorcycles are permitted, and cars are restricted to a few parking lots—the latter concealed by trees. The exceptionally well-marked foot trails are often shaded by conifer forests.

Picnic tables invite families, and there are meadows for kiters and butterfly fans. Lovers find privacy among the daisies, the scrub oak, and the spruce. Here, at 7,750 feet above sea level, a light breeze blows often. Summers are cooler here than in Denver, in the smog far below. For once you hear only the light Colorado wind. The traffic has been silenced.

Walker's fortunes ultimately waned: The Summer White House was never built, and the financier's own castlelike home was struck by lightning and burned in 1918. The stone walls and chimneys, and even the fireplaces, are still there—an interesting destination for hikers. A few minutes away, the stables do a good summer business. Cross-country skiers enjoy the park in winter; no charge.

Mount Falcon Park is accessible via Highway 8 to Morrison (turn west on Forest Avenue and north on Vine Avenue) or via US 285 and the Indian Hills exit (stay on Parmalee Gulch Road for 5 miles to Picutis Road, and then follow signs to the parking area). Be prepared for dusty roads to the park entrance. For more information contact Jefferson County Open Space at (303) 271–5925; www.co.jefferson.co.us/ext/dtp/comm_res/openspac/falcon.htm.

trivia

Long ago, a vast inland sea, which contained sediments that gradually built up on its floor, covered the Colorado area. After the sea receded, the sediments hardened and the forces of geology and erosion went to work over the next few million years to sculpt the formations you see at Red Rocks today.

TOP ANNUAL EVENTS

Bolder Boulder 10K race;
Boulder; May;
(303) 444–7223
www.bolderboulder.com

Colorado Music Festival;
Boulder Chautauqua Park;
June through August;
(303) 449–1397
www.coloradomusicfest.org

Colorado Shakespeare Festival;
CU–Boulder; July through August;
(303) 492–0554
www.coloradoshakes.org

Boulder Climbing Series;
Boulder Rock Club;
October through March;
(303) 447–2804
www.boulderrock.com

Surprise! Morrison, Mount Falcon Park, and Red Rocks are just twenty minutes west of Denver. As **Morrison Road** shoots through the foothills toward higher altitudes, many travelers will be preoccupied with reaching their goal: "the mountains or bust." Nonetheless, along the way there are jewels to be found.

One such jewel is the town of **Morrison.** On any given weekday small groups of congenial neighbors meet on the street corners to exchange pleasantries. A man with his dog drives a golf cart down the main thoroughfare toward the edge of town. Children maneuver mountain bikes onto paths that run along a rippling stream opposite the rushing Bear Creek. Indeed, at times, Morrison is very Norman Rockwellesque.

But more than a pleasant atmosphere, this community offers a treasure trove of antiques that will please collectors and browsers alike. A 1910 phonograph. A wooden wagonwheel, circa 1895. You might like to try **Lacey Gate Antiques,** 116 Stone Street; (303) 697–4407; **Little Bits of Yesterday & Today,** 309 Bear Creek Avenue; (303) 697–8661; or **El Mercado,** 120 Bear Creek Avenue; (303) 697–8361.

Whatever your pleasure—buying, selling, or window shopping—Morrison is a pleasant place to while away an hour or two. For more information call (303) 697–8749; or write P.O. Box 95, Morrison 80465.

A five-minute uphill drive from Morrison will take you to the much photographed locale of **The Fort,** which is a replica of Bent's Fort, an 1834 early Colorado fur-trading post. The thick, picturesque adobe building contains a small shop that sells authentic Indian jewelry, tomahawks, feathers, and other items. But The Fort is best known as a restaurant. The walls are covered with western oil paintings and original etchings celebrating the West. The cuisine features foods of the American West, both old and contemporary, with appetizers

Tracks in Time

A visit to the Morrison area would not be complete without a stop at the outdoor museum known as Dinosaur Ridge. View more than 300 dinosaur footprints, all preserved in the sandstone of the Dakota Formation on the east side of the hogback. This National Natural Landmark is open for free viewing year-round, with seventeen interpretive signs providing information about the tracks and other fossils found in the area. Visitors can also arrange for a guided tour with the Visitor Center ($3.00 per person) or call ahead to find out about the next Dinosaur Discovery Day, a day when part of West Alameda Parkway is closed to traffic and visitors can enjoy free guided tours and, sometimes, all-you-can-eat pancake breakfasts (for $5.00). For more information, call (303) 697–3466 or write Friends of Dinosaur Ridge, 16831 West Alameda Parkway, Morrison 80465; www.dinoridge.org.

such as roast bison marrow bones, delicate buffalo tongues, and Rocky Mountain "oysters" (bull testicles). The entree selections include Elk Chop St. Vrain, prime rib of buffalo, Tlingit-style cedar-plank salmon, and grilled quail, among others, all washed down with first-class, high-priced wines and followed by original desserts. The Fort is at US 285 and Highway 8. The restaurant is open for dinner Monday through Friday from 5:30 to 9:30 P.M. and Saturday and Sunday from 5:00 to 9:30 P.M. For reservations call (303) 697–4771; www.thefort.com.

trivia

Colorado's Front Range has an average of 300 days of sunshine per year—second only to Miami, Florida.

To the west of Morrison, as the crow flies, a mere 16 miles west of Denver on US 285, you suddenly see the sign for *Meyer Ranch Park.* Here are 397 quiet acres replete with almost 4 miles of well-maintained hiking trails. You climb gently through young aspen groves and pine forests. Your eyes are soothed by meadows filled with Colorado's state flower, the columbine, that give way to grasslands. Depending on the season, you spot shooting stars, lady slippers, and the purple Indian paintbrush. What remarkable serenity so close to the big city of Denver! The trail names fit perfectly: Owl's Perch, Lodge Pole, and Sunny Aspen.

Motorized vehicles are not permitted here, and dogs belong on a leash. The Meyer Ranch Park area has a history of homesteading, haying, and grazing. According to local legend, during the late 1880s the animals of the P. T. Barnum circus wintered here. The Victorian-style Meyer home—still occupied by the Meyers—stands proudly and handsomely across the highway. For more information about the park, call Jefferson County Open Space at (303) 271–5925; www.co.jefferson.co.us/ext/dpt/comm_res/openspac/meyer.htm.

The same US 285 will take you to a truly offbeat family destination. Denverites, twenty minutes down the valley, know about *Tiny Town;* out-of-town visitors probably haven't heard about this Lilliputian village and its miniature railway.

Tiny Town appeals to children. Imagine about one hundred toy-size, hand-crafted buildings to peek into, and sometimes to crawl into as well! This town has old miniature log cabins, a fire station, a post office, a water tower, a flour-mill, a bank, stables, a school-house, a roominghouse, farms, ranches, barns, windmills, mines, and miners' shacks. There's even a miniature train ride around the entire Tiny Town village loop.

The attraction is run on a not-for-profit basis by the Tiny Town Foundation, which donates a portion of its annual proceeds to local charities. The distance from Denver is about 12 miles via US 285, turning south at South Turkey

Creek Road. Bring a picnic and be prepared to pay $3.00 for adults and $2.00 for children ages two to twelve. Children younger than two get in free. There is a $1.00 train fare per person. Open every day from Memorial Day weekend through Labor Day 10:00 A.M. to 5:00 P.M. Open weekends in May, September, and October 10:00 A.M. to 5:00 P.M. For more information call (303) 697–6829; www.tinytownrailroad.com.

US 285 is sometimes narrow and curvy, so it's easy to miss an entrance to an offbeat retreat for vacationers. One example? The modest little wooden sign that reads *GLEN-ISLE RESORT.* These humble log cabins and a well-worn lodge are hidden by a tiny bridge and assorted bushes and trees off the highway between Grant and Bailey. This unpretentious holiday settlement dates back to 1900 and works out fine for families, couples, and singles who want to cook and who appreciate the silence of a 160-acre forest. The forest is honeycombed with footpaths for hikers; horse trails are nearby, too. A National Historic Site, Glen-Isle is nicely old-fashioned; don't be surprised if you don't find a television set. For folks who don't want to cook, a dining room offers homey food. The tab for everything seems reasonable enough. Expect basic (not luxurious) accommodations. Open June through mid-September. For more information call (303) 838–5461; www.caccl.com/glenisleresort.

Matthews/Winters Park derives its importance from its location: The park lies astride the entrance to Mt. Vernon Canyon, which is one of the early routes to the gold fields of Central City and South Park. Other canyons were also used, and at each portal a town was founded to try to get a share of the quick fortune the Fifty-niners were scrambling to uncover.

The big year here was 1859. The stagecoaches and wagons rolled through, and the new town of Mt. Vernon had a 150-horse corral. A local paper declared that "timber, stone, lime, and coal are abundant in the vicinity." For a while Mt. Vernon became a stage stop. An inn, a saloon, and a schoolhouse were built, used, and abandoned. Once "boasting forty-four registered voters," the town of Mt. Vernon lost its place in history after the railroads arrived.

Sunflowers, chokecherries, and willows now lean over the gravestones and crosses of long-gone pioneers: One marker reads I.I. DEAN, DIED AUGUST 12, 1860, AGED 31 YEARS, I AM AT REST. Not far from the few square gravestones, the crosses and picnic tables sit under leafy trees near Mt. Vernon Creek.

The rest of the park consists of undulating grasslands, trails, and fields of silver-green sage, purple thistles, wild roses, and wild plums. Trails run through rabbit brush and tall dill, and there's nary a sound, despite the nearby highways.

In recent years the park has become a popular after-work and weekend destination for hikers and mountain bikers. A fun, 7⁷⁄₁₀-mile out-and-back ride on the Village Walk Trail and the Red Rocks Trail is suitable for intermediate riders, with only a few moderately difficult sections. Serious mountain bikers can make the ride into a loop by crossing the street and testing their skills on the 1³⁄₁₀-mile Dakota Ridge Trail, a challenging ride across the hogback.

For more information contact Jefferson County Open Space at (303) 271–5925; www.co.jefferson.co.us/ext/dpt/comm_res/openspac/maw.htm.

The public parking area is located off Highway 26, just south of I–70, and lies within the Mt. Vernon town site. All Jefferson County Open Space parks are closed from one hour after sunset until one hour before sunrise unless otherwise noted by signage at individual parks.

The front-range mountain settings come with precious few dinner retreats—particularly when it comes to historic ones like the **Manor House Restaurant** in Littleton. From afar the white Georgian mansion makes its appearance on top of a green hill, amid footpaths and an equestrian center. White columns give the building a fairy-tale quality.

The Manor House was built on a vast ranch in 1914 by John C. Shaffer, industrialist, owner of the *Rocky Mountain News,* importer of Hereford cattle from distant points, and collector of antiques. Shaffer's wife, Virginia, hosted President Theodore Roosevelt and other notable figures, who raved about the magnificent fireplaces, elegant carpets, and valuable nineteenth-century paintings. Various ranchers raised cattle nearby, with a view to faraway Denver. Virginia Shaffer wrote a poem about the landscape: "Where the sunsets are entrancing / where one sees a sight sublime / Come again! Come again!"

Now the elegant ranch house serves distinctive food in sumptuous surroundings. The restaurant is a little hard to get to. Look for US 285 and exit at Highway 470, then to Ken-Caryl Avenue, to Mountain Laurel, and finally onto Manor House Road. It's a complicated trip, at least the first time. The thirty-minute drive from Denver is worthwhile, however. The Manor House has an imaginative chef who starts you off with meat-stuffed crab cakes or fresh green salad, followed by buffalo spareribs, savory salmon, or one of many more fine dishes, graced by elegant glassware and shining silver. Good service plus mountain views. Dinner is served Tuesday through Sunday. For more information call (303) 973–8064; www.themanorhouserestaurant.com.

If you travel west on U.S. Highway 40 out of Denver, you abruptly leave behind the plains of Denver and eastern Colorado and enter a long valley with the jagged foothills of the Rockies rising on both sides. As you proceed, you may see some horses grazing on the slopes.

Soon you reach the heart of **Golden.** First stop in at the **Golden Visitors Center,** located at 1010 Washington Avenue adjacent to historic downtown, for an overview of what to do while you're in town. Grab a cup of coffee and surf through the informational touch-screen kiosk. The center, run by the

Greater Golden Chamber of Commerce, is open Monday through Friday from 8:30 A.M. to 5:00 P.M.; Saturday and Sunday from 10:00 A.M. to 4:00 P.M. For more information call (303) 279–3113 or write P.O. Box 1035, Golden 80402; www.goldencochamber.org.

Consider a trip to **Heritage Square** to get a sense of Golden's history. The rustic artisan and entertainment village was built on the 1860 townsite of Apex, another mining boomtown. It has metalsmiths, jewelers, candy makers, and more, including horseback rides; an alpine slide and water slide; a narrow-gauge train trip; a large melodrama theater; tree-lined, lamplighted streets; and plenty of free parking. Take exit 259 off I–70 and go north 1 mile. Open daily 10:00 A.M. to 9:00 P.M. (summer); 10:00 A.M. to 9:00 P.M. Monday through Saturday and noon to 9:00 P.M. Sunday (fall, winter, and spring). For more information call (303) 279–2789.

trivia

Golden's Armory Building, built in 1913, is the largest cobblestone building in the country. Workers hauled 3,300 wagonloads of stream-worn boulders from nearby Clear Creek and quartz from Golden Gate Canyon to construct the building, which is located at Thirteenth and Arapahoe in Golden.

To the west you'll find range after range of mountains, each higher than the last. These mountains, besides having whatever aesthetic or spiritual value you may find in them, serve the practical purpose of limiting the size to which Golden can grow—it currently has about 17,000 inhabitants. But the Rockies have protected the city from becoming part of a growing urban sprawl.

The Golden story began back in 1859, when a man named Tom Golden set up a hunting camp with a couple of other men. Soon some representatives of the Boston Company passed by on a wagon train, looking for a suitable place to establish a trading and supply base for the prospectors who were flooding the mining areas to the west. They liked the site and stayed.

Golden grew rapidly. Within a year it had a population of 700. By 1862 it became the territorial capital but lost this honor five years later to Denver. There was sporadic gold excitement in the immediate area—people still occasionally pan Clear Creek, west of town—but there were no big gold findings. (The primary reward for panning here is the sight of gold in your pan. You can work all day for a dollar.) Its early economy was built on trading. It was the major supply center for the mining operations at Black Hawk, Central City, Idaho Springs, and other communities.

With the decline of mining, new economic bases emerged. Golden's present economy is based in part on two institutions, both of which have brought it international recognition: the Colorado School of Mines, for a century the

Golden Adventures

Seekers of unusual family fun will want to check out Heritage Square's *Alpine Action.* After riding a chairlift nearly 500 feet up the mountainside, visitors can cruise downhill for half a mile aboard a toboggan that fits on the tracks of the alpine slide. Those who can't get enough of heights can leap from a 70-foot tower—attached to a bungee cord, of course! Or they can slip and slide down a 330-foot water slide into a heated pool. Contact Alpine Action, Heritage Square, Golden 80401; (303) 279–1661; www.heritagesquare.info/businesses/alpine.html.

leading school in the world devoted to mining and minerals, and a brewery, one of the largest in the country.

The *Colorado School of Mines* has an interesting, kid-friendly museum that fits the theme of the school. The *Geology Museum,* on the corner of Sixteenth and Maple on campus, is almost an art gallery. Murals by Irwin Hoffman depict many periods in the development and history of mining. See minerals from around the world, Colorado's mining history, fossils, Colorado gem trails, and more. Regular hours are 9:00 A.M. to 4:00 P.M. Monday through Saturday and 1:00 to 4:00 P.M. Sunday; closed all CSM holidays and on Sunday during summer. Admission is free. Contact Colorado School of Mines Department of Geology and Geological Engineering; (303) 273–3823; www .mines.edu/Academic/geology/museum.

Golden greets its visitors with a sign arched across Main Street that reads: HOWDY FOLKS! WELCOME TO GOLDEN, WHERE THE WEST LIVES. *West* is the most basic word in American folklore. Its connotations extend well into the realms of history, morality, and philosophy. To the tourist out to see the country, it's obviously a matter of history. Golden, with its ten museums—a record for a town of its size—does not disappoint in the "History of the American West."

Start out at the *Colorado Railroad Museum,* which displays many ancient, narrow-gauge locomotives and even a small depot. The narrow-gauge railroads of Colorado made it possible for miners and other fortune seekers to access the mineral riches of the Rocky Mountains. These tracks also allowed the wealth to be carried out and spread. The history of railroads in Colorado is preserved in the fifteen-acre Colorado Railroad Museum. Here you will see the original rolling stock, including locomotives. A rail spur allows the facility to "steam up" different engines throughout the year.

The building itself, a masonry replica of an 1880 depot, houses some 50,000 photographs and artifacts. The basement contains one of the state's largest model railroad exhibits, open to the public on the first Thursday of each month. It re-creates some of Colorado's old rail lines, such as the one in Cripple Creek. Famous relics of the museum include the Rio Grande Southern 1931 Galloping Goose No. 2 and the steel observation car used on the Santa Fe Super Chief, the Navajo. A bookstore sells more than 1,000 specialized titles and magazines, tapes, gifts, and mementos, while the Robert W. Richardson Library, a reference library, holds more than 10,000 railroad-specific publications.

trivia

Golden once rivaled Denver; it was the capital of the Colorado Territory from 1862 to 1867.

Open every day except Thanksgiving, Christmas, and New Year's Day. Hours are 9:00 A.M. to 5:00 P.M., September through May; 9:00 A.M. to 6:00 P.M., June through August. The museum, library, and gift shop stay open until 9:00 P.M. on Thursday. Admission is $7.00 for adults, $6.00 for seniors, and $4.00 for children two to sixteen (children under two free); family admission (two adults and children under sixteen) is $16. Contact the Colorado Railroad Museum by writing to P.O. Box 10, Golden 80402, or call (800) 365–6263 or (303) 279–4591; www.crrm.org.

If the West remains here in Golden in any living sense, it can only be in the character of the people. What kind of people were they? As with all pioneers, they had to be extremely self-reliant. They were dissatisfied with what they had left behind and were willing to take all necessary risks to try to find something better. They were doers rather than theoreticians.

The current Golden folks love the outdoors. Everywhere there are campers, tents, jeeps. Backpackers can be seen heading out of town toward the mountains. Life here seems aimed at "doing" rather than the less demanding "appreciating."

It should come as no surprise that Golden is home to the 37,000-square-foot *American Mountaineering Center,* located at 710 Tenth Street. This center is the headquarters for the century-old American Alpine Club, the Colorado Mountain Club, the American Mountain Guides Association, the Colorado Fourteeners Initiative, and the nonprofit organization Climbing for Life, which uses rock climbing to have a positive impact on at-risk youth in the Denver metro area. Stop by the center for a visit to the *Henry S. Hall Jr. American Alpine Club Library.* The library, with more than 16,000 volumes specific to rock climbing and mountaineering, is open to the public for research (only club members can check out books). Hours are Tuesday and Thursday, noon to 7:00 P.M., and Wednesday and Friday, 8:30 A.M. to 4:30 P.M. For more information call

(303) 384–0112; www.americanalpineclub.org. A museum, tentatively scheduled for completion in 2006, will house numerous climbing artifacts from the United States and around the world.

Before you're done with Golden, ask yourself what could possibly epitomize "the West" more than the place where Buffalo Bill asked to be buried? Buffalo Bill was a unique character of the frontier. And the museum that bears his name, 12 miles west of central Denver, on Golden's Lookout Mountain, has a uniquely western character. Here are the mementos that bring a fascinating man to life: the paintings and posters that show him in full regalia on his white horse, the white of his beard, a cowboy hat jaunty on his head. You can see his clothes, saddles, old weapons, a mounted buffalo, and lots of artifacts at the **Buffalo Bill Grave and Museum.** It attracts more than half a million visitors annually, and is crammed with photographs that retrace his careers as a buffalo hunter, Indian fighter, and army scout (for U.S. Army General Sheridan, among others).

Born as William F. Cody, Buffalo Bill led an extraordinary life. As a longtime Pony Express rider, he was pursued by Indians, escaping (as he wrote), "by laying flat on the back of my fast steed. I made a 24-mile straight run on one horse." On another occasion he rode 320 miles in some twenty-one hours to deliver the mail. (En route he exhausted twenty horses for the journey.) He had few rivals as a hunter and was said to have shot 4,280 bison in a 1½-year period. His slogan: "Never missed and never will / always aims and shoots to kill."

The buffalo shooting had a purpose, of course; the meat was needed to feed some 1,200 men who were laying track for the railroad. And though William Cody had his battles with the Indians, he later learned the Sioux language and befriended the Cheyenne, among other tribes.

William Cody may have had his best times as a circus rider, actor, and showman, gaining fame all over the world. The first "Buffalo Bill's Wild West" show opened in 1883. The extravaganza toured for nearly three decades, spreading the myths and legends of the American West around the globe. Almost a hundred mounted Sioux Indians chased wagon trains and a stagecoach; Annie Oakley and Johnny Baker amazed audiences with their marksmanship; eighty-three cowboys rode bucking broncos, thereby formalizing a cowboy sport into rodeo; and the entire Battle of Little Big Horn was re-created. Spectators could see live elk and deer from Colorado. There were horse races and even a bison hunt complete with a charging herd. At its height Buffalo Bill's show employed more than 600 performers. In one year he traveled 10,000 miles, performing in 132 cities in 190 days. (He was particularly popular in Europe.)

Cody's flowing white hair, short white beard, and rifle-holding figure symbolized the Wild West in many European capitals. Buffalo Bill gave a command performance for Queen Victoria at Windsor Castle and amused Kaiser Wilhelm II in Berlin.

No fewer than 557 dime novels were written about Cody during his lifetime. His face beamed out from hundreds of thousands of posters. Even today the distinctive goatee and silver hair continue to make him as recognizable as the kings, generals, and presidents who may have honored him.

Cody made one of the first movie Westerns ever produced. Although near the end of his career, he also lived to see the start of the tourist industry as he opened the first hotel near Yellowstone National Park.

Toward the end of his life, he turned into an entrepreneur and author. He gave most of his life's savings away to various good causes. His money ran out; his fame did not.

When Buffalo Bill died, President Woodrow Wilson wired his condolences. Former president Teddy Roosevelt called Cody "an American of Americans." The Colorado legislature passed a special resolution ordering that his body lie in state under the gold-plated rotunda of the State Capitol in Denver. Nearly 25,000 people turned out to pay their last respects and march in his funeral on Memorial Day, June 3, 1917.

Buffalo Bill's grave is a few steps from the museum atop Lookout Mountain, with a good view of Denver and the plains. Anyone can come and see the burial place. It is marked by white pebbles. The simple legend reads: WILLIAM F. CODY 1846–1917.

The museum stands in a quiet conifer forest. First opened in 1919, it has been restored and improved over the years. The Pahaska Tepee Gift Shop sells original western artwork and western-themed toys, and serves food—including buffalo—in its large coffee shop.

Museum hours are 9:00 A.M. to 4:00 P.M. Tuesday through Sunday, November 1 through April 30; closed Christmas; open 9:00 A.M. to 5:00 P.M., May 1

Home on the Range

The city of Denver has continuously maintained a herd of bison since 1914 at Genesee Park, just down the hill from the Buffalo Bill Grave and Museum. The buffalo roam free in their natural habitat and are best seen in fall, winter, and early spring when park officials feed them daily. Take I–70 west to exit 254 (Genessee Park). The twenty-four adult cows and two bulls can be seen on either side of the highway—a tunnel under the road allows the animals safe passage.

Flying over Golden and Lookout Mountain

A bright weekend in the foothills. The air above Lookout Mountain sparkles. You get here via Highway 6; after the traffic light changes, you turn left on SR 68 and let your car curve uphill.

Suddenly, something catches your eye at the top of your windshield. A hang glider circles above calmly, quietly, like a bird of prey. He soars above the highway that brought you here. As you climb higher on Lookout Mountain, you spot two more human flyers just taking off. You stop the car and learn that this 7,000-foot mountain is the gateway for these daredevils. Do they belong to a club or organization? Apparently not. They're simply individuals who enjoy hang gliding.

through October 31. Call (303) 526–0747 or write to 987½ Lookout Mountain Road, Golden 80401; www.buffalobill.org. Admission is $3.00 for adults, $2.00 for seniors over sixty-five, and $1.00 for children six to fifteen (children under six free). For the most scenic drive, take U.S. Highway 6 west of Denver to Golden, turn left on Nineteenth Street, and proceed uphill via Lookout Mountain Road, also called Lariat Trail because it twists and turns all the way up Lookout Mountain.

As you continue south on Lookout Mountain Road after leaving Buffalo Bill's grave, a sign on Colorow Road will direct you to turn right toward the *Lookout Mountain Nature Center and Preserve.* Situated on 110 acres of a fenced nature preserve, the center has a Discovery Corner, Observation Room, plant and animal displays, and a self-guiding nature trail (all wheelchair-accessible). Admission is free. Nature Center hours are 10:00 A.M. to 4:00 P.M. Tuesday through Friday, and 9:00 A.M. to 5:00 P.M. Saturday and Sunday; the facility is closed Monday and holidays. The preserve is open 8:00 A.M. to sunset daily. Also offered are nature classes that range from "Tales of the Trail" to "Foxes in the City!" to night tours where you'll discover constellations and nocturnal animal activity. Most sessions require preregistration. The Nature Center is located at 910 Colorow Road, Golden. Call (303) 526–0594; www.co.jefferson.co.us/ext/dpt/comm_res/openspac/natstart.htm.

Step aside, you hardy mountaineers! Make room for some hiking tourists—the sort who can spare only a couple of hours for a gentle excursion into the Colorado front range. Easy, mountain flower–bordered trails abound in the foothills near the state capital.

One of the least-known paths curves around *Lookout Mountain,* which was first used by the Cheyenne and Arapaho Indians as a lookout. Now known

Mother Cabrini Shrine

On a 900-acre hilltop on Lookout Mountain sits the Mother Cabrini Shrine. There is no charge to enter the famous little chapel, which was built in 1954 and devoted to Saint Frances Xavier Cabrini. The setting includes lovely fields, surrounding forests, and quite a few steps that will make hikers happy. For more information call (303) 526–0758; www.den-cabrini-shrine.org.

as the ***Beaver Brook Trail,*** it is one of the state's most interesting paths, yielding views of the gorges below, dipping and climbing with a varied landscape of leaf trees and dramatic Douglas fir. Although you're close to Denver, you're quickly led away from civilization.

Instead of highways there are fields of asters, yucca, and wild roses under you. In the forests the path is moss bordered, and spring beauties show their heads in season.

The Beaver Brook Trail makes some demands on your balance because you need to maneuver across several small boulder fields. Due to the rock scrambling required, the trail is inappropriate for small children and mountain bikes. The trail, a little more than 14 miles out and back, remains blissfully quiet during the week. On Sundays, however, you sometimes see church groups and lines of scouts and other hikers coming up from the city. If you hike up here in July and August, you'll be surrounded by lots of color. On the trail you may also spot the state flower, the blue Rocky Mountain columbine.

Wildflowers bloom later at the higher elevations, so by the time plants have already wilted around Golden (elevation 5,675 feet), other flowers on the Beaver Brook Trail just begin to unfold. The higher you climb, the later the growth, the smaller the flower, and the colder the air.

Small Colorado plants appear and disappear with the seasons, go underground, or take many years to mature. Certain wildflowers can sleep peacefully under the thickest snow cover, biding their time until spring. In summer the large fields of mountain flowers on the Beaver Brook Trail give pleasure to your eyes.

The Beaver Brook Trail is within easy reach from Denver by car. Just take US 6, turn left at the first traffic light (Nineteenth Street) in Golden, then drive up the curvy Lookout Road for 3 miles. Before you get to Buffalo Bill's grave, you spot a sign on your right: BEAVER BROOK TRAIL: WINDY SADDLE ENTRANCE. Free, the trail is open one hour before sunrise until one hour after sunset year-round. For more information contact Jefferson County Open Space at (303) 697–4545; www.co.jefferson.co.us/ext/dpt/comm_res/openspac/windy.htm.

Finally, see Colorado's remnant of the Ice Age, called a glacier but actually an icefield, covering a steep year-round snowbowl of about ten acres. In summer, when Denver swelters in a 95°F heat wave, it's about 45°F on the glacier, and young people come to ski here in July and August. Other visitors to the famous snowfield bring platters or auto tubes or even race downhill on shovels. Hikers, campers, and backpackers can be spotted at the 11,000-foot level as they scramble uphill past the last scrub pines. A few tourists come to sit on rocks and soak up the Colorado sun.

All that eternal snow and ice make **St. Mary's Glacier** unusual, of course. The trip is a pleasant one, attracting Sunday drivers from the big city. Once you exit I–70, you follow a creek flanked by stands of conifers and aspen trees. After about 8 miles the road steepens and leads into a series of challenging curves and serpentines. Then the valley widens and the forest thickens. You see several rushing waterfalls. At an elevation of 10,400 feet you notice a free parking lot; leave your car and hike up the rocky jeep trail or follow the uphill footpaths through kinnikinnik (evergreen groundcover), past the many fallen trees that age gracefully in gray. On weekends you'll meet lots of families on your way up to the glacier. People are friendly and talkative. "Been to the top yet? How was it? Do we have far to go?"

After half an hour you see a cold lake, topped by the glacier. It's less harmless than most folks think. Mountain dwellers know the glacier's record: Almost every year someone who skis too fast or careens downhill on a shovel somehow gets bruised, bloodied, or even killed. On rare occasions cross-country skiers are buried by an avalanche up here. In winter, the ill-prepared, ill-clothed can get frostbitten on top of the glacier at the 11,400-foot level. The prudent know that mountains are unforgiving; these visitors come to St. Mary's only when it smiles.

From I–70 just past Idaho Springs, take exit 238, known as Fall River Road. A 12-mile drive brings you to the parking lot and the start of your St. Mary's Glacier adventure.

Richest Square Mile on Earth

At one point in history, **Central City** vied with Leadville for the bonanzas. They called Central City the Richest Square Mile on Earth. In all, some $75 million in gold was found there. Tourists can still do a bit of gold panning in nearby creeks. And through Labor Day you can ride a re-created narrow-gauge railway along the bleached mountainsides, past the old abandoned mounds of earth, the mines of yesteryear.

Sloping, winding **Eureka Street** has been kept up. The redbrick buildings look as well preserved as those of Denver's restored Larimer Square.

Central City's pharmacy and several other stores put their oldest relics into the windows.

For an overview of the area's history, visit the **Gilpin History Museum,** located at 228 East High Street. Housed in a brick building built in 1870 and used as a school until the 1960s, this two-story museum includes a replica of a classic Main Street of the past. The Gilpin History Museum is open 11:00 A.M. to 4:00 P.M. daily, Memorial Day through Labor Day. For another window into the days of yore, visit the **Thomas House Museum** at 209 Eureka Street. This Greek Revival frame house was built in 1874 around the entrance to a mine. The Thomas House Museum is open 11:00 A.M. to 4:00 P.M. Friday through Monday from Memorial Day through Labor Day. Entrance to each museum costs $5.00, or you can pay $8.00 for entrance to both. For more information call (303) 582–5283; www.coloradomuseums.org/gilpin.htm.

The Gilpin History Museum, the Thomas House Museum, and the well-appointed Central City Opera House contrast with the miners' dwellings. The latter are small, modest cubes scattered across the pale gold or ochre and russet slopes.

The first frame houses sprang up during the 1860s, along with the mine dumps. Gold! Not just in a river but in the mountain, too. A man named John Gregory had plodded to 8,500-foot-high Central City from Denver, a trip of some 35 miles with an elevation gain of more than 3,000 feet.

That was in 1859. Gregory soon dug up a fortune. The word raced as fast as the spring waters of Clear Creek. Horace Greeley, a New York editor, heard about Gregory Gulch and traveled west to take a personal look. Greeley reported: "As yet the entire population of the valley, which cannot number less than four thousand, sleep in tents or under pine boughs, cooking and eating in the open air."

A mass of prospectors swarmed into the hillsides. Some people had a grand time. A theater was built. Sarah Bernhardt and Edwin Booth came to perform. The **Teller House Hotel** rose in 1872, attracting the finest artisans.

allaboard!

The first train from Denver to Black Hawk rolled through on December 15, 1872. It took another six years for the line to extend to Central City. Regardless of the railroad's success, writer-explorer Isabella Bird once complained that she had never seen such "churlishness and incivility as in the officials of that railroad." She wrote of her disapproval in her 1875 book, *A Lady's Life in the Rocky Mountains.*

Back then, the train traveled a 200-foot-per-mile grade through Clear Creek Canyon. Black rock walls rose more than a thousand feet on either side. You can still look at the ominous walls if you travel Highway 6 through the area; it follows the same route as the railroad did.

Large, carved bedsteads, marble-topped commodes, and tall rosewood and walnut highboys were ferried across the prairies and up the rough roads by teams of oxen and mules and on wood-burning trains. Central City's hotel hosted famous people. President Ulysses S. Grant, Walt Whitman, Oscar Wilde, Baron de Rothschild, and assorted European noblemen and their wives all slept in Central City.

In 1874 most of the community burned down, but gold rebuilt it. Fewer than four years later there was a new opera house, which still stands. Built in 1878 by Welsh and Cornish miners, the ***Central City Opera House,*** located on Eureka Street, is home to the fifth-oldest opera company in the nation. This restored Victorian opera house holds an annual summer festival that draws patrons from nearly every state. Performances range from its popular one-act opera *The Face on the Barroom Floor,* which recounts the local lore behind the painting on the Teller House Bar floor, to classic operas such as Giuseppe Verdi's *La Traviata.* Central City Opera House invites opera buffs to sit back and relax in one of its 550 comfortable seats while taking in performances by known stars and future divas.

trivia

Sherill Milne and Beverly Sills both got their operatic starts in Central City.

For show dates (performances are in summer), prices, and times, write to Central City Opera at 621 Seventeenth Street, #1601, Denver 80293 or call (303) 292–6500 or (800) 851–8175; new.centralcityopera.org.

Opening night remains Colorado's great social event. Cars and busloads of operagoers from nearby cities climb the road along Clear Creek Canyon, the same route taken by John Gregory more than one hundred years ago.

Central City Opera House

Now masses of gamblers also swarm into the area, since gaming was approved some years ago for Central City and Black Hawk. New casinos have replaced many historic buildings and shops. Where parking was once hard to find it is now almost impossible, but shuttle services run from Golden and other areas in Denver on a regular basis.

If you want to try your luck, stop at these Central City establishments: Teller House, Famous Bonanza, and Fortune Valley. Down the road in Black Hawk, try Bullwackers and Colorado Central Station.

Central City is about an hour's drive from Denver via US 6 and Colorado Highway 119. For more information, contact the Central City Marketing Office at (303) 582–5251; P.O. Box 249, Central City 80427.

Rock Canyons and Boulders

As you descend into **Boulder** the towering Flatirons, huge slabs of metamorphic sandstone lifted up by the same geologic forces that account for the birth of the Rocky Mountains, will command your view to the west. Now the city's trademark, the Flatirons—some of which reach heights of more than 1,000 feet—offer ample opportunities for rock climbers of all abilities. These monoliths also beckon to hikers and trail runners due to the abundance of trails interwoven among the tree-lined hills that surround them. Forming the abrupt border between the plains and the Rocky Mountains, this stunning assortment of rock formations in all shapes and sizes is a true paradise for the outdoor enthusiast. Located 22 miles northwest of Denver, Boulder is easily reached in about half an hour via the Boulder Turnpike, U.S. Highway 36.

Arguably in possession of the highest population of rock climbers per capita of any city or town in the United States, Boulder enjoys its status as one of the centers of U.S. rock climbing. This reputation becomes even clearer when you drive up Boulder Canyon or consider the proximity of Eldorado Canyon—a mere ten-minute jaunt from South Boulder. A vast amount of world-class climbing areas within several hours' drive only beefs up the city's appeal, not to mention two of the best indoor climbing facilities in the country.

trivia

Boulder is the only U.S. community that uses its own city-owned glacier, Arapahoe Glacier, for its water supply.

Added to this, rock climbing's popularity has witnessed a tremendous explosion since the early 1990s. Those seeking more rock to climb tend to flock to areas rife with quality cliffs—like Boulder—while those living in such places find the transition from nonclimber to climber relatively painless.

Eldorado Canyon is counted among the birthplaces of rock climbing in the United States. Gorgeous sandstone cliffs soar above the canyon floor in shades of red speckled with greenish and golden-hued lichen that appears to take on its own luminescence when viewed in the right light. Formed of the same type of hardened sandstone that makes up the Flatirons—known as the Fountain Formation—the world-class walls of Eldorado Canyon enjoy international prestige within the rock-climbing community.

trivia

President Dwight Eisenhower and his wife, Mamie, spent their honeymoon in Eldorado Canyon.

Hundreds of established routes await rock climbers of all abilities on the canyon walls, but none should be taken lightly. "Eldo," as climbers affectionately refer to the place, is known for its stiff grades, polished rock (especially on popular climbs), and sometimes scanty protection. All of these factors mean that climbers should take caution when they first start out climbing in the canyon, perhaps choosing an easier route to allow themselves time to grow accustomed to the area.

Once a bastion for some of the state's hardest routes, Eldorado Canyon's heyday as far as pure difficulty for climbing moves has passed, but that doesn't relegate its challenges to second-tier status by any means. Exposure—that sensation you get when you can truly feel just how high above the canyon floor you are—is the name of the game on classic routes like the Naked Edge, the Yellow Spur, and even Bastille Crack. Easily identified as the crack that divides the Bastille formation (the crag that sits on the left of the auto road as soon as you start to drive up the canyon), it is an ever-popular classic; more likely than not you will see someone climbing it any given day, at any given time.

Seeing the climbers in Eldorado Canyon, you might wonder what—if anything—the kind of climbing they're doing has in common with reaching the summit of Mount Everest. The answer, simply put, is, "not much!" These days, the term climbing encompasses a variety of subdisciplines. Among these disciplines is rock climbing, which itself can be broken down into even more categories, from bouldering to big wall climbing to free climbing. Free climbing, by the way, is not soloing—the term free climbing means that the climber uses his or her own physical ability to climb the rock, with the safety gear and rope serving only as a backup should he or she slip and fall (this does happen more often than you might think and usually has no serious consequences). Climbing without ropes or gear is called soloing.

Modern rock climbers revel in an abundance of varied challenges, from less-than-vertical slabs of rock (like the Third Flatiron) that require precision footwork and perfect balance to overhanging ceilings that demand explosive

Traditional vs. Sport Climbing

Most of the rock climbing done in Eldorado Canyon falls under the definition of traditional climbing, meaning that climbers place and remove virtually all the pieces of protection that they utilize on any given climb. More recently, "sport climbing" has taken off in a variety of locations, including Boulder Canyon. In sport climbing, climbers hook devices called quickdraws into preplaced expansion bolts that are relatively permanent fixtures to the rock face, meaning that the bolts remain in the rock for the use of future parties.

power and the ability to literally leap dynamically from hold to hold. Even more amazing (to nonclimbers) is that a climb of 15 feet or less in length can pose a far greater challenge, in terms of pure difficulty level, than a climb of 100 or even 1,000 feet! Rock climbs in this country are rated for difficulty on the Yosemite decimal scale, which assigns a rating of 5 to any rock climb that requires ropes for safety, and then a number following the decimal point telling how hard the route is. Starting at 5.10, climbs are further broken down into ascending degrees of difficulty with the letters *a* through *d* placed after the decimal (so a climb rated 5.10a will be significantly easier than a climb rated 5.10d). On this open-ended scale, climbs currently range from 5.0 to 5.15a. Bastille Creek is rated 5.17, Yellow Spur 5.10a, and Naked Edge 5.11a.

The type of rock climbing that you will most likely observe in Eldorado Canyon will be free climbing of the "traditional" sort. The climbing here generally requires forearm and calf endurance, poise under stress, the ability to place gear quickly and effectively, a strong sense of balance and technique, and, of course, experience. Climbers utilize modern, specialized equipment, from virtually unbreakable nylon ropes to soft, formfitting shoes soled with "sticky rubber" that gives them greater purchase on tiny dime-edge footholds.

trivia

Tightrope walker and all-around daredevil Ivy Baldwin made 86 journeys across Eldorado Canyon on a tightrope suspended 582 feet above the ground. He made his last walk (and survived!) in 1948, at the ripe young age of 82.

Strong, lightweight, removable pieces of protection—including passive metal wedges called stoppers or nuts and active mechanical gear known as camming devices—are placed in cracks and other aberrations in the rock as a climber (the leader) works his or her way up the rock. The climber then attaches his or her rope to these pieces, thus ensuring that any fall will be relatively short and safe, so long as the piece is properly placed to arrest the fall. The following climber (the second) then removes the pieces as he or she climbs the route, as the rope is now attached to a safety anchor above.

If scaling the walls isn't your idea of fun, Eldorado Canyon has plenty to offer in the way of alternative recreation. Tourists flock to the canyon in at least as many numbers as rock climbers, often clogging the narrow road up the canyon as they stop to gawk at their vertically inclined brethren. At the end of the canyon's road lies a lovely streamside picnic area with tables, barbecue grills, and individual campsites, perfect for a family outing. Numerous hiking trails allow those who prefer to keep their feet on the ground a chance to explore the canyon's deeper realms. Kayakers and anglers delight in South Boulder Creek, which burbles its way down the canyon for most of the year, freezing over during winter months.

Mountain bikers, too, are not left out—they can be seen slogging their way up the unrelenting ***Rattlesnake Gulch Trail,*** a strenuous but short trail that challenges the rider with 1,200 feet of elevation gain in 2 miles, not to mention some tight, technical single track. To find the trail, turn left on the Fowler Trail after passing through the first parking area in Eldorado Canyon State Park.

To reach Eldorado Canyon State Park, 25 miles northwest of Denver, take the Boulder Turnpike to the Superior exit; turn south at the light and then turn right onto Highway 170 which will take you to Eldorado Springs. From Boulder, head south on Highway 93 and then take a right (west) on Highway 170 (Eldorado Springs Drive). The visitor center is located 1 mile up the canyon. Eldorado Canyon State Park is open from dawn to dusk year-round. A $5.00-per-vehicle charge is required for entry from the day after Labor Day through April 30; from May 1 through Labor Day a vehicle pass costs $6.00 per car. For

Eldorado Enchantment

While the parking lot in Eldorado Canyon bustles with activity on the weekends, on weekdays the canyon tends to see far less traffic. For rock climbers, this is the preferred way to enjoy the fabulous Eldorado classics. One magical weekday morning, I set out with a partner in the brilliant Colorado sunshine. We hiked the steep hill up to the base of Red Garden Wall, the largest crag in the entire Boulder area. As we rapidly danced our way up one of the area's classic routes, I reveled in the vastness and beauty of the canyon as it swept away beneath me. Sitting on the top of the buttress, I watched my partner surmount the final arête, dazzlingly outlined by the morning sun just as it started to envelop the cliffs—caught up for a moment in the magic of Eldo.

more information write 9 Kneal Road, P.O. Box B, Eldorado Springs 80025, or call (303) 494–3943; parks.state.co.us.

Make sure you don't miss out on **Eldorado Springs** as you leave the canyon. This tiny, eclectic town not only serves as a gateway to the park but also is home to the Eldorado Springs Pool at the historic **Eldorado Springs Resort,** which makes for a great place to cool off during hot summer months. Once a major tourist destination known as the "Coney Island of the West," more than 60,000 guests flocked to the Eldorado Springs Resort every summer during the early 1900s. The pool, built in 1906 and then advertised as the largest pool in the country, is filled to the brim with artesian water from the springs. Open from 10:00 A.M. to 6:00 P.M. daily from the Saturday before Memorial Day through Labor Day. Admission is $6.00 for adults, $4.00 for children five to twelve; children under five free. Call (303) 499–1316 for more information; www.eldoradosprings.com.

trivia

The pure, 76° water of Eldorado Springs flows at a constant rate of 200 gallons per minute. Bottled at the source, Eldorado Springs drinking water is available for purchase at local grocery stores.

To find out more about the history of rock climbing, as well as mountaineering and skiing, stop by **Neptune Mountaineering** on your way into Boulder. There you can explore owner Gary Neptune's impressive collection of climbing and skiing artifacts while you stock up on hydration packs, hiking boots, and energy bars. Make sure you grab an event schedule—Neptune Mountaineering hosts weekly slide shows, bringing some of the most famous names in the climbing community to Boulder. Usually held on Thursday nights, the slide shows are generally low in cost and high in fun.

The store (633 South Broadway, Suite A) is located on the upper level of the Table Mesa Shopping Center at the corner of Broadway and Table Mesa in Boulder. From Eldorado Springs, take Highway 93 north (it turns into Broadway). Open Monday through Friday, 10:00 A.M. to 8:00 P.M.; and Saturday and Sunday, 8:00 A.M. to 6:00 P.M. For more information call (303) 499–8866 or check the Web site at www.neptunemountaineering.com.

After stopping at Neptune's, continue along Broadway to Baseline Road, turning west to head up **Flagstaff Mountain,** the perfect place to mingle with some rock climbers while taking in some beautiful scenery. Bouldering—a type of rock climbing that involves short, intense movements up the sides of the rocks, with the climber normally staying low to the ground—is a popular pastime on Flagstaff, and for good reason. As plentiful as the spots on a dalmatian's back, high-quality boulders dapple the flanks of Flagstaff, serving up myriad boulder problems that both delight and frustrate the numerous rock climbers who flock to test their skills on the sharp, rough sandstone. Pull out at any of a number of locations along the road and follow the paths back to the boulders where you'll likely find some climbers who have come to test their skills for an afternoon. You can either continue strolling along one of the mountain's marked trails, or just grab a seat on one of the surrounding smaller boulders and relax in the shade of ponderosa pines while you watch the boulderers. The jagged ridge of the First Flatiron pokes out above the trees to the south, and obstructed views of the city of Boulder can be seen to the east.

For more information on Flagstaff Mountain contact the City of Boulder Open Space and Mountain Parks Department, P.O. Box 791, Boulder 80306; (303) 441–3440; www3.ci.boulder.co.us/openspace. Open year-round, 5:00 A.M. to 11:00 P.M. (midnight for Panorama Point parking lot). Daily permits can be purchased for $3.00 from any of the six well-marked, self-service stations located along Flagstaff Road.

For a big treat, make dinner reservations at the *Flagstaff House Restaurant,* one of Boulder's finest dining establishments. Nestled on the side of Flagstaff Mountain, this lovely restaurant is a sure bet to delight even the most discriminating of palates. Expect to shell out a bundle (think $60 to $70 per person) for gourmet New American cuisine complete with impeccable service, complimentary appetizers from the chef, and a terrific wine list, not to mention the stupendous views of Boulder. The Flagstaff House Restaurant (1138 Flagstaff Road; 303–442–4640) is on the right as you drive up the mountain. Visit them on the Web at www.flagstaffhouse.com.

After dinner walk off your meal with your date by taking a romantic moonlit stroll at *Panorama Point* (1 mile up Flagstaff Road from the base of the mountain) or one of the many other overlooks that line Flagstaff Road. If you're still feeling guilty about your marvelous dinner the next morning, you can always come back and bike up Flagstaff Road; it's one of the most popular workouts for local bikers of both breeds: mountain and road.

The tree-lined campus of the University of Colorado at Boulder (known to locals as simply "CU") warrants a visit, particularly in the summer when the university stages its annual *Colorado Shakespeare Festival.* During the season, you'll notice banners proclaiming the performances—and telling you to keep quiet—along Broadway as you head toward downtown Boulder. The festival performs several

trivia

CU-Boulder's mascot is a live buffalo named "Ralphie." Four Ralphies—all females—have trotted around the football field since the original Ralphie made her debut in 1966.

Boulder Creek Path

From Eben G. Fine Park at the base of Boulder Canyon to Fifty-fifth Street on the east side of town, the 7-mile-long wooded Boulder Creek Path winds its way through. You can run it, walk it, bike it, or blade it. You never have to stop for a second; underpasses protect you from car traffic at every intersection. And there's plenty to see along the way: Xeriscape gardens, a fish observatory, and a fishing pond for the kids. (The pond is actually designed for children.) A network of other paths connect with this main artery, allowing for easy access to virtually all areas of Boulder. West of town, the path follows Boulder Creek up Boulder Canyon for a ways, turning to dirt before it ends.

Shakespeare plays in July and August. National auditions attract actors from all over. Contact the festival organizers at (303) 492–0554 or write Colorado Shakespeare Festival, 277 UCB, Boulder, 80309; www.coloradoshakes.org.

Macky Auditorium Concert Hall, also on the CU campus, hosts performances by the Boulder Philharmonic, the College of Music, visiting musicians participating in the Artists Series, and concerts by nationally known groups. For information call (303) 492–8423; www.colorado.edu/Macky.

Boulder also hosts the *Colorado Music Festival* from June through August. Visiting performers and composers lend their talents and energy to the festival. Reservations are required. Call (303) 449–1397 or write to 900 Baseline Road, Boulder 80302 for details; www.coloradomusicfest.org.

Hopefully you haven't tired of rock formations yet—Boulder still has more to offer in this department. Turn your sights north and then west for a drive up *Boulder Canyon,* with a stop, of course, at beautiful *Boulder Falls.* Tall, granite outcroppings line Highway 119 as it wends its way up toward the rustic town of Nederland and the Peak-to-Peak Highway. Find the canyon via Broadway (Highway 93) in Boulder. Head west on Canyon Boulevard (Highway 119)—you can't miss it! Stop at the pullout 11 miles up the canyon on your left to park, and then cross the street for a short walk back to the falls. Free; open from dawn to dusk. Contact City of Boulder Open Space and Mountain Parks Department, P.O. Box 791, Boulder 80306; (303) 441–3440; www3.ci.boulder .co.us/openspace.

You'll probably catch glimpses of rock climbers here and there on the formations as you drive up the canyon, weather permitting. Of course, come winter, you're more likely to see people with crampons (metal-toothed attachments) on their boots and ice axes in their hands hacking their way up frozen waterfalls and sheets of ice—Boulder Canyon attracts ice climbers, too. But with its classic rock climbs, both traditional and sport, the canyon most likely sees far more traffic from those who like to feel the rock beneath their fingers and under their feet in warmer weather. After all, some claim that the canyon's famous Country Club Crack (5.11a) was the hardest rock climb in the country for a period of time!

Seeing all the rock climbing around Boulder might spark your interest in trying out rock climbing yourself—but don't head out there uninformed. Though rock climbing is a relatively safe sport—despite the media's perpetual desire to portray it as "extreme" or "death-defying"— you should receive proper instruction and learn the safety basics before trying it out on your own. Rock climbing also requires specialized equipment that can take a big bite out of your wallet. Though rock climbing these days is a relatively safe endeavor when properly undertaken with an understanding of ropes and gear, novices must take a lesson or find an experienced mentor to show them the ropes, so to speak. Boulder has a number of local services that cater to the needs of newcomers to the sport.

trivia

Boulder has no shortage of trails to explore: The city's Open Space and Mountain Parks Department maintains 120 miles of trails.

One of the best places to learn rock climbing in Boulder is ***Boulder Rock School.*** Affiliated with ***Boulder Rock Club,*** the AMGA-accredited school offers a wide range of classes for all ages and ability levels. The school teaches a two-hour class called Introduction to Indoor Climbing for $45. After this lesson, the novice climber should be able to go to any gym around the

Boulder Hiking

The **Mesa Trail,** one of Colorado's most scenic introductions to year-round hiking and trail running is easily accessible. From Denver, drive the Boulder Turnpike (US 36) until you get to the Superior exit; Highway 170 will take you toward Eldorado Springs. Slow down until you notice the picnic tables and a small parking area on the right. The Mesa Trail is well marked. You cross a little bridge and soon zigzag through a landscape enhanced by sumac bushes, ferns, and sedges. The uphills are gentle enough, leading you before long into impressive pine forests, with glades to view the Flatiron citadels. (You see climbers here all summer.) The Mesa Trail winds up in Boulder's Chautauqua Park, from where some people actually embark on the same journey in the other direction and head back down. *Note:* In winter, the terrain is delightful for cross-country skiers.

country and pass the belay test, the rope safety skills test required by all climbing gyms.

Pretty much anybody can take a beginning climbing class—rippling abs or bulging biceps are not prerequisites. It's not unusual to see couples enroll for a climbing class together only to discover that the female partner can immediately climb harder routes than her brawny male counterpart, much to his surprise. This only goes to show that, especially at the more moderate levels of the sport, technique, balance, and flexibility count just as much as, if not more than, sheer strength.

More adventurous novices can try an outdoor lesson. Generally, experienced rock climbers use the gym for training and workout purposes but find that the indoor environment does not compare to the outdoor experience of climbing on real rock. Most guiding services, Boulder Rock School included, offer beginning climbing courses, with the option for private instruction (more expensive). As with indoor classes, the service provides all the necessary climbing equipment, allowing the student to sample rock climbing without making any monetary investment beyond the price of the class.

Contact the Boulder Rock Club/Boulder Rock School for details by calling (303) 447–2804 or (800) 836–4008; www.boulderrock.com. The facility is located at 2829 Mapleton Avenue. Take US 36 into Boulder, and then head east on Mapleton. The club is on the north side of the street. You must call for class schedules and to reserve a space.

The mood of Boulder can perhaps be felt most at the ***Pearl Street Mall,*** easily found by taking Broadway north from Canyon; the mall intersects

South Boulder Creek Trail

Rain or shine, summer and winter, at least once a week I venture out to run along my favorite stretch of trail in all of Boulder. Located east of the main part of town, South Boulder Creek Trail doesn't tackle any of Boulder's hilly terrain but rather offers a nice, flat, 3½-mile dirt trail alongside South Boulder Creek. This path winds through trees and grasslands, offering interpretive signs along the way as well as the opportunity to see wildlife, from coyotes to entire prairie dog towns. To me, this trail always seems to epitomize the season—in fall, the trees lining it burst into glorious shades of orange and yellow, while winter finds them stark and bare as my feet crunch the packed snow and ice on the trail. Spring brings with it budding greenery and the most fragrant smells of new growth, and summer bursts with bountiful life. From Broadway in Boulder, head east on Baseline, passing Foothills Parkway. The trailhead, with plenty of parking, is on the right side of the street. Located on City of Boulder Open Space.

Broadway a few blocks up. Both locals and visitors mingle among boutiques and restaurants, many of which feature outdoor patios. Some people simply hang out on the mall's strip and watch the eclectic crowd. Besides the shoppers and the leisurely crowd of patrons, Pearl Street has musicians, jugglers, and many other types of street performers (some of whom may not necessarily intend to perform, but perform nonetheless). The mall's sidewalk is a street that has been closed to traffic since the 1970s, and this street never fails to excite.

Don't miss out on a cool treat from locally based *Glacier Homemade Ice Cream,* located a block north of Valmont at 3133 Twenty-eighth Street, (303) 440–6542. Glacier Ice Cream has a wide variety of tantalizing flavors, all of which are made fresh in the store using premium ingredients. Popular flavors include peanut butter cup, pralines 'n' cream, and mocha almond fudge. The chocolate-dipped waffle cones are coated in real, mouth-watering dark chocolate, which only adds to the sinful delight of the large helpings served up by the friendly staff.

Places to Stay in the Colorado Foothills

(All area codes 303 unless noted otherwise)

The rating scale for hotels is based on double occupancy and is as follows:
Inexpensive:
Less than $75 per night
Moderate:
$75 to $100 per night
Expensive:
$100 to $150 per night
Deluxe:
More than $150 per night

BLACK HAWK

Gold Dust Lodge,
5312 Highway 119;
582-5415
Moderate

BOULDER

Alps Boulder Canyon Inn,
38619 Boulder Canyon Drive;
444-5445
www.alpsinn.com
Expensive to deluxe

Boulder Mountain Lodge,
91 Fourmile Canyon Drive;
444-0882
Inexpensive to moderate

Briar Rose Bed and Breakfast Inn,
2151 Arapahoe Avenue;
442-3007
www.briarrosebb.com
Moderate to expensive

Broker Inn,
Thirtieth and Baseline;
444-3330
www.boulderbrokerinn.com
Moderate to expensive

Courtyard by Marriott,
4710 Pearl East Circle;
440-4700
Moderate to expensive

Earl House Historic Inn
2429 Broadway;
938-1400
Expensive to deluxe

Hotel Boulderado
2115 Thirteenth Street;
442-4344 or (800) 433-4344
www.boulderado.com
Deluxe

Sandy Point Inn
6485 Twin Lakes Road;
530-2939 or (800) 322-2939
www.sandypointinn.com
Moderate to expensive

CENTRAL CITY

Fortune Valley Hotel/Casino
321 Gregory Street;
582-0800
Moderate

GOLDEN

Glen-Isle Resort,
Bailey;
838-5461
Inexpensive to expensive

La Quinta,
3301 Youngfield Service Road;
279-5565
Inexpensive to moderate

OTHER ATTRACTIONS WORTH SEEING IN THE COLORADO FOOTHILLS

BOULDER

Boulder Museum of History,
(303) 449–3464
www.boulderhistorymuseum.org

University of Colorado,
(303) 492–1411
www.colorado.edu

CENTRAL CITY

Coeur d'Alene Mine,
(303) 582–5283
www.coloradomuseums.org/
coeurdal.htm

GOLDEN

Coors Brewing Company,
(303) 277–2337
www.coors.com

Golden Gate Canyon State Park,
(303) 582–3707
parks.state.co.us

Table Mountain Inn,
1301 Washington Avenue;
277–9898 or (800) 762–9898
www.tablemountaininn.com
Moderate to deluxe

Places to Eat in the Colorado Foothills

(All area codes 303)

The rating scale for restaurants is as follows:
Inexpensive:
Most entrees less than $10
Moderate:
Most entrees $10 to $15
Expensive:
Most entrees $15 to $20
Deluxe:
Most entrees more than $20

**BLACK HAWK/
CENTRAL CITY**

Tony Roma's,
321 Gregory Street;
Central City;
582–0800
Inexpensive

BOULDER

Cafe Gondolier,
1738 Pearl Street;
443–5015
Moderate to expensive

Dandelion,
1011 Walnut Street;
443–6700
Deluxe

Flagstaff House,
1138 Flagstaff Road;
442–4640
Deluxe

Q's,
2115 Thirteenth Street;
442–4880
www.qsboulder.com
Deluxe

Royal Peacock,
5290 Arapahoe Avenue;
447–1409
Expensive

Sunflower,
1701 Pearl Street;
440–0220
Expensive to deluxe

GOLDEN

Chart House,
25908 Genessee Trail;
526–9813
Deluxe

**Coburn's Steak
and Spirits,**
800 Eleventh Street;
279–2010
Expensive

Cody Inn,
866 Lookout Mountain Road;
526–0232
Moderate to expensive

Hilltop Cafe,
1518 Washington Avenue;
279–8151
Moderate to expensive

Table Mountain Inn,
1310 Washington Avenue;
277–9898
www.tablemountaininn.com
Expensive

LITTLETON

Manor House Restaurant,
1 Manor House Road;
973–8064
www.themanorhouse
restaurant.com
Deluxe

MORRISON

The Fort,
19192 Highway 8;
697–4771
Deluxe

SELECTED COLORADO FOOTHILLS
GENERAL INFORMATION RESOURCES

BOULDER

Boulder Convention
and Visitors Bureau,
2440 Pearl Street, 80302;
(303) 442–2911 or (800) 444–0447
www.bouldercoloradousa.com

GOLDEN

Greater Golden Chamber
of Commerce,
P.O. Box 1035,
Golden, 80402;
(303) 279–3113
www.goldencochamber.org

CENTRAL CITY/ BLACK HAWK

Central City–Black Hawk
Chamber of Commerce,
281 Church Street,
Central City, 80427;
(303) 582–5077

Gilpin County,
203 Eureka Street,
P.O. Box 366,
Central City, 80427;
(303) 582–5214
www.ccionline.org/counties/gilpin.html

Northwestern Mountains

Rocky Mountain National Park Territory

If you happen to come to **Estes Park** during the high summer season—and want to be above the melee—you might consider the short uphill drive to the **Stanley Hotel and Conference Center.** It stands above the busy town like a white castle. The one-hundred-room Stanley reminds you of those old Swiss Grand Hotels—aristocratic, flawlessly kept up, frequently restored, a monument to good taste and good manners.

The hotel is all stately white columns, Victorian furniture, fireplaces crackling in the lobby, rooms with impeccable white linen, polished cherrywood furniture, and antique dressers. The handwrought leaded-glass windows, the spotless white tablecloths in the (deluxe) dining room, and the comfortable bar add to a feeling of being on vacation. Miles of walks surround the hostelry, which is at an elevation of 7,500 feet.

The historic hotel was built by the inventor of the Stanley Steamer automobile. Back in 1905, doctors gave F. O. Stanley, the inventor, only a few months to live. Stanley gathered his wife, her maid, and his controversial Steamer and headed for

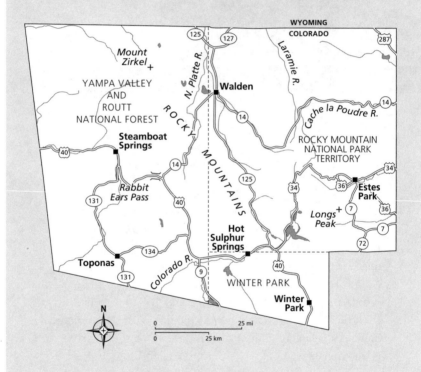

WYOMING
COLORADO

Mount
Zirkel +

YAMPA VALLEY
AND
ROUTT
NATIONAL FOREST

N. Platte R.

Walden

Laramie R.

Cache la Poudre R.

Steamboat
Springs

ROCKY MOUNTAINS

ROCKY MOUNTAIN
NATIONAL PARK
TERRITORY

Rabbit
Ears Pass

Estes
Park

Longs +
Peak

Hot
Sulphur
Springs

Toponas

Colorado R.

WINTER PARK

Winter
Park

N

0   25 mi

0   25 km

the Colorado Rockies. The undaunted old gentleman was determined to drive his vehicle to Estes Park, Colorado, regardless of roads declared impassable. He victoriously covered the 20-mile stretch in a record one hour and fifty minutes. The inventor suffered from tuberculosis, and his doctor had sent him to Estes Park with the hope of prolonging his patient's life "for a year or so." The sturdy old gentleman was to live for another thirty-seven years. (He reached the age of ninety-one.)

The ingenious, eccentric millionaire ran his lavish hotel facility with a style all his own. In order to bring chamber music to Estes Park for his guests, he had a huge New York Steinway piano shipped to Colorado by oxcart. His resort, located on 160 acres of land, was part of the 6,000-acre Lord Dunraven hunting estate.

Most of the guests arrived by train, to be picked up in Stanley's steaming ten-horsepower automobile. The "all-electric" hotel charged $8.00 a day, gourmet meals included.

The Stanley Hotel opened in June 1909. It had cost $1 million to build and was described as "simply palatial." The materials had come by horse teams on

AUTHOR'S FAVORITES IN THE NORTHWESTERN MOUNTAINS

Beaver Village Condos,
(970) 726–8813 or (800) 824–8438
www.beavercondos.com

C Lazy U Ranch,
(970) 887–3344
www.clazyu.com

Grand Lake,
(970) 627–3402 or (800) 531–1019
www.grandlakechamber.com

Ponderosa Lodge,
(800) 628–0512
www.estes-park.com/ponderosa

Rocky Mountain National Park,
(970) 586–1206
www.nps.gov/romo

Stanley Hotel,
(970) 586–3371 or (800) 976–1377
www.stanleyhotel.com

Strawberry Park Hot Springs,
(970) 879–0342
www.strawberryhotsprings.com

Trail Ridge Road
(Rocky Mountain National Park between Grand Lake and Estes Park),
(970) 586–1206
www.nps.gov/romo

Vista Verde Ranch,
(800) 526–7433
www.vistaverde.com

Winter Park,
(800) 979–0332, (970) 726–5514, or (303) 892–0961
www.skiwinterpark.com

Aspen Lodge Ranch Resort at Estes Park

What a contrast! Estes Park, the stylish community that became famous with the Stanley Hotel, also gave us the *Aspen Lodge Ranch Resort at Estes Park,* a rugged, typically western log-cabin lodge with sixty spacious rooms. The main year-round focus here is on the outdoors. In winter, you skate or play ice hockey or broomball, go sledding or tubing, enjoy a sleigh ride or rent snowshoes or cross-country skis. In summer, there are short or long hikes (this writer required three hours to reach the summit of the Twin Sisters peak), hot tubs, mountain bikes, and a weight room, all to stimulate your appetite. There's also a restaurant on the premises. The Aspen Lodge Ranch Resort at Estes Park is located at 6120 Highway 7, (970) 586–8133 or (800) 332–6867; www.ranchweb.com/aspenlodge.

roads that Stanley himself designed. A magnificent white edifice with dormers and flagpoles and elegant porches welcomed the hotel guests. Once inside the lobby, the arrivals were dazzled by the hand-carved wooden staircase, the ornate brass elevator, and the carpeted halls that led to rooms with lead-glass windows and four-poster beds.

Stanley, who'd made huge sums with the invention of his automobile and later with photo-dry plates, personally designed the hotel's electric kitchens. He ordered the decor of a music room, arranged for a gentlemen's smoking room (even though he never touched tobacco himself), and enjoyed showing up in the billiard room. The legendary Stanley Hotel eventually attracted such celebrities as Theodore Roosevelt, John Philip Sousa, and Molly Brown.

trivia

The Stanley Hotel earned some of its more recent notoriety as the setting that inspired Stephen King's novel, *The Shining*. King wrote roughly half of the manuscript for the novel while staying in room 217 at the hotel. He returned to the Stanley Hotel in 1997 to make the ABC miniseries version of The Shining (the motion picture was filmed elsewhere).

Remarkably enough, F. O. Stanley's creation still stands; indeed, it prospers. It can be found in the National Register of Historic Places. The music room is still there, as is a writing room. Picture windows and restaurant views look out on the mountains, including Longs Peak. Sunning and swimming are available in summer. A professional theater flourishes; in fact, the hotel stays open through the winter as well. Rates are expensive even when the snow falls, and summer accommodations are more expensive, as they should be at this palace.

Contact Stanley Hotel and Conference Center by writing to P.O. Box 1767, Estes Park 80517; or call (970) 586–3371 or (800) 976–1377; www.stanleyhotel.com.

On a July day in 1982, a flood roared into one of Colorado's most visited tourist centers. The water raged through Elkhorn Avenue, Estes Park's main street, breaking shop windows and causing wholesale destruction. The Fall River rose, tearing into motels and mountain cabins. Three people drowned. The damage was estimated at $31 million. For the remainder of that season—and part of the next—the flood stopped tourism in its tracks.

Estes Park has long been rebuilt. The reborn main street offers prettily painted benches, trees and planters, new sidewalks, and souvenir stores. A church has become an array of shops. Someone coined the slogan "The Gutsiest Little Town in Colorado!" Some 250,000 to 300,000 tourists come to stay here each year. They enjoy themselves in myriad ways. Rock climbers flock to climb not only on aptly named **Lumpy Ridge,** which rises above the town to the northwest but also to attempt some of the other, more remote cliff faces so abundant in Rocky Mountain National Park. You may see them in town picking up a coffee in the morning, or more likely after a climb, when, dirty and tired, they'll stop in at a restaurant to fill their bellies. Other visitors carry fishing tackle; trout are plentiful (Colorado license required). Wildlife abounds, and the air is pure in the surrounding mountains.

TOP ANNUAL EVENTS IN THE NORTHWESTERN MOUNTAINS

Winter Carnival,
Grand Lake; last weekend of January;
(970) 627–3402 or (800) 531–1019
www.grandlakechamber.com

Steamboat Springs,
Chamber Annual Marathon, early June;
(970) 879–0880
www.steamboatchamber.com/events/
marathon.htm

Music in the Mountains,
early June through late August;
(970) 586–4031
www.estesnet.com

Cowboy Roundup Days,
Steamboat Springs; July 4 weekend;
(970) 879–0880
www.steamboatchamber.com

Rooftop Rodeo,
Estes Park; mid-July;
(970) 586–6104
www.estesnet.com/events/rooftop
rodeo.htm

Estes Park: The Best Views

The Estes Park Aerial Tramway, west on US 34 to Moraine Park Road, carries passengers to the 8,896-foot summit of Prospect Mountain for an unmatched look at the community and surrounding mountains. Sit on one of two suspended cabins and view the Continental Divide, and then picnic at the summit. For more information call (970) 586–3675; www.estestram.com.

Estes Park has two golf courses, including one that occupies land once owned by the famous Earl of Dunraven, an Irish nobleman who discovered the area in 1827 while on a hunting trip. The American homesteaders followed during the 1870s. Nowadays Estes Park has about 4,000 permanent inhabitants, plus 25,000 others who own mountain cabins, show up briefly in summer, and often keep to themselves.

To be sure, the town is ideal for vacationing families. Estes Park makes boredom impossible. In summer, the **Estes Park Aerial Tramway** ascends the flank of Prospect Mountain, located a few blocks from Elkhorn Avenue. **Catch Wild Trout,** also close by, features rainbow-filled Peter's Pond, plus gear for rent. On nearby **Lake Estes** lie boating possibilities and free access to terrific family hiking terrain. For more information contact Estes Valley Recreation and Park District, 1770 Big Thompson Avenue, P.O. Box 1379, Estes Park 80517; (970) 586–2011; www.estesvalleyrecreation.com/marina.html.

The reborn Estes Park presents some contrasts: new and old, serene and loud, natural and artificial. The touristy aspects of the town will disturb the sensitive traveler. Mountains don't seem to suffice. Your children can race noisy little go-karts. On Elkhorn Avenue, a store prints handbills with headlines ("The Smiths having a Ball in Estes!" or "Patsy Saw Her First Snow!!") and sells T-shirts with silly messages ("Colorado is owned by Canadians").

For all visitors there are rodeos, parades, chamber music concerts, and Rocky Mountain National Park talks, walks, and campfire programs. Still other possibilities: You can shop for Native American crafts or jewelry, sporting goods, western wear, or mineral specimens.

When should you come to Estes Park? Avoid July and August. Elkhorn Avenue then turns into a tourism circus, with thousands of people descending upon the town. Early June and September are good months. A tranquil time begins after Labor Day.

Accommodations? The redecorated **Ponderosa Lodge** overlooks the now peaceful Fall River; some units were damaged by the flood but were rebuilt (1820 Fall River Road; 800–628–0512; www.estes-park.com/ponderosa). The Ponderosa also features a large cedar log cabin for families or groups.

The YMCA in the Rockies rents rooms in lodges. Estes Park has a Holiday Inn with a large indoor swimming pool. The Stanley Hotel is the most elegant and historic in town. Except for the moderately priced YMCA, the tariff for summer accommodations is high.

Estes Park is 65 miles northwest of Denver and easy to reach via the Boulder Turnpike and U.S. Highway 36 through Lyons. For more information contact the Estes Park Chamber Resort Association, 500 Big Thompson Avenue, Estes Park 80517; (970) 586–4431 or (800) 443–7837; www.estesparkresort.com.

For those who prefer to do their nature exploration by automobile, a drive along the spectacular ***Trail Ridge Road*** (U.S. Highway 34) in Rocky Mountain National Park shouldn't be missed. Lying within the park, Trail Ridge Road winds along for 48 miles through the high country, connecting the towns of Estes Park and Grand Lake. Eleven miles of the road are above tree line, with the high point at 12,183 feet. Take some time to enjoy your passage along the highest continuously paved highway in the United States, but make sure you plan your trip with the weather in mind.

The season is short for a visit, though. Deep snows and snowdrifts cover Trail Ridge all winter and spring; indeed, the famous road is open only from Memorial Day until the first heavy snowfall, usually in mid-October.

Starting from Estes Park, you climb for some 4,000 feet on a highway that has serpentines like those of Alpine passes. Reaching 12,183-foot (3,713-meter) level, you find that the air is thin and the ultraviolet rays are strong. Eventually you descend through the clouds to Grand Lake, which is 4,000

Estes Park Specialty—Fly Fishing

Even the most avid of anglers will want to cast their attention toward the Estes Park area.

For fly fishing, the **Colorado River,** west of Estes Park, cannot be faulted. Your frying pan will be kept busy, because the fish thrive in the chilly waters here. Indeed, the "Colorado," as it's called, has been named a Gold-Medal trout stream. The reason? The high number of trout over 14 inches long that have been pulled from its waters.

If you prefer to drop your line in a lake, you won't want to miss **Grand Lake,** south and west of Estes Park. This is the largest natural lake in Colorado and is home to Kokanee, brown, rainbow, and lake trout.

One more tip: **Catch Wild Trout** (510 Moraine Avenue, 970–586–5171; www.eto nnant.com/catch_wild_trout) may just be your ticket for a fun time fishing with the kids without any hassle: No license is required—and the proprietors will clean and pack your catch on ice.

feet below. In between you spot some of Colorado's highest mountain ranges. When you park, you find yourself in view of rock piles, known as moraines, deposited here during the Ice Age. There's the Iceberg Lake View at 12,080 feet, and there's high meadowland known as tundra, which is reminiscent of Alaska.

Your family can learn much about forestry below timberline. The lovely aspen tree stands at elevations of about 9,000 to 10,000 feet. Trail Ridge Road also provides a home for alder trees and Douglas fir. In the conifer family you find blue spruce, lodgepole pines, and the beautiful *Pinus ponderosa*. At some higher levels, 9,500 feet and up, grow the subalpine fir and the Engelmann spruce.

How do you distinguish between the many species of conifers? The differences are noticeable. Spruces, for example, can be identified by cones that stand up straight like candles, and spruce needles are attached singly to the twigs. By contrast, ponderosa pine needles come in clusters of two to three; the bark is a dark brown. Lodgepole pine needles are attached in pairs.

Like most important Colorado highways, Trail Ridge has a long history. First came the Utes and other Native American tribes, who actually followed the already marked trails of wild animals. Miners used it in the 1880s. In 1929, Congress appropriated almost $500,000—a large sum in those days—to build a highway over the Continental Divide. Engineers called it Tombstone Ridge, which became Trail Ridge Road. The paving was finally completed in 1935.

The government engineers, normally cool and scientific, became eloquent enough in their final analysis, which mentioned the "deep canyons, many lakes, and perpetual snow." The route report concluded: "Below lie streams, valleys, forested slopes, and the realms of civilization. All around are mountains and peaks, no longer towering above but close at hand or seen across some mighty valley."

Break the Ice: Ice Climbing near Estes Park

Estes Park is home base for the ***Colorado Mountain School*** (CMS), the sole concessionaire permitted to guide rock and ice climbs in nearby Rocky Mountain National Park. Wintertime is the perfect season to test yourself on the park's frozen waterfalls under the watchful eyes of one of CMS's expert guides. From introductory one-day courses to an intensive, multiday advanced course, CMS has classes appropriate for all skill levels. Contact CMS at 341 Moraine Avenue, P.O. Box 1846, Estes Park 80517; (970) 586–5758 or (888) 267–7783; www.cmschool.com.

Coping with the Altitude

Most out-of-state visitors need a day or two to become accustomed to the altitude. Los Angeles, New York, and Dallas are at sea level. Colorado's resorts and the lifts are from 8,000 to 12,000 feet up. Some midwestern skiers may fly to Vail and immediately storm the slopes. The abrupt altitude change will affect flatlanders, of course. They'll probably ski their initial runs with knees made of Jell-O. And they'll tire more easily. A suddenly transplanted midwesterner or southerner may not sleep well the first night in the high mountains. And, if one were to ask the ski patrol about the acclimatization of older visitors, the advice is always the same: Please don't overdo it on the first day! According to the patrol, people with chronic heart or lung problems should take it especially easy at the higher elevations.

Doctors claim that it takes one day to get used to each additional thousand feet. An exaggeration? The point seems valid enough, however. A New York skier needn't rush up to his final Colorado destination as though he were trying to catch a commuter train or subway at home.

Travel some 70 miles north and west from Denver (Interstate 25 north to Highway 66, west on 66 until it joins US 36) to Estes Park and Trail Ridge Road (US 34).

One hundred and twenty years ago, an Englishwoman named Isabella Bird waxed enthusiastic about this Colorado landscape. She came upon the nearby Longs Peak region on horseback. What expressions of wonder! "Exquisite stretches of flowery pastures dotted with trees sloping down-like to bright streams full of red waistcoated trout or running up in soft glades into the dark forest, above which the snow peaks rise," wrote the lady, and the description still fits.

The peaks and lakes of **Rocky Mountain National Park** have present-day names that bear witness to it all: The tourist can view Deer Mountain, Isolation Peak, Snowdrift Peak. Those who come afoot—and more people do every year—may head for Dream Lake, Lone Pine Lake, Fern Lake, and up to Chasm Lake.

All belong to the impressive 415-square-mile span of Rocky Mountain National Park. Established by the federal government in 1915, the park now encompasses more than one hundred upthrusting peaks higher than 11,000 feet above sea level. Longs Peak is the highest mountain in the park at 14,255 feet.

There are lots of things to *do* here, yet the expanse also brings happiness to the inactive. Nearby resort hotels are inviting with clean rooms and deck chairs, and the area appeals to the most sedentary motorist.

Nature studies, lectures, and tours are conducted by park rangers. The many summer doings make this part of Colorado especially attractive to visitors. There are not only campfire programs, but also a number of short, self-guiding nature paths for the benefit of families. (You can bring small children, too.) A Colorado fishing license entitles you to angle for trout in the park's many lakes; some 350 well-marked trails invite the hiker. Wildflowers abound in late spring. Bring your camera.

Walking is the best way to see this national park. One of the most scenic and easily accessed trails is the one to **Bear Lake.** Nine different hikes begin here. Difficulty ratings range from the half-mile "easy" stroll around the lake to the 8⁹⁄₁₀-mile round-trip to Flattop Mountain that is rated "strenuous." Rocky Mountain National Park is especially popular with backpackers, who need a permit, and with rock climbers.

The Park Service exacts a fee ($15 per vehicle) to enter the mountainous domain; if you plan to visit other national parks and sites managed by the U.S. Fish and Wildlife Service, the U.S. Forest Service, or the Bureau of Land Management, it will be worth your while to buy a Golden Eagle sticker for your National Parks Pass ($65). It's good for your car and its occupants for the entire year. Travelers age sixty-two and older may ask for the Golden Age Pass—a lifetime pass to all federal recreation areas for a onetime $10 charge. Hikers can reach the park gratis by setting out from the main parking lot of the Longs Peak Trail toward Chasm Lake, below the summit of the peak. The trails are marked and not too steep.

trivia

The 1,000-foot east face of Longs Peak, a vertical granite cliff known as the Diamond, attracts rock climbers from all over the world.

Please note that the Rocky Mountain National Park has become so popular that every year more than 3 million people stream through four entrances, especially in summer. The major highway, Trail Ridge Road, closes from mid-October through Memorial Day.

Rocky Mountain has only five campgrounds, fewer than a third of Yosemite's or Yellowstone's. No hookups are available for trailers; the big ones, like Airstreams, are hard to navigate on the curvy park roads. Some tents go up early in the morning, and at the peak of the season—June through Labor Day—accommodations may be hard to come by, even in neighboring towns.

There are several ways to avoid the crowds and still enjoy the Rockies' pleasantly cool summers; the green of pine, spruce, and fir; the mosaic of wildflowers; and the water that cascades down those Rockies. For instance, you can arrive early in the season or after the children are back in school. You can relax by renting a mountain cabin.

Autumn is the best time of all, bringing with it a seemingly endless string of clear, warm days. The evenings turn crisp and the nights are chilly, so bring an overcoat. Mid-September seems the best period. Come after Labor Day and you'll find less competition for the area's good rooms, restaurant tables, and traffic lanes.

In winter, cross-country skiing is plentiful. In summer, the patient animal watcher can see deer, elk, sheep, beaver, pikas, and many birds as well.

The Englishwoman was right about the park and its "exquisite stretches."

From Denver you can arrive at this ultrascenic region via several routes. Some summer motorists head west from the Mile High City on Interstate 70, cross Berthoud Pass via U.S. Highway 40, and then get to Rocky Mountain National Park via Grand Lake (altitude 8,367 feet and icicle-cold). You can also come on the spectacular Peak-to-Peak Highway (Highways 119, 72, and 7) from Black Hawk. The drive is especially enjoyable in late fall when the aspen trees burst into gold. Earmark at least half a day to get to the national park via this route. To save time, you can drive through Boulder and Lyons instead (use US 36); from Boulder it's about 34 miles to Estes Park and the Rocky Mountain National Park gates.

For more information contact Rocky Mountain National Park, 1000 Highway 36, Estes Park 80517, (970) 586–1206; www.nps.gov/romo.

If you've decided to spend a day driving along Trail Ridge Road from Estes Park, the end of your journey will deposit you in the town of **Grand Lake,** which skirts the shores of Grand Lake itself. This unusually blue lake—the largest glacial lake in the state—will be dotted with sailboats in August, its marinas filled up with yachts. At an elevation of almost 8,400 feet above sea level, Grand Lake boasts the "World's Highest Yacht Club." The mountain giants of Rocky Mountain National Park cast a watchful presence over the stunning, Swiss-like scene.

The slightly offbeat location doesn't prevent the international sailing elite from competing here for trophies. Regattas are frequent. During the summer marinas get busy with vacationers who rent rowboats, paddleboats, or motorboats.

You see sailboarders. The lake and the nearby streams are populated by anglers. River-rafting companies take you out on various excursions. You have limitless opportunities for hiking. Stables with horses beckon. The surrounding peaks are forested by healthy aspen trees, ponderosa pine, and Douglas fir. You will find waterfalls and mountain flowers.

trivia

Rocky Mountain National Park's annual budget is about $10 million—which may seem like a lot, until you consider that the park has nearly 3.4 million visitors each year!

In winter the handsome, wooden, lakeshore summer homes are abandoned by their rich midwestern and Texan owners. The souvenir shops along the boardwalk close down; only a few saloons, a tiny grocery, and the pharmacy stay open. Trail Ridge Road is closed. At the same time, the cross-country ski possibilities are plentiful. The Rocky Mountain National Park entrance is only a mile away, and you see Nordic skiers even on the golf course. Noisy snowmobile enthusiasts show up with their machines. Most winter tourists stay in nearby Granby; the wealthy ones repair to the C Lazy U Ranch.

For those who wish to enjoy the deep silence that winter in the Rockies can bring, the smell and roar of snowmobiles shatter any attempt to enjoy the deep quiet of winter. One escape from the snowmobiles: the *Grand Lake Touring Center* (Box 590, Grand Lake 80447; 970–627–8008; www.grandlake colorado.com/touringcenter). Although few people know about it, the location is easy to find; just turn left on County Road 48 and proceed to the west entrance of Rocky Mountain National Park. The Ski Touring Center is more scenic than most, and the 30 kilometers of trails are immaculately kept up. Some of the runs are surprisingly steep—especially for a golf course!—but other trails are gentle enough for beginners. Among the many runs, experts will enjoy the Spirits Haunt; good skiers can be seen on Ptarmigan Tuck.

trivia

Legend says the Ute shunned Grand Lake, believing its mists were the spirits of women and children killed during an attack by the Cheyenne and Arapahoe Indians.

Actually, you rarely see many people up here in this pristine territory; Grand Lake just doesn't get many visitors in winter. And, of course, snowmobiles are verboten in the Ski Touring Center. Full-moon ski adventures and spaghetti dinners take place throughout the season; call for details. The center is open daily from 9:00 A.M. to 4:00 P.M.

Grand Lake's history is also worth writing about. The Native Americans called it Spirit Lake. According to local historians, the first Indians arrived around A.D. 900 to 1300. They no doubt stayed during the summer and late fall. Game, fish, and other food were plentiful.

The earliest legend of the region tells of Ute, Arapaho, and Cheyenne squabbles. Apparently, the Utes living in this summer paradise were suddenly attacked by marauding Cheyennes. Fearing for their women and children, the Ute braves hastily loaded them on rafts and shoved the rafts onto the lake for safety. As the battle with the Cheyennes raged among the trees and along the lakeshore, a storm came up, blowing the rafts far out onto the 400-foot-deep lake. The Indians watched helplessly as the rafts were overturned and the women and children drowned. After this time the Utes regarded the lake as dangerous and stayed away, naming it Spirit Lake.

The first white visitors probably showed up in 1855 to hunt for furs and catch the plentiful trout. Although he is best known for his discovery of the Gore Range near Vail, Sir George Gore, the Irish nobleman, also explored the Grand Lake wilderness for a couple of years. He arrived with a party of fifty people and thirty supply wagons. He brought guides, secretaries, and hunt-and-fish-supply artisans. The country then abounded with game, including elk, bear, deer, and buffalo.

Other hunters and trappers of lesser stature came next, and some, attracted by the remote beauty of the area, remained to become the region's first settlers. Among these was Joseph L. Westcott, who became the first postmaster of Grand Lake in 1877. Westcott, later known as Judge Westcott, remained here most of his life.

In 1881, the little hamlet of Grand Lake got its first sizable general store, and the Grand Central Hotel was completed. It was a decade of summer residents building homes that looked out on the water. The first big regatta took place here in 1912, on the 12-mile-long lake. It is measured only a mile across, so you always see the other shore. The mountain backdrop is as stunning as any in Switzerland.

trivia

Grand Lake is also known as the "Snowmobile Capital of Colorado," due to its more than 300 miles of trails.

While a somewhat lengthy trek is required for a summer visit (via Trail Ridge Road), winter renders Grand Lake an even more out-of-the-way destination. A circuitous route can be followed from Denver, taking I–70 to U.S. Highway 40 north, then breaking off after Granby onto US 34 to head farther north. For more information contact Grand Lake Area Chamber of Commerce, P.O. Box 57, Grand Lake 80447; (970) 627–3402 or (800) 531–1019; www.grandlakechamber.com.

The **C Lazy U Ranch,** ensconced in its own Willow Creek Valley some 100 miles west of Denver, is no ordinary guest ranch.

At the stables, the wranglers assign you a personal horse for your stay, and you and your group set out into a quiet, slightly remote, truly relaxing 5,000 acres of mountains and hillsides, forests and rivers, ponds and lookout points.

In winter, the ranch turns into Grandma Moses scenery, all white, with brown barns and fences and the children—colored dots—playing ice hockey, skating, and tubing. At the Nordic shop, one hundred pairs of cross-country skis and boots and poles await the lucky guests. Some 30 miles of trails are packed and ready; you share these winter woods with elk and deer, which show up in the meadows, stealing the horses' hay. You ski in privacy, in a private preserve. When the snow falls, some summer wranglers turn into cross-country guides. No extra charge for lessons or rentals.

Rates are high and commensurate with the ranch's amenities and all-inclusive package. C Lazy U is closed in October and November and in April and May. Take I–70 to exit 232, then along US 40 to Highway 125. You'll see the sign. For more information and to make reservations, contact C Lazy U Ranch, Box 379, Granby 80446; (970) 887–3344; www.clazyu.com. Don't be surprised if the ranch is sold out in July and August.

Spend a day traveling a little farther west along US 40 to reach ***Hot Sulphur Springs Resort,*** located between Granby and Kremmling. This tiny resort has reinvented itself after having been practically forgotten for decades. Recently restored, the handsome resort is now outfitted with a half-dozen tiny pools, a massage room, and a solarium. Anyone age sixteen or older can soak in the outdoor pools for $14.50 a day ($16.50 in summer); the price is $11.50 for kids age six through fifteen and free for children age five or younger. Reservations are highly recommended for all services; call for details. Hot Sulphur Springs Resort, P.O. Box 275, Hot Sulphur Springs 80451; (970) 725–3306 or (800) 510–6235; www.hotsulphursprings.com.

South of Granby beckons the ***Devil's Thumb Ranch Resort,*** P.O. Box 750, Tabernash 80478; (970) 726–5632 or (800) 933–4339; www.rkymtnhi.com/dev thumb. The 400-acre Shangri-la is idyllic in summer, picturesque in fall, and one of Colorado's best places for horseback riding, trail hiking, and trout fishing. In winter, the ranch reinvents itself as a first-class cross-country center with rentals, instruction, and 105 kilometers of varied, lone trails. Most of the accommodations can be described as rustic, even primitive, without TV or the bathroom down the hall. The scenic beauty—pure Colorado!—makes up for the lack of hotel-style amenities or the feeling of loneliness. The price is right, though, and the Devil's Thumb Ranch Resort guarantees memories. You get here via US 40 past Fraser. About 2 miles after Fraser, turn right on Highway 83. The road forks a short distance after this; turn onto the right-hand fork and follow it for 3 miles.

Winter Park

How does a large ski area come to be? Where did it all start? To understand ***Winter Park*** and its landscape better, some historical background may be in order.

A few hardy Denverites already skied in the region around 1920. Winter Park (then West Portal) consisted of sawmills and railroad shanties; a tunnel construction shack served as a warming house to skiers who sought their thrills in forest glades and down logging roads. They climbed the Winter Park hills under their own steam, all the while dreaming of real trails. The dream became a reality in the mid-1930s when several ski clubs laid out better runs.

Denver's manager of parks and improvements was among the first to see the potential. He appropriated the funds for a first ski tow, a "T-bar of sorts," built with staves from old whiskey barrels. In March 1937 the Denver official told an astonished Colorado audience, "We'll create a winter playground unequaled in the world!" He brought in Otto Schniebs, then one of America's most famous skiers. Schniebs, who spoke of the sport as "a way of life," was enthusiastic about the runs.

Winter Park's official dedication took place on January 28, 1940. A ski band played. Hans Hauser, a handsome ski school director, had been commandeered from Austria. Alf Engen, a jumper, came from Utah to show his stuff. A ticket for the ½-mile-long lift cost $1.00 (50 cents for students).

By 1947, Winter Park (which got its name from its designation as a winter park in Denver's park system) had three T-bar lifts and four rope tows. Owned by the city of Denver, the area made good progress during the early 1950s; soon there were numerous chairlifts, which multiplied every season. (The area now has twenty lifts.)

The history of this ski mecca was crowned in 1975 when its capacity was almost doubled. To drum up $6 million for lift construction and base facilities seems an even greater feat when you consider the tight money situation of the early 1970s.

Twin factors—fairly easy access and adequate accommodations—always helped Winter Park's cause.

To avoid the hassle of renting a car, many families take advantage of **Home James Transportation Services'** frequent shuttle vans that run from Denver International Airport (DIA) directly to lodging properties in Winter Park. The cost is $43 per person age twelve or older for one way in winter; $23 for children two to eleven. Children younger than two ride free if sitting on an adult's lap. Advance reservations are required. Contact Home James Transportation Services, P.O. Box 279, Winter Park 80482; (970) 726–5060 or (800) 359–7503; www.homejamestransportation.com.

Winter Park always attracted customers of every age and ability. The slopes are well groomed. The lifts run without fail. A large ski school teaches beginners in record time; three days of lessons should get you up and down many slopes. The area boasts more than 120 ski runs that satisfy the most fanatic mogul skier as well as the rank novice.

Winter Park vies with Colorado's top resorts, yet it has none of the poshness, the celebrity parade, the hectic atmosphere of other international ski resorts, or the wild nightlife of the Beautiful People. The resort works out well for nonskiers also. Resort managers make it possible for anyone to reach the Winter Park summit (elevation 10,700 feet) in comfortable, heated vehicles called snowcats. For $30, a nonskiing vacationer can take a two-hour scenic tour, and thus mingle with the fast downhill crowd, take pictures of the deep sun-flecked woods, and lunch al fresco. Several ski lodges offer heated swimming pools, and even older people like to spend a few unstrenuous hours on light cross-country skis or guided snowshoe tours.

You can also turn a snowcat adventure into a lunch to remember by signing on for a mountain dining tour. A snowcat will take you to dine in style at the mid-mountain **Snoasis** (for $10 per person) or at the award-winning **Lodge at Sunspot,** Winter Park's mountaintop restaurant (for $25 per person). Call (970) 726–1564 or (800) 729–7756 for details and reservations.

Other resort activities include moonlight snowmobile dinner tours, nighttime gondola rides, and fun experiences in the **Gravity Zone,** such as summertime rock climbing for groups on the 30-foot **Base Camp 9000 Climbing Wall,** located in Winter Park's West Portal Station. Call (970) 726–1564 for more information.

trivia

Winter Park's Mary Jane area offers seventy trails on three mountains for more advanced skiers, including the mountain known as Mary Jane itself, which has been voted the best mogul mountain in North America.

The 67-mile drive from Denver across Berthoud Pass to Winter Park won't take much longer than two hours on I–70 and US 40. The roads are kept sanded. Winter Park Resort opens in November and closes in April. Resort hours are 9:00 A.M. to 4:00 P.M. Monday through Friday and 8:30 A.M. to 4:00 P.M. Saturday, Sunday, and holidays. Call for information about summer activities. For more information contact Winter Park Resort, 150 Alpenglow Way, P.O. Box 36, Winter Park 80482; (970) 726–1564 or Denver direct (303) 892–0961; www.skiwinterpark.com.

Wake up to a winter morning in the Colorado ski country. Outside your windows, the sun slants through the conifers; from the condo cross-country ski tracks take off for the snow-covered forest. You're on the quiet edge of Winter Park. You gratefully set out, skiing through light and shade, breathing deeply. Ah, to be alive! To be in motion!

Later you return to the comfortable condominium for lunch. Some people are unaware that they can rent these vacation apartments for a night or a weekend, solo, coupled, or even as a family of six. Kristine Meyer, the manager at the **Beaver Village Condominiums,** puts it this way: "Your time with us will be special. You can cross-country ski outside your door or catch a free shuttle to Winter Park's downhill runs. Afterward, you can sit in our sauna, enjoy a whirlpool, or swim in the indoor pool. It's all included."

Beaver Village is typical for Colorado's condo pleasures: a well-equipped kitchen, matching dishes, pots and pans, ironed sheets, clean towels, shiny glassware, and cozy, generous furniture in mountain hues. The more than 120 units contain moss-covered fireplaces, plus free wood. And each *room* has its own thermostat. The management hands honeymooners a gratis bottle of vintage wine. For reservations call (800) 824–8438; www.beavercondos.com.

Alpine Resort Properties' **Hi Country Haus** occupies a multiview hillside above the little hamlet of **Fraser,** which was President Eisenhower's favorite. Year-round lodging here exudes charm. For reservations call (970) 726–8822 or (800) 797–2750; www.alpineresortproperties.com.

Size doesn't mean impersonality. In the Hi Country Haus unit 1510, for instance, the coffee mugs come with greetings:

> *My best to you*
> *Each Day*
> *My best for you*
> *Each Day*

The little-known **Pines at MeadowRidge** sits astride a promontory. MeadowRidge enjoys an outdoor swimming pool plus outdoor and indoor hot tubs. The condos are attractive and come with maid service and gratis ski area shuttles. It is very quiet on the promontory. Arrange a rental through Alpine Resort Properties (see previous entry for contact information).

Several times each winter the slopes of this giant area are alive with multicolored pairs of flags, and through these gates, at intervals, there descend a succession of skiers. In a downhill race they're clocked at 40 miles an hour.

Nothing unusual? Not for the ordinary ski racer. But these people are not ordinary. Many of the competitors have only one leg. Others have only one

Grand Adventure Balloon Tours

Passing through Winter Park in the summer and looking for a fun adventure? Try out a hot air balloon flight. The tour takes you and your companions up, up, and away, soaring up above the treetops with astounding views of the surrounding mountainous terrain. For reservations and information about prices, contact *Grand Adventure Balloon Tours,* P.O. Box 3423, Winter Park 80482; (970) 887–1340 or (888) 887–1340; www.grandadventureballoon.com.

Winter Park: Rail Trips

The U.S. west and Colorado always appreciate a ski train; for some sixty years, Denverites have supported the rail trip to Winter Park. It starts at Denver's Union Station and ends on the ski area's slopes. Tradition! The first such train ran in 1936. Nowadays, skiers welcome the reliable schedule, departing on weekends from Denver at 7:15 A.M. and leaving Winter Park to return to Denver at 4:15 P.M. The two-hour adventure covers 56 miles, travels through 29 tunnels, and climbs almost 4,000 feet. For guests who arrive in Winter Park by train, Beaver Village Condos has arranged a complimentary pick-up and drop-off service. For more information call (303) 296–4754; www.skitrain.com.

arm or no hands. The rest fly down the Colorado mountain despite paralyzed joints, missing kneecaps, absent toes, or stiffened backs.

The skiers are all disabled, the result of disease, accidents, or their conditions at birth. Yet these people show that you can conquer almost any barrier. Eyes shining, cheeks glowing, the racers speed through the finish line.

Colorado's Winter Park Ski Resort offers the **National Sports Center for the Disabled (NSCD),** the world's largest teaching program for physically challenged skiers. More than a thousand volunteers and a staff of fifty-four participate in it. Each ski season, nearly 30,000 lessons are given here to people with cerebral palsy, spina bifida, polio, multiple sclerosis, and paraplegia. Some of the students are blind. The NSCD provides services for people with almost any disability.

Skiing requires perfect coordination and good balance. To hurtle down a snowy slope, two-legged sighted skiers use all of their God-given limbs—their feet to direct the two skis, and their hands and arms to hold the poles, which act as stabilizers.

The loss of an arm throws the body out of kilter. With only one ski pole, it's more difficult to make the turns or to walk up a hill. Yet, where there's a will, there's a way, and practice and determination will make a one-armed skier as good as a two-armed one.

The sudden loss of a leg is more serious, yet even that can be overcome. At first there will be pain, and when the stump has healed, the person will feel off-balance. Then come the weeks of learning the use of crutches. The amputee must strengthen the remaining leg—and how the muscles will ache for a while! There's also the self-consciousness. But only at first.

A positive mental attitude will put the disabled person onto the right track within a few weeks. The individual realizes that one can do many things with an incomplete body. Winter Park simply calls it "rehabilitation through recreation." The students themselves often see it as a lark. "Skiing on one leg is easier than on two," chuckles one participant. "The trouble with *two* skis is that they don't go in the same direction for the beginner!"

The NSCD started in 1970 and has become the largest program of its kind in the world. The program began with twenty-three amputees from the Children's Hospital in Denver, and each year more lessons were added. Most of the students are now adults. One of the highlights has been the introduction of mono skis and a sledlike device used by paraplegics or any individual confined to a wheelchair.

Skiers with one good leg and two usable arms are taught the three-tracking technique, which means skiing with small outriggers. The outriggers consist of a ski tip attached to the bottom of a modified crutch. In full gear, the three-tracker has contact with the snow on the bottom of the full-length ski and balances with both ski tips. In due time, amputee skiers become so proficient that they can enter races.

How is it possible to teach skiing to the sightless? In some countries instructors ring a little bell at every dip of a mountain. Winter Park has used bamboo poles that link instructor and pupil; the key teaching elements, however, are touch and verbal contact. The sightless individual has to begin from the beginning: He or she has to learn all about ski boots (and how to put them on) and then about the skis them-selves. The feeling of standing on skis comes next, with the feet parallel to each other, then walking to the sound of the instructor's ski poles tapping.

Next, the pupil sidesteps up a gentle slope, constantly in communication with the instructor. Chairlift loading has to be taught, too. Again, with proper instruction and good communication, it proves to be no problem.

The sightless person eventually moves on to steered turns, parallel turns, and, finally, mogul skiing. Oftentimes a sightless skier will progress down the hill to the sound of the instructor calling, "Turn, turn, turn!" In due time, a close bond develops between student and instructor.

A member of the National Sports Center for the Disabled (NSCD)

How is this large Colorado program financed? Funds come from general donations, program fees, grants from private corporations and foundations, and special events. A large Denver bank finances a major race. The participants also pay a small daily fee toward lessons and equipment rental.

The learning experience isn't too difficult for athletic individuals who already skied before injury or illness hit them. Thanks to the use of special gear, people can now take up skiing despite physical problems.

One good example is Larry Kunz, who was born with spina bifida, a condition that gave him little muscle control from the knees down. Thanks to the Children's Hospital in Denver, Larry was introduced to Hal O'Leary, a Winter Park coach who specializes in teaching the physically impaired. "At first Larry couldn't even walk," O'Leary says. "But in a week, he was able to use his crutch skis and get around in heavy ski boots. Today, he soars down the slopes despite his spina bifida."

Some of the most exciting moments occur on the racecourse. At one competition a Winter Park official handed out trophies to the three fastest skiers. "You three won this slalom," he said. "But actually, all you people were winners. You won over your disability."

More information on the program can be obtained by writing or calling National Sports Center for the Disabled, P.O. Box 1290, Winter Park 80482; (970) 726–1540 or (303) 316–1540; www.nscd.org.

Honestly now, did you ever dream of a family ski vacation? Various condos and lodges offer a memorable family diversion—a nighttime sleigh ride. The sleighs are pulled by sturdy draft horses. You glide through spruce forests, bundled up in warm blankets. The destination, 2 to 3 miles yonder, may be an old homesteader's cabin or a bonfire, where a western steak dinner awaits. The various Winter Park–based sleigh teamsters have been at their trade for many years, including **Dashing Through the Snow** (970–726–5376 or 888–384–6773; www.winterpark-info.com/activities/91.html), **Devil's Thumb Ranch Resort** (970–726–8231; www.rkymtnhi.com), and **Grand Adventures** (800–726–9247; www.grandadventures.com). Rates are reasonable for all.

High up, a ski jumper pushes off, sinks into a crouch, chest tight against his knees. He accelerates in the two steep snow grooves toward the platform. Suddenly, his body uncoils, straightens, dives upward. He is airborne. Seconds tick away. The spectators gasp. Still he soars through the Colorado sky, then a smooth landing. Judges note the distance. The audience roars.

Ski jumping is sensational to watch. Especially in this case. The competitor was six years old! His leap was the result of a unique school for youngsters at Winter Park. For the past several decades, thousands of kids have been trained in human aviation here at the **Nordic Program at the Winter Park**

Playground for Cross-Country Skiers

A ten-minute drive north from Winter Park, near Tabernash, you come upon the year-round **Snow Mountain Ranch/YMCA** of the Rockies. Thanks to its 100km of cross-country skiing, the ranch is popular with large groups—especially religious and educational groups. True, you find yourself in a somewhat remote country: no shops or restaurants or movies in the vicinity, no television in the spartan rooms; and for dinner you line up for simple, wholesome meals. Who comes here? Lots of midwestern folk to whom spiritual values and prayer are important. Recreation makes for a better Colorado vacation. Apart from cross-country skiing, you can try showshoeing, swimming in an indoor pool, or guided hiking in summer.

For more information contact YMCA of the Rockies, P.O. Box 169, Winter Park 80482; (970) 887–2152 or (303) 443–4743; www.ymcarockies.org.

Competition Center, where children begin training at the age of six. The upper limit for competitors is eighteen. Even middle-aged parents have turned up for lessons. And why not? The school is for first-timers. There is a fee to enroll on a regular basis.

During the season's first get-together, anxious parents ask: Could a child come to harm here? Ski jumping is actually safer than downhill skiing. For one thing, the special hills are well prepared. For another, the youngsters jump in a straight line, and training is worked out with great care. No person, therefore, has ever suffered a serious accident at this Colorado school.

Before being taken on, a youngster must know how to ski at least a little. The coach gives a brief test for this purpose. The youngest jumpers join the Winter Park Grasshoppers program, while more experienced skiers ages eight to eighteen enter the Winter Park Flyers program. Fortunately, Winter Park's Nordic Program is lighthearted enough for an occasional snowball fight, and there are neither roll calls nor other regimentation.

How do you create a young ski jumper? The novices first learn the basic aerodynamic position for the inrun, meaning the short chute spurt before take-off. They're taught the precise instant for leaping. They're shown how to stop safely and gracefully. When the youngsters are ready to make actual jumps, they always start with the smallest hills.

They only fly for a few feet at first, but they nonetheless get an idea of what it's like. A few novices may have their hearts in their throats. After a single leap, though, the kids like the flight so much that they come back for more. Most of the little jumpers feel like conquerors. "I'm a pilot!" they cry. "I'm a bird!" "Look at me! I'm a kite!"

A few jumps later they graduate to bigger hills, where they can zoom 30, 40, or more feet. In all, Winter Park has five jumping installations. The largest allows distances of 200 feet; here speeds of 55 miles per hour are normal. And from time to time, the winners battle it out at other Colorado ski areas as well. To be sent to Steamboat Springs or Summit County is a great honor, of course.

The jumping meets pack the greatest excitement, both for the young athletes and for the spectators. The eager, freckled faces, the colorful suits, the splashes of reds, greens, and blues of parkas and ski pants and caps are a delightful sight. Before each leap tension fills the thin, sweet mountain air. Up on top the eyes squint under big goggles. Competitors get last-minute advice from coaches. Six-year-olds wonder: Will they jump far enough? Will they look good enough in the air? Will they beat the competition?

These junior affairs are staged much like adult championships: The entrants wear bibs with starting numbers. The reporters are there; the ski patrol stands by in case of the rare sprain; the judges sit sternly in a tower, ready to compute results. The jumpers are judged not only by what distances they can reach but also by their style. They lose points, for instance, by standing straight after takeoff. (The jumper must be forward while in flight.) They lose points if their skis flutter in all directions. (The skis must be together.) They cannot win if their arms go like windmills. And they're evaluated for their landing—which should be steady—and for the ease of coming to a halt (no flailing hands).

This is the real thing, and even the tiniest of the fifty to seventy-five youngsters try to do their best. Afterward the kids get ribbons, and the year's final championship means a trophy for at least one jumper.

Some of the jumpers keep training until the sun goes down behind the darkened fir trees. The youngsters struggle upward to fling themselves into the sky, soaring and soaring. At a time when we're often told that the American youth is going soft, Winter Park must command attention. Soft? The fresh, scrubbed, entrancing faces may look it. But after one or two winters, these leaping children become as hard as the steel edges under their skis. Surely, some of them will do us proud in future Olympics!

For more information contact Competition Center, Winter Park Recreational Association, P.O. Box 36, Winter Park 80482; (970) 726–1588 or (303) 316–1588; www.skiwinterpark.com/competition/nordic.html.

Yampa Valley and Routt National Forest

In 1875 James Crawford, the first white settler of **Steamboat Springs,** arrived here from Missouri with two wagons, his family, his horses, and a few head of cattle. He was attracted to the area by a newspaper article. The author of the piece described his view from the top of the Park Mountain Range as "a wilderness of mountain peaks and beautiful valleys, dark forests and silvery streams—a deserted land except for immense herds of elk and deer and buffalo which had not yet learned by experience to shun the presence of man."

The Yampa Valley's idyllic setting and mild climate made the eventual "presence of man" inevitable. Even before Crawford built his log cabin along the west bank of Soda Creek, the Yampa Valley had sheltered Ute Indians and, later, French and English fur trappers.

Cattle ranchers had found Steamboat's emerald-green slopes ideal for fattening their herds en route to market. Hot and cold running water in the forms of three creeks, numerous hot springs, and the flow of the Yampa River lured more and more settlers to the valley.

Recreational skiing first came here in the early 1900s, when Norwegian Carl Howelson introduced the sports of ski jumping and ski racing to the community.

Before the turn of the century, they skied in "Ski Town U.S.A." facing Main Street on long boards, with a long staff, the women in long skirts. They jumped here from a giant hill before many other people thought of such things.

For years they've taught Steamboat youngsters to ski from kindergarten up, all through high school, and through the small local college. Men with first names like Alf, Ansten, Lars, and Ragnar showed off their telemark turns way back when, and Steamboat Springs skiers—immigrants as well as natives—showed the world what they were made of. Many Olympians cut their ski teeth here.

A Tour of Steamboat Springs

The giant **Steamboat Ski Area** caters to skiers of all abilities and to four-season travelers. Massive mountains with almost countless lifts, a prestigious ski school, and a top-notch ski patrol all add to this ski area's quality. All kinds of accommodations await in or on the edge of this handsome community, which sticks to its western image: You'll see plenty of jeans, Stetsons, cowboy boots, and saddles here.

Steamboat, also known as "Ski Town U.S.A.," is closer to Denver (153 miles) than Aspen (205 miles). From Denver, the three-hour drive follows I-70 west to the Silverthorne exit (exit 205). Head north on Highway 9 to Kremmling, and then west on US 40, which takes you over Rabbit Ears Pass and into Steamboat. Arrival by air is also possible; daily direct flights land at Yampa Valley Regional Airport, near Hayden, which is 22 miles from the ski area. The skiing starts in November and runs through April; open 8:30 A.M. to 3:30 P.M. daily. For more information contact Steamboat Ski & Resort Corporation, 2305 Mt. Werner Circle, Steamboat 80487; (970) 879-6111 or (877) 237-2628; www.steamboat.com.

Steamboat has an excellent ski school, of course, which operates 2 miles away on Mt. Werner and Storm Peak. A Ski Marching Band unfurls every February with an "oompah-oompah" during the **Steamboat Springs Winter Carnival,** one of the country's oldest ski festivals. It features skijoring, ski obstacle races, ski jumping, skiing with torches, ski parades, and ski balls. Call (970) 879–0880 for details.

> ## trivia
>
> Steamboat Springs probably received its name in the early 1800s from French trappers, who mistakenly thought that they heard the chugging steam engine of a steamboat. In fact, they were hearing a natural mineral spring.

At last, in the 1960s, the town was discovered by tourism, first by a giant Texas conglomerate, then by some private investors. In 1981 the real boom began.

Millions of dollars have since been invested in new ski lifts, new trails (and reshaping old ones), and other amenities. A Swiss gondola's eight-passenger car, the Silver Bullet, carries loads of skiers an hour up Thunderhead Mountain. The downhill skier can choose from 142 different trails, including the lengthy **Why Not Trail,** which meanders toward the valley from 9,080-foot Thunderhead Mountain. You ski along gentle logging roads and hiking trails that cut through sound-muffling conifer forests. The same trails make dandy walking paths in summer.

> ## trivia
>
> More Olympians—more than 50 in all—have emerged from Steamboat Springs than from any other town in the United States. The reason? World-class skiing, including the area's famed trademark, its Champagne Powder.

While downhill skiing is taught on a big scale here, cross-country skiing isn't neglected. The many programs even include a Citizens Cross-Country Race Camp for would-be competitors, many of them in their fifties and sixties.

The **Scandinavian Lodge** has varied but often pricy rates, commensurate with its facilities and prestige. For more information contact Pioneer Ridge Management at (800) 233–8102; www.steamboat-springs.com/resreq.html.

Steamboat does have springs. A walking tour downtown will take you past ten hot springs, easily identified by their pungent smell.

For a rustic hot springs experience, check out **Strawberry Park Natural Hot Springs,** located about 7 miles outside of downtown Steamboat Springs. With three main pools varying in temperature and gorgeous masonry construction—including five waterfalls—this special place warrants a visit. Recent additions include a stone steam house, a warm changing area, and picnic areas.

Strawberry Park has a small, warm pool for Watsu (water massage) and offers conventional massage services as well (both cost extra).

Reservations for cabins, a renovated train caboose, covered wagons, and tenting sites are available but should be made in advance. Strawberry Park Natural Hot Springs is open from 10:00 A.M. to 10:30 P.M. (admission until 9:30 P.M.) Sunday through Thursday, and 10:00 A.M. to midnight (admission until 10:30 P.M.) Friday and Saturday. Admission to the pools is $10.00 for adults, $5.00 for teenagers, $3.00 for children three to twelve. (Children younger than three free.) After dark, only adults are admitted. For more information call (970) 879–0342; www.strawberryhotsprings.com.

trivia

Ten national ski-jumping records have been set on Howelsen Hill.

Steamboat Springs is also home to one of the country's best automobile driving schools. But don't expect to learn how to parallel park here. The **Bridgestone Winter Driving School** is patterned after similar facilities at European ski resorts. In operation since 1983, the school is open from December 15 through March 10. The track is a snow-and ice-covered course with enough turns, loops, and straights to satisfy anyone who envisions being a race-car driver.

But this is not play. You often share your class with law enforcement officers and ambulance personnel. Although these people are professional drivers, they recognize the need for practice, and many return every year. But the novice is welcome here, too. One winter student was a homemaker from Atlanta, Georgia, who had never seen snow before.

For safety, the track is surrounded by high walls of soft snow. In case of a spinout—and there will be spinouts!—the snow guard walls catch the car and hold it safely with no injury to driver or machine.

Students are put into threatening positions and must learn how to stop on glare ice on a downhill slope and what to do when the car spins out of control. (No, you don't apply the brakes for this one, but the gas—and hard! It works.) After the one-day class, you will feel confident in your ability to avoid collisions due to ice- and snow-covered roads. Costs start at $155 for a half-day of instruction. For more information contact the Bridgestone Winter

trivia

Steamboat boasts more than 100 natural hot springs.

Driving School at (800) 949–7543; www.winterdrive.com. Classes are available in half-day and full-day sessions. Count on personalized small groups and video

Steamboat Water Sports

The Steamboat area is renowned for its variety of water sports options. It offers river floats, churning whitewater rafting, canoeing, sailing, and more.

Anglers will love **Steamboat Lake State Park,** which allows fly, lure, and bait fishing for its cutthroat and rainbow trout year-round with a Colorado fishing license. Take US 40 west through Steamboat Springs for 2 miles, and then turn north on County Road 129 and go another 26 miles. Cost is $5.00 for a vehicle day pass. For information call (970) 879–3922; www.parks.state.co.us.

Fishing licenses may be purchased from most sporting goods and convenience stores in Colorado. A one-day license costs $5.25 and a five-day license costs $18.25 for both residents and nonresidents. An annual fishing license costs $20.25 for residents and $40.25 for nonresidents.

Whitewater rafting is great on the nearby Yampa and Elk Rivers during the summer. There are a number of guiding services available. In Steamboat Springs contact the **Steamboat Rafting Company,** call (888) 888–7238 or (970) 879–6699; www .steamboat-rafting.com. Kayakers, too, can join in the fray. Contact **Mountain Sports Kayak School,** (970) 879–8794; www.mtsportskayak.com.

presentations. Instructors remain in constant contact with pupils by two-way radios. Well-qualified teachers monitor every movement from their separate cars, so the students are on their own. Cars spin and skid down a 1½-mile ice circuit. In fact, instructors claim that the more you spin, the more you learn!

Though Steamboat Springs has grown over the years (permanent year-round population is now nearly 9,000), it has retained its scenic beauty and western charm. Cattle ranching is still important, too. Lots of saddles, boots, and Stetsons are for sale in downtown Steamboat.

Typical for this western community is the ***Annual Cowboy Downhill,*** which takes place in January. Some one hundred genuine cowboys compete in a "ski rodeo" on the famous ski slopes. This involves a slalom on skis, the lassoing of pretty hostesses, and the saddling of a horse.

Those who come to visit or stay are drawn to many of the same qualities that caused James Crawford to settle in the valley.

Steamboat Springs is 170 miles west of Denver via US 40. For information on year-round Steamboat Springs, write or call Steamboat Springs Chamber Resort Association, P.O. Box 774408, Steamboat Springs 80477; (970) 879–0880; www.steamboatchamber.com.

The ***Vista Verde Guest & Ski Ranch*** sits at the end of a rugged road, 30 miles north of Steamboat Springs. It's one of the best such vacation places in the state. The staff is warm, helpful, eager to please, and experienced. Apart from horseback riding, this dude ranch offers supervised hiking, cycling, fly fishing, white-water rafting, and even rock-climbing instruction. Almost every Thursday balloon rides zoom the guests heavenward. In winter, you can cross-country ski here.

The summer staff consists of a small group of people who take care of the horses, the housekeeping, the office, and the kitchen, plus they are hiking guides. Every spring the application letters cascade onto owner John Munn's desk.

trivia

One of North America's largest elk herds ranges near Steamboat Springs.

The hiring procedure is by telephone—long interviews and reference checks. What does Munn look for? "The work ethic," he says. "The love of the outdoors. Real caring for the guests." Much of the staff is versatile and interchangeable; the Vista Verde's bookkeeper, for instance, helps clean the rooms. The staff brings strong background experience to their jobs, guaranteeing that you'll be in the care of experts.

The typical wrangler knows how to shoe horses, how to treat the sick ones, and how to please the others. He or she knows a dozen horse tricks. One Oklahoman spends so much time around the hoofed creatures—his real love—that he has been stepped on, backed into, and severely kicked by horses. A few years ago, three of his ribs were broken by one of his animals. The rancher spent a week in the hospital, cursing and cussing. Yet he wouldn't

Downhill All the Way

No, I'm not talking about skiing, but about the annual *Steamboat Springs Marathon,* which takes place in early June. Starting out at an elevation of 8,128 feet and finishing at 6,728 feet, the marathon really is mostly downhill, but don't let that fool you. Though *Runner's World* cited this course as one of the "10 Most Scenic Marathons of the Year" (February 1996) and one of the "Top Ten Destination Marathons in North America" (March 1999), it's still quite a challenge. I found this out when I ran my first marathon here in 1998. After finishing, I soaked my aching body at nearby Strawberry Park Natural Hot Springs—a destination of choice for many marathoners, who were easily discerned by their stiff-legged gaits as they staggered and groaned their way down the stairs and into the pools.

Sign up early for the marathon, which is limited to 500 runners. For more information call (970) 879–0880 or visit www.runningseries.com.

give it all up for anything. His nostrils love the sweet smell of hay and manure, and his ears like to pick up the comforting, caressing sound of horses feeding.

Munn bought the 600-acre former homestead with the environment in mind: He immediately buried the power lines and other utilities underground to enhance the beauty of the high-altitude landscape. Guests sleep in a dozen authentic log cabins or in a deluxe lodge room. John's wife personally decorated these spacious units.

Shortly after dawn one morning, Vista Verde's chief wrangler and an assistant headed up the hill past the golden aspen trees to the pasture where the horses grazed. "Time for the corral!" the wrangler told them, as though the creatures could understand. Later, the horses saddled, the red-shirted dude-ranch staff helped the guests mount for a morning ride. To the staff's surprise, this group of ten new arrivals had lots of riding experience. The wrangler trotted ahead, cantering along the winding trail. The western sky was perfectly blue, and a smell of sage was in the air. The colored mountains ascended gently toward more forests. "Lucky you," one of the guests said to the head wrangler, "spending your summers up here!"

For more information contact Vista Verde Guest & Ski Ranch, Inc., P.O. Box 465, Steamboat Springs 80477; (800) 526–7433; www.vistaverde.com.

Steamboat Springs is 170 miles west of Denver; if you keep driving west on US 40 past Craig and Maybell, you will eventually reach the out-of-the-way *Dinosaur National Monument.* It straddles the Utah border. You get to it via the small town of Blue Mountain, or via Dinosaur, another small town. On US 40 the signs will proclaim the WELCOME CENTER AT DINOSAUR. You soon see the visitor center; as you keep driving north, you'll understand why some Colorado folk call the area a Jurassic Park. This is dinosaur fossil bone country. Of course, not everyone is overwhelmed by skeletons of sauropods, stegosauruses, or other dinosaurs. But it's hard to ignore a magnificent natural landscape of giant

Sans Skis—Summer in Steamboat

Summers guarantee an adrenaline rush. The breaking in of wild horses, the barrel-racing on horseback, the sound of galloping hooves through forest clearings, are all exciting. Climbers have scaled the rock faces of *Rabbit Ears Pass.* And of course you can reach the Mount Werner summits in style by gondola and then test your leg muscles against the long downhill walks—or runs—through knee-high meadows or on logging roads.

sandstone cliffs, gray-green sage bushes, juniper, and piñon pine. Moreover, this land is laced with hiking trails. And the spectacular Yampa River is never far away. The visitor center in Colorado for Dinosaur National Monument is open daily in summer, closed on weekends and holidays in winter (hours vary according to season) and requires no entry fee (but no fossils can be seen here). Exhibits and a ten-minute orientation are available for viewing. For more information contact Dinosaur National Monument, 4545 East Highway 40, Dinosaur 81610; (970) 374–3000; www.nps.gov/dino. An entry fee ($10 per vehicle) is required only in Utah at the Dinosaur Quarry area.

Places to Stay in the Northwestern Mountains

The rating scale for hotels is based on double occupancy and is as follows:
Inexpensive:
Less than $75 per night
Moderate:
$75 to $100 per night
Expensive:
$100 to $150 per night
Deluxe:
More than $150 per night

ESTES PARK

Holiday Inn,
101 South Saint Vrain Avenue;
(970) 586–2332
Inexpensive to expensive

Ponderosa Lodge,
1820 Fall River Road;
(970) 586–4233 or
(800) 628–0512
www.estes-park.com/
ponderosa
Moderate to expensive

The Stanley Hotel,
333 Wonderview;
(970) 586–3371 or
(800) 976–1377
www.stanleyhotel.com
Deluxe

YMCA of the Rockies,
Estes Park Center;
(970) 586–3341 or
(303) 448–1616
www.ymcarockies.org
Inexpensive to moderate

GRANBY

C Lazy U Ranch,
from Granby, 3 miles west on US 40, then 4 miles northwest on CO 125;
(970) 887–3344
www.clazyu.com
Deluxe

Devil's Thumb Ranch,
P.O. Box 750,
Tabernash 80478;
(800) 933–4339
www.devilsthumbranch.com
Inexpensive

GRAND LAKE

Grand Lake Lodge,
15500 US 34;
(970) 627–3967
www.grandlakelodge.com
Inexpensive to deluxe

Western Riviera Motel and Cabins,
419 Garfield Street;
(970) 627–3580
www.westernriviera.com
Moderate to expensive

STEAMBOAT SPRINGS

Alpiner Lodge,
424 Lincoln Avenue;
(970) 879–1430 or
(800) 340–9169
www.rockymountainfun.com/
alpinelodge.html
Inexpensive to expensive

Best Western Inn,
2304 Apres Ski Way;
(970) 879–1730 or
(800) 538–7519
Inexpensive to deluxe

Scandinavian Lodge,
2883 Burgess Creek Road;
(800) 233–8102
www.steamboat-springs
.com/
resreq.phtml
Moderate to deluxe

Sky Valley Lodge,
31490 US Highway 40;
(970) 879–7749 or
(800) 538–7519
Moderate

OTHER ATTRACTIONS WORTH SEEING IN THE NORTHWESTERN MOUNTAINS

ESTES PARK

Big Thompson Canyon,
(970) 498–1100
www.fs.fed.us/r2/arnf/

Cascade Creek Miniature Golf,
(970) 586–6495
www.rideakart.com

Enos Mills Cabin Museum Center,
(970) 586–4706
www.home.earthlink.net/~enosmillscbn/
index.htm

Estes Park Area Historical Museum,
(970) 586–6256
www.estesnet.com/museum

Estes Park Ride-a-Kart,
(970) 586–6495
www.rideakart.com

GRANBY

Arapaho National Forest,
(970) 498–1100
www.fs.fed.us/r2/arnf

SolVista Golf & Ski Ranch,
(800) 757–7669
www.solvista.com

STEAMBOAT SPRINGS

Haymaker Golf Course,
(970) 870–1846
www.haymakergolf.com

Howelsen Ice Arena (ice skating),
(970) 879–0341
www.rockymountainfun.com/
iceskate.html

Routt National Forest,
(307) 745–2300 or (970) 879–1870
www.fs.fed.us/r2/mbr

Tread of Pioneers Museum,
(970) 879–2214

WINTER PARK

A Maze'n Winter Park
(two-level giant labyrinth),
(888) 909–6293

Children's Center
(ski center for children),
(970) 726–1551
www.winterparkresort.com/activities/
familyresortactivities.html

**Vista Verde Guest &
Ski Ranch,**
(800) 526–7433
www.vistaverde.com
Deluxe

WINTER PARK

Alpine Resort Properties,
P.O. Box 66, 80482;
(800) 797–2750 or
(970) 726–9690
www.alpineresort
properties.com
Moderate to deluxe

**Beaver Village
Condominiums,**
P.O. Box 349, 80482;
(800) 824–8438
www.beavercondos.com
Moderate to deluxe

**Hi Country Haus Resort
Condominiums,**
P.O. Box 66, 80482,
(800) 797–2750 or
(970) 726–8822
www.alpineresort
properties.com
Moderate to deluxe

**MeadowRidge
Condominiums,**
P.O. Box 66, 80482;
(800) 797–2750 or
(970) 726–8822
www.alpineresort
properties.com
Moderate to deluxe

The Vintage Resort,
100 Winter Park Road;
(970) 726–8801 or
(800) 472–7017
www.vintagehotel.com
Moderate to deluxe

**YMCA of the Rockies,
Snow Mountain Ranch,**
P.O. Box 169;
(970) 887–2152 or
(303) 443–4743
www.ymcarockies.org
Inexpensive to moderate

Places to Eat in the Northwestern Mountains

The rating scale for restaurants is as follows:
Inexpensive:
Most entrees less than $10
Moderate:
Most entrees $10 to $15
Expensive:
Most entrees $15 to $20
Deluxe:
Most entrees more than $20

ESTES PARK

Mama Rose's, (Italian)
338 East Elkhorn Avenue;
(970) 586–3330
www.mamaroses.com
Moderate to expensive

Nicky's, (Greek, Italian; near park entrance)
1350 Fall River Road West;
(970) 586–5376
Inexpensive

Timberline Family Restaurant,
(American food; kids' menu)
451 South Saint Vrain Avenue;
(970) 586–9840
Moderate to expensive

Twin Owls Steakhouse at Black Canyon Inn
(continental),
800 MacGregor Avenue;
(970) 586–9344
Expensive to deluxe

GRANBY

Longbranch Restaurant,
(German-American; eclectic menu)
185 East Agate;
(970) 887–2209
Inexpensive to moderate

GRAND LAKE

Waconda Restaurant and Bar, (fondue, pasta, Chinese buffet)
725 Grand Avenue;
(970) 627–8312
Moderate to expensive

STEAMBOAT SPRINGS

Antares, (continental)
57½ Eighth Street;
(970) 879–9939
Expensive to deluxe

L'Apogée, (French)
911 Lincoln Avenue;
(970) 879–1919
www.lapogee.com
Expensive to deluxe

La Montaña,
(Mexican, Southwestern)
2500 Village Drive;
(970) 879–5800
Moderate to expensive

Mazzola's Italian Restaurant,
(large portions; well-known; authentic Italian)
917 Lincoln Avenue;
(970) 879–2405
www.mazzolas.com
Moderate

Ore House at the Pine Grove
(steak, seafood, game)
1465 Pine Grove Road;
(970) 879–1190
www.orehousealpine grove.com
Expensive to deluxe

WINTER PARK

Carlos and Maria's,
(Mexican)
Cooper Creek Square;
(970) 726–9674
Moderate

Dezeley's at Gasthaus Eichler
(European, continental)
78786 US Highway 40;
(970) 726–5133
www.gasthauseichler.com/restaurant.html
Expensive to deluxe

Rome on the Range Restaurant & Saloon,
(steak, wild game, pasta, 20 beers on tap)
78491 US Highway 40;
(970) 726–1111
Moderate to expensive

SELECTED NORTHWESTERN MOUNTAINS GENERAL INFORMATION RESOURCES

ESTES PARK

Estes Park Chamber
Resort Association,
500 Big Thompson Avenue, 80517;
(970) 586–4431 or (800) 443–7837
www.estesparkresort.com

GRANBY

Greater Granby Area Chamber
of Commerce,
P.O. Box 35, 80446;
(970) 887–2311 or (800) 325–1661
www.rkymtnhi.com/granbycoc

GRAND LAKE

Grand Lake Area Chamber
of Commerce,
P.O. Box 57, 80447;
(970) 627–3402 or (800) 531–1019
www.grandlakechamber.com

STEAMBOAT SPRINGS

Steamboat Springs Chamber Resort
Association,
P.O. Box 774408, 80477;
(970) 879–0880
www.steamboatchamber.com

WINTER PARK

Winter Park/Fraser Valley Chamber
of Commerce,
P.O. Box 3236, 80482;
(800) 903–7275 or (970) 726–4118
www.winterpark-info.com

Western Mountains

Beyond the Front Range

"The forests are shouting with color," John Steinbeck once wrote. It's the sudden September frost that produces the spectacle that exalts Coloradans and brings them out of their homes and offices autumn after autumn. Look into the local newspapers; follow the color photographers, the Sunday painters, the young couples. Exodus to the Rockies! See the aspen trees! The leaves suddenly turn on like so many bright lights. They dazzle. They glow among the deep green of the firs. There are entire aspen forests in these mountains.

The largest groves generally are found between elevations of 8,000 and 10,000 feet. Colors start at the higher elevations and spread their way down as the season progresses. A bright golden yellow predominates, with varying shades of brilliant reds, browns, and oranges interspersed with the green of the slower-changing leaves and the surrounding conifers.

There is something lyrical about these "quaking" trees when you're alone among them; the golden leaves tremble in the slight breeze, make a gentle sound of applause, talk to themselves, or send messages to the wild raspberry bushes. You'll see gold and copper all over the state from the end of

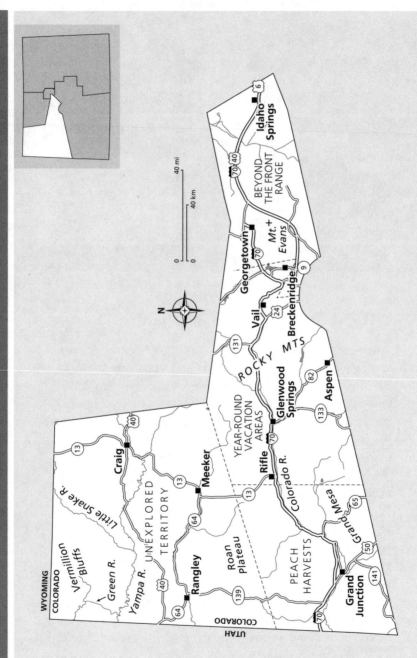

September through early October. In Aspen itself, in Winter Park, along the Rampart Range Road from Colorado Springs to Sedalia, beside the Peak-to-Peak Highway between Nederland and Allenspark, west of Boulder. "Aren't the aspen beautiful?" people ask, setting out to see them before winter blows down from the Rockies. Of course, it depends on how much time you have. Six hours? A day? Two? Then consider a good circle tour: Denver, Idaho Springs, Silver Plume, Breckenridge, Fairplay, Denver. No toll roads. Easy motoring.

Begin with U.S. Highway 6, all the more spectacular because it's been carved out of deep canyons, where the upper rocks are highlighted by the sun. It takes you up to the little mountain community of Idaho Springs (altitude 7,540 feet), on Interstate 70, with the peaks rising on both sides. The aspen trees shine like so many lamps among the fir and spruce, and after you're through Georgetown (which is well worth a visit), you seem to be in the Alps.

The mountains go up steeply now, and the valley is narrow. For a breath-taking experience, skip the Eisenhower Memorial Tunnel—weather permitting, of course—and break off again onto Highway 6, climbing up to **Loveland Pass** and the Continental Divide (11,990 feet). The views are unbeatable from up here, so take some time to get out of your car and take in the sights. After-ward, cruise down toward the Dillon Reservoir. The sun skips across these lake

AUTHOR'S FAVORITES IN THE WESTERN MOUNTAINS

Clark Family Orchards,
(970) 464–5385
www.palisadecoc.com

Georgetown,
(303) 569–2840
www.historicgeorgetown.org

Glenwood Canyon,
(888) 4–GLENWOOD
www.glenscape.com

Gore Range/Pass,
(970) 638–4516
www.fs.fed.us/r2/mbr/about/districts/
yampa.shtml

Lake Dillon Recreational Area,
(970) 468–5100
www.dillonmarina.com

Mt. Evans,
(303) 567–3000
www.mtevans.com

Museum of Western Colorado's Cross Orchards Living History Museum,
(970) 434–9814
www.wcmuseum.org/crossorchards.htm

Rifle Falls State Park,
(970) 625–1607
www.parks.state.co.us

Town of Vail Library,
(970) 479–2184
www.vaillibrary.com

Tumbling River Ranch,
(303) 838–5981 or (800) 654–8770
www.tumblingriver.com

Colorado Dangers

Colorado is renowned for its afternoon thunderstorms, which proliferate during the early summer months but are possible year-round. For this reason, outdoor activities—particularly those that involve a long time commitment away from safe shelter—should be undertaken only with careful planning and attention to time. If you do happen to find yourself caught in a thunderstorm, take refuge in a car (with the windows up) or a substantial building—not a shallow cave or rock outcropping. If no safe shelter is available, seek a low-lying area or trench with shrubs or trees of similar stature. Avoid lone trees, open spaces, higher ground, water, and contact with two different objects (such as rock and ground). Also maintain a 15-foot distance from others. Crouch low to the ground with both of your feet together and cover your ears. For more safety tips, visit the National Lightning Safety Institute's Web site at www.lightningsafety.com.

Flash flooding can pose a real danger in narrow canyons, even on days that begin with clear skies and sunny weather. Be sure to check weather reports for thunderstorm predictions and always have a backup plan. Disastrous flash flooding is a real danger.

As you probably know, drinking water from lakes, rivers, and streams is not exactly the same wilderness treat it once was. Unless you want to find out just how nasty a bout of giardiasis can be—think diarrhea, violent stomach cramps, and hospital visits—avoid drinking water from lakes, streams, or rivers unless you purify it first. Try to bring adequate drinking water (minimum of two liters per person per day), as well as effective water purification paraphernalia, which can be purchased from area sporting-goods stores. You can also purify water by boiling it for at least twenty minutes to kill all disease-causing organisms.

waters with their small marina sailboats, fishing boats, and canoes. In Frisco swing left onto Highway 9, which circles this handsome reservoir. You encounter grasslands now, in shades of gold, brown, and green, which lead to the pivot of the tour—Breckenridge!

This little mining community is once more on the verge of a bonanza. In 1859, it was gold. Now it's real estate and second homes for airline people or retired corporation presidents, and skiers. Yet, you couldn't tell this boom from the looks and feeling here. Breckenridge remains congenial, unpretentious, informal, western. Children run across silent brown-pine needles, and teenagers fish for trout in the transparent Blue River.

It's peaceful again as you drive through thick forests past beaver ponds to little-known, ever-so-gentle **Hoosier Pass.** Golden brown-yellow meadows and faded green lichened rocks provide a feast for the eyes, and there's hardly a house in sight. Impressive 14,000-foot peaks surround you—Quandary Peak,

Mt. Lincoln, Mt. Sherman—as you head into Placer Valley, where the aspen trees brighten the pine woods. With a population of 500, Fairplay is the "big" town now, but you're through quickly, heading north on U.S. Highway 285. Suddenly, clouds darken this bright-blue sky; a quick autumn rain. The horses and cows and sheep stand patiently in these darkening fields while the water pours down. Half an hour later, along the South Platte River, the sun bursts through the trees again. At Grant, US 285 narrows and curves along the river past nice campsites that you'd expect to be full but aren't. (There are few tourists after Labor Day.) All the way to Denver, the names spell nature, forest, Colorado: Pine Junction, Deer Creek, Conifer, Indian Hills, Aspen Park.

A few last golden aspen trees are followed by the russets and reds of maples and oaks. Then Morrison, where the orchards are thick with purple apples. At the lower altitude, and out of the mountains, the air warms you once more. After some 175 miles the Colorado circle tour ends where it began. But what a six-hour world between!

TOP ANNUAL EVENTS IN THE WESTERN MOUNTAINS

Wintersköl Carnival,
Aspen; mid-January;
(970) 925–1940
www.aspenchamber.org/htdocs/
winterskol.cfm

Aspen Music Festival,
June through August;
(970) 925–9042
www.aspenmusicfestival.com

Breckenridge Music Festival,
June through August;
(970) 547–3100
www.breckenridgemusicfestival.com

Strawberry Days,
Glenwood Springs; mid-June;
(970) 945–6589
www.strawberrydaysfestival.com

Annual XTERRA Off-Road Triathlon,
Keystone; mid-July;
(877) 751–8880
www.xterra.net/race/

Gold Rush Days Festival,
Idaho Springs; mid-summer;
(303) 567–4660

Peach Festival,
Palisade; mid-August;
(970) 464–7458
www.palisadecoc.com/

Beaver Creek Oktoberfest,
Vail; mid-September;
(970) 845–9090
www.beavercreek.snow.com

Annual Fall Art Festival,
Glenwood Springs;
last week in September;
(970) 945–2414
www.glenwoodchamber.com

Little-Known Facts about Idaho Springs

Some of Colorado's earliest gold strikes took place here in 1859.

The Ute Indians were the first to discover and use its famous hot springs.

Idaho Springs is home to the world's longest mining tunnel. The 5-mile-long tunnel once ran all the way to Central City, another gold-rush town. Unfortunately, only a portion of the tunnel remains, and it is not open to the public.

The highway that runs to the summit of Mt. Evans from Idaho Springs is the highest paved driving road in North America.

From US 6, west of Denver, follow I–70 to US 6 to Frisco, then Highway 9 through Breckenridge to Fairplay, from where you return to Denver via US 285.

From Denver, it's a nearby trip to *Idaho Springs.*

Stroll along Idaho Springs's short main street. Step into a leather shop that features beaver hats and into a little rock store that also sells gems and beads.

Late-hour drivers should keep in mind that the local motels, while not fancy, are among the lowest-priced in Colorado. If you reach the area around dinner time, Idaho Springs's *BeauJo's Pizza* is well-known in Colorado for its varieties and its "pizza by the pound." You can build your own pizza here as well. 1517 Miner Street; (303) 567–4376; www.beaujos.com. Open Sunday through Thursday from 11:00 A.M. to 9:00 P.M. and Friday and Saturday from 11:00 A.M. to 10:00 P.M.

Another dinner option is the historic, western-style *Buffalo Restaurant and Bar,* which serves up wholesome Colorado-style fare. Try any of the buffalo entrees. Salads are also fresh and tasty. 1617 Miner; (303) 567–2729; www.buffalorestaurant.com. Open Monday through Friday from 11:00 A.M. to 10:00 P.M. and Saturday and Sunday from 10:30 A.M. to 10:00 P.M.

Strike Gold! At the *Phoenix Gold Mine,* located at the west end of Idaho Springs, you and your children can try your hand at what brought thousands of men to Colorado back in the 1800s . . . gold panning!

The only working gold mine in Colorado that is open to the public, here you can do it all. Take a tour guided by the actual miners. Better yet, dig your own samples—you even get to keep what you score! Gold panning costs $5.00 per person, which is included in the price if you take a tour. Walking tours cost $5.00 for children under twelve and $9.00 for adults. Open from 10:00 A.M. to 6:00 P.M. daily, weather permitting in winter. Added bonuses: There is a picnic area for those who work up their appetites panning all that gold, and bring your camera—you're allowed to take pictures.

NOTE: The temperature in the mine is only 50° to 55° F, so you'll need to dress accordingly.

To get to the Phoenix Gold Mine, take I–70 eastbound to exit 239, and then take Stanley Road southwest to Trail Creek Road. For more information call (303) 567–0422 or write P.O. Box 3236, Idaho Springs 80452; www.phoenixmine.com.

"It was awesome," commented one visitor. "We looked down at the passing clouds. You felt as though you'd reached the top of the world."

The traveler was referring to the highest paved auto road in the United States, which leads from Idaho Springs, west of Denver, to the top of 14,264-foot-high **Mt. Evans.** The mountain first attracted gold-hungry prospectors during the nineteenth century and was named in 1870 after Governor John Evans. A few years earlier, the famous artist Albert Bierstadt and a friend had climbed it. The climb inspired Bierstadt, whose paintings express the grandeur of this and other high Colorado peaks.

The road to the top of the mountain is usually opened in May and stays open until the first significant snowfall of the year—meaning that if you want to tackle the peak in winter, you'll need to plan accordingly by packing snowshoes or cross-country skis and having the necessary wilderness skills to do so safely. Once the road has been opened for the season, it is accessible twenty-four hours a day. Cost is $10.00 for a three-day vehicle pass, on sale at the entrance station. There is also a mechanical collection station that accepts cash ($1.00, $5.00, $10.00 bills) and credit cards; it will issue you a valid pass. Any sunny summer day will do to make your drive up to the summit, but weekdays are preferable if you want to avoid the crowds. In addition, visiting very early or very late in the day ups your odds of seeing the abundant fauna that call Mt. Evans home.

If you're starting your journey in Denver, you can choose to approach the mountain via Bergen Park and return via Idaho Springs, or vice versa. Expect to see stunning Colorado scenery along the way, including large, fertile meadows, dense lodgepole pine forests, aspen trees, ponderosa pine, Douglas fir, and thick bushes of wild raspberries, as well as the occasional chipmunk or squirrel.

Placid **Echo Lake** makes for a nice stopping point en route to the summit. Get out of the car, stretch out your legs, and perhaps enjoy a picnic lunch while you watch families angling for trout and hikers setting out for the trails that captivated Bierstadt so many years ago. If you're visiting after Thanksgiving, expect to see a vast frozen expanse—the lake freezes completely, and you can skate across it on narrow cross-country skis, reaching numerous trails that yield great views. But even in summer, it gets cool up here, so dress warmly and bring extra layers. Theoretically, for every 1,000 feet of elevation gain in the Rockies, you can compare your journey to traveling 200 miles north. Of course, this means you get to experience the cooler air in each zone on the way up, not to mention the shifting vegetation. Above Echo Lake, you can follow trails through alpine tundra, stopping to study the small grasses, sedges, herbs, and the almost microscopic plants with their teeny flowers.

If you take a close look at the ancient bristlecone pines, you will read the story of their struggle for survival in these unfriendly high-altitude settings. Each and every dwarfed bristlecone or leaning Douglas fir shows the signs of withstanding blizzards and summer storms as well as coping with blazing sunlight followed by rains. This harsh weather destroys most exposed buds and conifer seeds, limiting the trees' reproduction. Some trees are bent and twisted from the relentless wind, while others are bleached from the sun or blackened and split by lightning strikes. At timberline, the already small array of trees becomes even sparser, with only single, isolated soldiers standing to face the sky's hail cannons.

Above timberline, in Colorado's alpine life zone, the fauna changes, too. Marmots often show themselves, as well as the occasional ptarmigan. Mountain goats are frequently seen up here, and once in a while you'll spot a bighorn sheep. ("Don't feed them," advises the U.S. Forest Service. "They sometimes bite.")

Mt. Evans' upper reaches are also dotted with lakes. At 11,700 feet, you'll spot Lincoln Lake; it's 800 feet below the highway. Then at 12,830 feet, Summit Lake awaits, complete with a short trail overlooking the picturesque Chicago Lakes, some 1,400 feet below. The Forest Service warns parents not to let their children run around in this area due to the sudden drop-offs—the highway has few guardrails.

Finally, complete the motorized journey by pulling into the parking lot at 14,130 feet. Get out of your car and hike that last 134-foot gain in altitude to the summit via a ¼-mile hike along a trail. Catch your breath—the air is much thinner up here than it is on the plains, so visitors from the flatlands should walk slowly and take in the scenery. From the summit, the views are tremendous.

Start your tour on I–70. Take exit 240 in Idaho Springs onto the Mt. Evans Highway (Highway 103). After Echo Lake, head onto Highway 5, which will take you to the summit. For a change of pace, continue west along Highway 103 to Bergen Park, and then take Highway 74 and I–70 to Denver. The distances are moderate—it's only 28 miles from Idaho Springs to the summit of Mt. Evans. For more information call the Clear Creek Ranger Station at (303) 567–3000 or write to the CCRD Visitor Information Center, P.O. Box 3307, Idaho Springs 80452; www.mtevans.com.

Idaho Springs is home to the ***Edgar Experimental Mine,*** where students and faculty from the Golden-based Colorado School of Mines try their

hands at traditional mining methods and put to use the most recent technological advances. Open to the public for tours from early June through late
August. Admission is $6.00 for adults, $4.00 for seniors, and $3.00 for chil-
dren ages six to sixteen. Call ahead to reserve a tour: (303) 567–2911 or visit
www.mines.edu/academic/mining/edgar.html. Write to 365 Eighth Avenue,
P.O. Box 1184, Idaho Springs 80452

In autumn the wind whistles through the well-kept streets of **Georgetown,**
rattling the windows of the impeccable Victorian houses. The winter snows
pile up high here, and spring is slow to come at an elevation of 8,500 feet
above sea level. The mountains rise so steeply on all four sides of Georgetown
that even the summers are cool; the sun shines for only a few hours a day.

Yet, this community 45 miles west of Denver has more ambience, more
sightseeing, and more genuine concern for its own history than most other
Colorado cities. It is special in its own way. The city officials have spent six-
figure sums to rebuild and preserve the pink-brick houses, the old-time
saloons, and the museums that conjure up the nineteenth century of gold and
silver riches. The antiques shops, silversmiths, and weavers are among the best
in the state. The craft shops are different, real, worth browsing in, and much
better than those of Vail or other fancy ski resorts to the west.

Loveland in Wintertime—or All Year Long

Loveland Ski Area—which is not near the city by the same name—has always been
a favorite ski spot for Denverites. And for good reason. A big plus is Loveland's
proximity—just 55 miles from Denver via I-70. There are no passes to cross and
no Eisenhower Tunnels, either (which Loveland publicists call "a big bore").

Snowboarding sure can wake you up, and Loveland Ski Area has excellent instructors.
So, if you've been skiing your whole life, try it! Skiing and snowboarding, though
related, are different experiences, and it's definitely worth it to discover the distinction.
For information on taking lessons in snowboarding from Loveland's friendly and
skilled instructors call (303) 571–5580, ext. 163.

Do it before it's too late, though—the ski center shuts down in late spring, and
since Loveland Ski Area does not operate hotels or offer condominiums, the area
essentially shuts down when the snow melts. It's still worth a day trip, though. In
summer the slopes fill up with mountain flowers and freelance hikers.

For more information contact Loveland Ski Area, P.O. Box 899, Georgetown 80444;
(800) 736–3754; www.skiloveland.com. Loveland Ski Area is open from November
through April; lift ticket prices run from $20 to $43.

Unlike Vail, which rose from a cow pasture, Georgetown is a historic community. And proud of it.

On a clear spring day in 1859, two prospecting brothers, George and David Griffith, struggled their way up Clear Creek searching for minerals. Unsuccessful at the other mining camps in Colorado, the two prospectors reached out for new, untried land, and this time they had luck—they found gold.

After the discovery the Griffith brothers did a highly unusual thing for gold or silver seekers—instead of just digging up the mountain and leaving with their wealth, they brought their entire family out from Kentucky to live permanently in their valley. The tiny settlement they founded became known as George's Town, and although no more significant strikes were made, it grew steadily for five years.

trivia

Two historic Georgetown homes, the Bowman-White House and the Hamill House, exemplify the city's Victorian style. See the Web site www.historicgeorgetown.org.

Then in 1864 assays showed an extremely high silver content. The boom was on. Over the next thirty years, the mines in and around the town produced more than $200 million worth of silver. The town became known as the Silver Queen of the Mountains—and in 1868 it was renamed Georgetown.

By 1880 some 10,000 people made the city their home. Fortunes, houses, and reputations flourished. Elaborate mansions attested to wealth. Hotels served the finest cuisine in gilt rooms with elegant furniture. An opera house brought Broadway productions and favorite classical operas to the wealthy.

All this came to an abrupt end; the silver panic of 1893 hit hard, with silver prices dropping to almost nothing. Mines, mills, and livelihoods vanished. The town became a ghost of its past glory.

Georgetown languished this way for more than six decades. Then tourism came, and interstate highways transported millions of travelers to the high mountains.

A historic transportation mode was reconstructed to bring these tourists to Georgetown. The **Georgetown Loop Railroad** was originally completed in 1877. The goal of the railroad company was to reach another mining boom town—Leadville.

They never made it. Instead, the workers pushed on just another 2 miles to Silver Plume, a mining camp up the valley. Even this short distance created difficult engineering problems.

Just 2 miles away, Silver Plume was 600 feet higher in elevation. To complete the spur to the next mountain stop, the rail tracks had to cover 4½ miles.

As the automobile gained popularity and the mining industry collapsed, the Loop was abandoned. The bridge and rails were used as scrap metal. The spur was forgotten and overgrown with weeds for thirty-five years.

Then the Colorado Historical Society stepped in, bought the land, and set about the major task of rebuilding the tracks and the bridge. In 1984 the new Devil's Gate Bridge was opened. The Georgetown Loop ran until October 2004 under one company's ownership; a new owner may take over the rail line. For more information visit www.georgetowncolorado.com.

Unlike other Colorado mining towns, Georgetown was never totally destroyed by fire, so today it has more than 200 carefully preserved historic buildings.

Luckily, too, Georgetown passed a historic preservation ordinance many years ago. The local historical society is serious about its purpose. One of Georgetown's landmarks is the French-style **Hotel de Paris Museum,** full of Tiffany fixtures, lace curtains, and hand-carved furniture. Open from Memorial Day through September 10:00 A.M. to 5:00 P.M., and on weekends from October to Memorial Day 10:00 A.M. to 5:00 P.M. Donations requested. Call (303) 569–2311; www.georgetowncolorado.com/museums.htm.

Georgetown has several Victorian mansions worth seeing. During the first two December weekends, a well-known Christmas market with small booths and outdoor stalls beckons.

Georgetown enjoys a good location for travelers who plan to explore the Continental Divide in summer or Colorado ski country in winter. A one-night stay in fall or spring is equally worthwhile. Consider the **Alpine Hideaway Bed and Breakfast** for its coziness, attention to detail, peace and quiet, and mountain vistas. The decor here includes sheepskins, potted palm trees, dollhouses, orchids, and a fireplace in every room. Dawn Janov, the enthusiastic owner, fairly showers guests with goodies like Swiss chocolates and bedtime

trivia

A mysterious Frenchman named Louis Dupuy originally ran the Hotel de Paris; some Georgetown people say he left a large family in France.

liqueurs. Breakfast pampering includes guava, papaya, ripe cantaloupe, kiwi slices, pancakes, quiches, and strong coffee—all left discreetly in front of your door. The Alpine Hideaway is located on a lone 8,500-foot promontory at 2045 Blue Bird Drive. Write to P.O. Box 788, Georgetown 80444 or call (303) 569–2800 or (800) 490–9011; www.georgetowncolorado.com/alpinehideaway.htm. Hikers will be delighted with nearby trails to old mines; drivers can motor to the 11,600-foot Guanella Pass, which is visible from the bed-and-breakfast.

Georgetown Fishing

The lakes in this area are often crowded during the summer, with the exception of **Silver Dollar Lake.** A somewhat steep jaunt on foot leads off the beaten path to the lake, which yields good catches and offers peace and quiet. From Georgetown, head 8½ miles south on Guanella Pass Road. Turn right at the SILVER DOLLAR LAKE sign.

Georgetown is about an hour west of Denver via I–70. For information about Georgetown, write to the Downtown Georgetown Community Center, 613 Sixth Street, P.O. Box 834, Georgetown 80444; (303) 569–2888 or (800) 472–8230; www.georgetowncolorado.com.

Want to taste a real flavor of life in the Old West? Then plan to take your vacation at one of Colorado's dude ranches.

The horse trip leads to a sunny meadow full of wildflowers, passing a few ghost houses, with caved-in roofs and sagging walls, the wood evenly bleached by the sun. Later the party rides on. There is an excited breathlessness about the journey as it takes them across two brooks, through thickets of willows and other bushes, and then slowly down a steep, rocky slope. The riders move with caution, savoring a touch of the primitive. They are in tune with the mountain and alone with their thoughts. It is quiet except for the slight creak of the leather saddles and the clicking of the hooves.

The vacationers are far away from the high-rises and superhighways. The riders arrive for breakfast at a sunny forest clearing. Everyone sits down on long logs. The coffee steams. The cowboys fry eggs for all. The mountains say good morning.

Ask other travelers to share their experiences with you. They'll speak about the informality, the privacy, and the utter friendliness of Colorado's guest ranches. What with an average of fifteen to about one hundred guests, the mood is calm and relaxed, and the owners really care about you. Families, couples, and newlyweds are pampered. If you arrive with a large party, you can write ahead for spacious quarters. At some hostelries you can also rent cabins.

The names say much: C Lazy U Ranch, Tumbling River Ranch, Peaceful Valley Ranch. They are all endearing places set in romantic, isolated Colorado locations. Some of them still breed cattle or horses.

A Colorado dude-ranch vacation is one of the most satisfying, genuine holidays available today. The air is clean, days are warm, evenings cool, and the mountain scenery absolutely spectacular.

At first primitive, the accommodations now range from rustic to deluxe ratings, such as Five Star by Mobil travel guides and Exceptional by AAA (American Automobile Association).

Colorado boasts some forty dude ranches, generally located in the scenic mountain regions. Activities are varied and informal. Life on the ranch resort is geared for the ultimate in easy relaxation. Guests are encouraged to set their own pace.

The essence of these cowboy-style vacations becomes clear when you read the greeting on a wall of one typical guest ranch on the Wyoming–Colorado border:

> GUEST, YOU ARE WELCOME HERE;
>
> DO AS YOU PLEASE.
>
> GO TO BED WHEN YOU WANT TO
>
> AND GET UP AT YOUR EASE.
>
> YOU DON'T HAVE TO THANK US
>
> OR LAUGH AT OUR JOKES.
>
> SAY WHAT YOU LIKE,
>
> YOU'RE ONE OF THE FOLKS.

You may ride all day every day or merely lounge by the heated pool and take in the pure mountain air. You don't even have to swim if you don't want to. Trail rides can be a few hours to half a day or full day with a picnic. Steak-fry rides are popular, too. At night the dudes head down a pine-scented trail in the moonlight; you gaze up at the Milky Way.

A Colorado dude ranch is a small, self-contained world where you ride away from city life as well. There are lots of horse trails for novices, guided breakfast rides, ghost-town rides, and even six-day rides into the wilderness. Some dude ranches arrange river-rafting trips, or you can rent a jeep. Archery, boating, and even golf are possibilities. Chaises abound.

The phenomenon is uniquely western and especially enjoyable in the Colorado mountains, where summers are never too hot or too cold. You're therefore outdoors much of the time. While adults rest or play, children have their own supervised programs. Much of the clientele returns every year. Most stay at least a week.

How much does a dude-ranch vacation cost? Much less than you'd expect. If you settle on an average western place, you can have an unforgettable week for half or a third of what an ocean cruise would cost. Everything is included. Such vacations mean honest value; the customers can always rely on meals that are well cooked and served family style, which allows you to get acquainted with other guests. At one ranch, about a two-hour drive from Denver, the breakfasts and dinners consist of huge eat-all-you-want buffets. In the morning, you'll want to ride off some of those calories—and get some sun in the process.

The *Peaceful Valley Ranch* near Lyons is best known for its summer square-dancing activities; the dude ranch employs a caller. This establishment has a special teenage program, scout trips to ghost towns, and even English riding instruction. Lyons is easy to reach from Denver via the Boulder Turnpike; then continue via Highway 7 and Highway 72. For more information contact the ranch at 475 Peaceful Valley Road; (303) 747–2881 or (800) 955–6343; www.peacefulvalley.com. Open year-round.

The *Tumbling River Ranch* in Grant seems hewn out of native rock and local wood. At night you can hear the tumbling river under your window. The ranch stands at 9,200 feet above sea level, and, overhead, the stars stand out clearly. The ranch features not only horse activities but also a handsome outdoor pool sheltered by glass panes. The food is excellent, and you get lots of personal attention from the owners.

Grant is a short trip southwest from Denver via US 285. For more information contact Tumbling River Ranch, P.O. Box 30, Grant 80448; (303) 838–5981 or (800) 654–8770; www.tumbling river.com. Open from June 1 through September 30.

Chapel at Peaceful Valley Ranch

Make a note of the Colorado Dude and Guest Ranch Association for more ranches: P.O. Box 2120, Granby 80446; (970) 887–3128; www.coloradoranch.com.

If you're driving east on Highway 6, you see the artificially created lake after you're out of the steep Glenwood Canyon, over Vail Pass, en route to Summit County. If your approach is from the west, you cross the 11,992-foot Continental Divide; then the highway suddenly straightens, and there it is—*Lake Dillon.*

With its 24½-mile shoreline, on a summer day the water can be a deep blue, dotted by white triangles of sails, and alive with small motorboats, cabin cruisers, and canoes skimming the surface. Now and then an angler fishes for rainbow trout in good privacy.

From the beaches, beyond the encircling highways, the mountains sweep upward—the domain of climbers, hikers, and horseback riders. Streams are everywhere: Blue River, Snake River, Ten Mile Creek, all agleam in the sun. The much-needed waters splash across rocks into the reservoir, flowing toward Denver, through the unseen Roberts Tunnel, not far from Dillon.

The highway has two lanes here, and if you're in a hurry, you may well sweep past the sign that reads: DILLON, ELEVATION 9,156. DENVER, 78 MILES.

trivia

In the early 1960s, the original town of Dillon—the whole town!—was moved in order to make way for the Dillon Lake reservoir.

The town is concealed by pines. But a surprise awaits the driver who heads into these woods. For all at once there is silence. The trucks rumbling toward Utah or Nebraska are no longer heard. And among the trees stands the new Dillon. The town officials and the city planners conceived it well. Buildings can be no higher than 30 feet, for instance, so that all comers can see the lake. Only natural materials—the stone and wood of the Rockies, plus glass—are permitted for the houses. The wood may be stained but not painted. The lots and homes have to keep their distance, for utmost peace. And timber was cut sparingly, for conservation's sake.

You notice other things. Dillon's signs are subdued, modest, inviting. Neon doesn't splash here; no beacons explode in the traveler's eyes. There are no unsightly shacks or dead auto carcasses. A cluster of stores—hardware, supermarket, drug—and a post office have been fashioned into a tidy shopping center. Built of native pine, it blends with the forest.

The old town was named after an early prospector. There was off-and-on gold mining, a little railroading, lumber trading, and much ranching. The first post office opened here in 1883. With the advent of the car came garages and service stations. Roads improved, and more tourists showed up "to breathe the exhilarating Rocky Mountain air," as one man put it. A longtime resident remembers the Dillon of the 1930s: "Ranchers picked up their mail here," he says, "and it was a place for a beer on Saturday night."

But on the other side of the mountains, Denver was growing, and it desperately needed more water. All through the forties and early fifties, the Denver Water Department bought up lands and ranches with water rights. Then, in 1955, Dillonites were told about the coming storage reservoir. It would inundate their town.

How Colorado's Ski Areas Respect the Environment

Competence is one of the Colorado ski area's earmarks. The mountain crews, the ski patrol, and the ski school are all carefully selected from some of Colorado's most experienced ski experts. Even the original forest workers fit the picture: Special crews of French-Canadian sawyers hand-cleared and close-cut stumps on most Summit County trails to avoid major disturbance of the underlying soil. (The newer mountain developments were seeded for proper ground coverage to avoid severe erosion problems during the spring runoff.) Thanks to forestry know-how, most of the utility poles from the valley to the summits were installed by helicopter in order to avoid excessive clearing. The utility poles were given a green hue to blend in with the natural vegetation. The trails, highways, and support facilites thus coexist with nature.

After many meetings and complex legal work, the machinery ground into high gear. There would be no turning back—Dillon had to move. Some of the old people left for warmer climates; others settled in nearby villages. But the young, sports-minded citizens decided to create a new Dillon on a hill of pine and evergreen. Here was a chance for a model town.

Down in the valley the old community was dismantled stick by stick. Because the water supply had to be pure, all the ancient buildings had to go. Some were cut in half and hauled elsewhere by trucks. Others had to be burned down. The Water Board uprooted telephone lines, removed old pipes, buried the last rusty tin cans. Even the peaceful graveyard, with its rococo stones and metal crosses, had to be shifted to higher ground. For a while there were still the busy swings in the school yard, and a church belfry pointed its white wooden finger into the sky. Then the school was moved, and the church found a new home in the reborn Dillon.

Slowly, the dam rose until it stood 231 feet high at some points and was capable of backing up 257,000 acre-feet of water. The Harold Roberts Tunnel, more than 23 miles long and costing $50 million, was completed to connect the reservoir with rivers flowing into Denver. Water from thawing snows and the mountain streams steadily accumulated in the reservoir behind the dam.

One August day, the waters rushed over the top and through the "glory hole" spillway into the outlet tunnel. By then nothing was left of the old Dillon town site. The roads that led to it now lay under about 150 feet of water. Unlike the fabled Atlantis, the sunken city that resurfaces, the ancient Dillon would never emerge again.

Instead of dwelling on its past, the new town has forged ahead quickly, enthusiastically redefining itself as a community rooted in nature. Tourists come to relax and experience the unique flavor of this exquisitely planned and orchestrated settlement. They can take a front row seat by renting a condo at the Lodge at Dillon Lake, known for its spectacular views. After eating at the Arapahoe Cafe and Pub, a charming, wood-paneled restaurant on Lake Dillon Drive, they can take a stroll through the peaceful town.

In the years ahead, Dillon and the entire vacationland around the 3,300-acre lake will witness even more development. Many agencies are involved, including the U.S. Forest Service of the Department of Agriculture; the Bureau of Land Management; the Denver Board of Water Commissioners; the Colorado Game, Fish, and Parks Department; and, of course, the town of Dillon itself. On the horizon are more motels, hotels, condos, restaurants, clothing stores, and curio and art shops.

The **Dillon Marina** hosts a number of fun community events annually, including regattas throughout the summer. For details call (970) 468–5100; visit www.dillonmarina.com or write P.O. Box 1825, Dillon 80435. Free Saturday night concerts take place throughout the summer at the Lake Dillon Amphitheatre; call (970) 262–3400 for details.

For more information about events and attractions in Dillon during your stay, call (970) 468–2403; visit www.ci.dillon.co.us; or write Town of Dillon, P.O. Box 8, Dillon 80435.

Denver is a mere seventy minutes from Lake Dillon when you use the time-saving **Eisenhower Tunnel**, which is a story in its own right.

"Nearly impossible!" a geologist said when a Colorado financier first suggested a long tunnel through the Continental Divide during the 1930s. "Unpredictable rock!" other geologists warned in 1941. The drilling of a pilot bore already gave a clue to the unstable rock strata of the area in the Colorado Rockies. Steel linings buckled in the exploratory shaft. For three decades tunnel builders battled the mountain some 58 miles west of Denver. Lack of money, politics, explosions, fires, and, most of all,

trivia

The utility bill for the Eisenhower Tunnel runs about $70,000 a month—each tunnel (one for eastbound and one for westbound traffic) has 2,000 light fixtures, and each light fixture contains an eight-foot bulb!

geological problems all thwarted the builders. A tunnel engineer later summed it up better than anyone else. "We were going by the book," he said. "But the damned mountain couldn't read!"

Fortunately, the 8,941-foot-long Eisenhower Tunnel was eventually drilled despite the obstacles. The tunnel saves the motorist 10 miles over the twisting and turning highway that crosses Loveland Pass. Since the tunnel opened in 1973, drivers need no longer expose themselves to the fierce storms and howling winds of the pass. No more jackknifed trucks, stranded cars, or vehicles swept off the highway ledges by avalanches, rock slides, or icy curves taken too fast. One of North America's best-known mountain passes was finally tamed.

For one hundred years, since the days when railroads were first reaching across the continent, men had worked and dreamed of tunneling through the Continental Divide here, where it's narrowest.

Everyone agreed that the existing roads across the 12,000-foot-high mountain crests presented some perils and inconveniences. In the 1920s and 1930s, a motor trip was still considered a major undertaking on the 12-foot-wide Loveland Pass road. The local papers claimed that such travel resembled a stunt and called the motorists undaunted. One eyewitness reported, "Mud and a steep grade combine to balk all but the highest built cars." In summer, automobiles sometimes plummeted from the steep road, and hikers could see old hulks rusting in the valleys. The worst times were in winter, when Colorado's east and west slopes became cut off from each other. Eventually, irate citizens put placards on their auto bumpers that read, WE DEMAND A TUNNEL!

It became clear that only a tunnel would make travel possible during all seasons, besides reducing distances across the Rockies. In January 1937, a mountain community leader proposed a 10-mile tunnel. It took four years until the Colorado Highway Department began to drill a 5,483-foot pioneer bore. World War II brought the work to a halt, despite much clamor in the mountain towns and in the Colorado state capital. One November day in 1947, a large group of marchers showed up at the statehouse in Denver, calling for action. At the same time, signs appeared in Front Range cafes and restaurants that demanded a LOVELAND PASS TUNNEL NOW!

Before long the tunnel idea moved into high gear. The project was advertised and bids were to be opened. Unfortunately, only one bid was received, which brought the tunnel idea to another standstill.

In short, the mountain giant had won. No one wanted to take it on. In the pilot bore the ceilings gradually caved in, and inspectors reported gushing water and musty odors. Engineers told the press that men would have to work and live under impossible climatic conditions at an 11,000-foot altitude and that it would be extremely difficult to transport materials to the site. Attention-seeking politicians showed up in the tunnel bore, garbed in yellow slickers, rubber boots, and impressive miner's hats. The test shaft's air quickly ended the visit.

Work progressed only slowly. The Continental Divide would not bow to the nine firms that had been welded into one contractor. Sometimes as many as 1,100 men sweated and coughed in three shifts inside the mountain. Mounted on three-tiered drilling platforms, a dozen giant drills poked into the tunnel's brain. The attack of these massive drilling machines was followed by blasts of water to wash out the fresh holes. The racket was tremendous, and bearded, hard-hatted miners wore thick plastic earmuffs lined with sponge rubber.

After just three months of penetration, workmen noticed that a large area had shifted, buckling some steel linings. Total costs soon soared above the original bids of $49 million to $100 million, with the tunnel still acting up. On February 13, 1969, miners had to run for safety as some walls 600 feet inside the west portal started to disintegrate. Dismay was equally great when the granite resisted altogether. The contractor requested permission to attack one fault zone with a specially designed shield. The five-story, twelve-drill, 22-foot monster weighed 670 tons with its tailpiece. The machine was capable of exerting a push of twenty million pounds.

The shield was first housed in a mammoth chamber near the west portal. Then came the historic day when the engineering wonder began its journey into the tunnel. The highway department's fanfare—and the newspapers' excitement—proved to be somewhat premature: The shield advanced only 70 feet in less than a month. On September 4, 1969, the device ground to a

Car Camping

When my youngest son was ten or eleven, we decided to explore the 10,000-foot level of the Continental Divide; we headed for the Rainbow Lakes, which can be accessed via a rutted, bumpy road. The famous Colorado weather was uncooperative. It rained. We had underestimated the length of the drive from Nederland, plus the long hike to the campground.

Strangely enough, the campground was empty. We were on our own. What's more, it had started to pour again. Hungry now at 8:00 P.M., we unpacked one hamburger each, crumpled up some paper, and topped the paper with the thinnest conifer branches. Then we struck some matches, which was still permitted in that particular area at that time. No luck. The rain had gone into high gear. It poured. Under its wet onslaught, the little, moist matches refused to participate. We ate the edible: the hamburger bun, the two onion slices, an apple.

The next morning, the sun greeted us from the sky. It would be a beautiful Colorado day.

sudden standstill; its thirty-four roller bearings were stuck. The shield was redesigned to move on skids. This time, alas, the machine budged just 7 inches. The earth pressures were too much, and the expensive colossus had to be abandoned in the tunnel, where it still lies today, cemented into the walls.

No further progress was made for more than a year after this multimillion-dollar failure. The tunnel designers brought in qualified consultants at stiff fees from all over the United States—to no avail. Finished sections still threatened to fall apart. On occasion the whole mass of granite, gneiss, and schist seemed to be moving. In some areas the rock resembled clay, and dust kept squeezing through every crevice. In the collapsing areas some rock could be "nailed" to a more stable surface; in other sections, curved supports helped distribute the pressures. Sometimes the only solution was to double the support beams. All these unforeseen emergencies and the additional materials consumed a fortune in man-hours.

There were other problems. About sixty miners walked out when a woman was hired as an engineer. Twice the workmen walked out to protest poor ventilation.

One December day a fire brought work to a complete stop. No one knows for sure how the flames started some 4,000 feet inside the western tunnel section. An acetylene torch—and some straw—may have touched off the fire. To smother it the outside air supply had to be shut off, and the smoke assaulted the men's lungs. Would gas pockets cause an explosion? The possibility seemed real enough. Almost a week passed before work could continue.

Barely three months later a $200,000 explosion rocked the concrete operation at the west entrance. This time there may have been an equipment malfunction. The mishap destroyed the huge boiler, the concrete-mixing machinery, 5,000 gallons of oil, a large propane tank, and the company ambulance.

The job had been enormous on all levels: The excavation alone had taken 524,000 cubic yards out of a mountain bent on creating mischief and causing deaths. The tunnel actually took five lives—three in accidents and two from heart attacks at the high elevation. There were more than fifty broken arms, legs, and ankles. No one could count the hours of anguish felt by the contractors, engineers, and workmen about whether the job would ever get finished. The mountain giant constantly held out its fist for more money. The original highway department estimate—made in 1937—was $1 million. The cost exceeded $115 million for one bore.

Yet, all this effort and expenditure represented a mere start, because the tunnel could at first accommodate only one lane of traffic each way. The interstate highway system must be four lanes, so a second section was dug by some

500 workers at a cost of another $225 million. The complete Eisenhower Tunnel opened for traffic on December 21, 1979. Lots of bad rock gave the engineers and drilling crews plenty of trouble.

But the job was at last accomplished. "The damned mountain finally knew the score," said one engineer. "Like it or not, we did get through!"

The Eisenhower Tunnel is 58 miles west of Denver via I–70. Visit www.dot .state.co.us/Eisenhower/description.asp for more information.

Year-Round Vacation Areas

Breckenridge is the perfect Colorado frontier town—one of the few that was rebuilt and is now well preserved and thriving.

In 1859, a group of fourteen prospectors discovered gold in the Breckenridge area. A town was quickly built by miners who were hopeful that they would strike it rich. One such miner, Tom Groves, walked away a big winner when he discovered "Tom's Baby," a 136-ounce gold nugget. But, like all areas rich in minerals, the mines eventually played out. Breckenridge citizens wouldn't give up, and they found another moneymaker when Summit County's first ski area opened in 1961.

trivia

Gold was first panned in Breckenridge's Blue River in 1859.

When a group of European journalists visited many of the state's resorts, Breckenridge seemed to delight them more than most others. Why? Here were all the earmarks of the old Gold Rush West: the little Victorian houses with their columns and crenellations; the clapboard structures of the miners, beautifully repainted; and store windows filled with antiques. Midwesterners and easterners feel the same way; they get the chance to let children (and themselves!) relive U.S. history.

The ski slopes are still named for the old mines in the area: Gold King, Wellington, Bonanza, Cashier, Silverthorn—these were the names that excited the gold hunters more than a century ago.

Breckenridge is actually one of Colorado's oldest towns. In August 1859 the first gold seekers came streaming across the Continental Divide to pan gold in the waters of the Blue River. Later, a silver lode started a second boom.

By 1861 some 5,000 people lived in and near Breckenridge. Summit County then extended as far as the Utah line and was one of seventeen counties composing Colorado Territory. It has since been whittled down to 600 square miles. Then, as now, Breckenridge was the county seat.

Breckenridge

More than $30 million in gold was taken out of the district during its heyday. Most of that was from placer and lode mining. Later on, gold dredges came to tear up the countryside, leaving the great piles of rocks still to be seen along the Blue and Swan rivers, as well as along French Creek. Dredging came to a halt about 1942.

In the early 1960s, Breckenridge became a year-round resort, at the same time maintaining its century-old status as a former mining community.

Development moved ahead when the ski area opened in the early 1960s. The runs were at first short, but fairly varied, and always aimed at families who could meet for lunch at the handsome Alpine base lodge. Soon the town attracted a number of people who built second homes in the serene forests.

Breckenridge, located 88 miles west of Denver via I–70 and Highway 9, is a good choice for the family in search of a winter vacation without pretense. Snowmobiling, ice fishing, easy skiing on the simply laid-out ski runs, as well as tobogganing, snowshoeing, bowling, and nightly sightseeing all add to satisfaction. Rates and ski lift tickets in Colorado can be expensive, however.

Do you like to snowboard? Breckenridge has 1,915 acres of snowboardable terrain. "Extreme" snowboarders can try to conquer Peak 7, which is above the timberline and offers abundant obstacles, or try Peak 8's Freeway Terrain Park, home to a Superpipe previously ranked as one of the top four in North America by *Snowboarder* magazine. For a neater, well-groomed run, try Peak 9. For a messy run with lots of bumps and trees, go to Peak 10. And novices, have no fear—Breckenridge offers snowboarding lessons at every level of skill. Opening date is usually in late October or early November; the season runs until the snow is gone sometime in the spring. For more information call the Breckenridge Resort Chamber (311 South Ridge Street) at (970) 453–2913 or (888) 251–2417; www.gobreck.com. You can also contact the Breckenridge Ski Resort (P.O. Box 1058, 80424) at (970) 453–5000 or (800) 789–7669; www.breckenridge.com.

trivia

Breckenridge features several ghost towns worth checking out: Lincoln City, Swandyke, Dyersville, and others.

Mining—an important part of Colorado's past—is alive and well and can be glimpsed at the **Country Boy Mine,** 2 miles from downtown Breckenridge. This working mine is one of the few that offer travelers the same experience that hard-rock miners had more than one hundred years ago when the mine was established. At the Country Boy Mine you can don a hard hat and venture 1,000 feet underground, seeing what actual miners saw, feeling what real miners felt. After the tour you can try your hand at gold panning in Eureka Creek or take a hay ride past the authentic mine buildings. Indeed, here you are the miner. There is plenty to see at Country Boy. Wonder at the dredge boat display or wander through the museum exhibit.

From Denver take I–70 west to exit 203; drive south on Highway 9, 10 miles into Breckenridge. Turn left on Wellington Road and stay on it until it comes to a final fork. Turn right, and then drive a mile east on French Gulch Road. Admission costs $16 for anyone thirteen and older, $11 for children four to twelve, children three and younger free. Open year-round. Call (970) 453–4405 for hours; www.countryboymine.com.

Where else but in Colorado would you expect to find an extensive ski museum? Founded in 1976, the **Colorado Ski Museum** in **Vail** reaches back

Breckenridge Horseback Riding

Tired of walking? *The Kingdom of Breckenridge Stables* offers ninety-minute rides along the Breckenridge Trail, which passes some of Colorado's finest scenery. Also available is a breakfast ride, departing at 7:00 A.M. daily. The stable's most popular ride since 1983, the breakfast ride includes scrambled eggs, sausages, "Cowboy Coffee," hot chocolate, orange juice, and all-you-can-eat pancakes. Dinner rides are available as well, particularly for larger groups. Reserve all rides at least one day in advance. Ride prices range from $40 to $75, with children age six or younger paying half price for any ride.

Call (970) 453–4438 or write P.O. Box 1816, Breckenridge 80454; www.colorado-horses.com/kingdom.htm/.

to the old miners of the nineteenth century who raced in the Rockies surrounding their camps, competing against one another on long wooden boards,
holding a long staff in one fist for braking. The museum contains a magnificent, enlarged 1859 etching of Snowshoe Thompson, the Norwegian who skied
from camp to camp in severe blizzards. He delivered the mail, candy, and
medicines to the marooned miners.

Here are the photos and artifacts of skiing clergymen like Father John
Lewis Dyer, who brought the gospel to Colorado's historic gold towns, as well
as the stories of sheepherders and trappers who braved the snows in the nineteenth century on 9-foot enormous wooden contraptions with crude leather
straps holding their boots. (Some of the men used baling wire to keep the ski
shovel curved during summer storage.) Mementos of the first long-ago jumpers
will fascinate viewers; photos show them taking off from knolls or flying
through the air, equipment sometimes falling off high above ground.

Do you want to learn more about the first ski lifts? The Colorado Ski
Museum displays the drive mechanism, pictures of the first rope tows, and
photos of funny "grippers," which latched onto the moving ropes. The local-
ized history of chairlifts, gondolas (including a gondola rescue), ski patrol
toboggans, the first U.S. Army Snow Tanks, and the first ski area snow-packing
and grading gear can all be seen here. Any student of ski equipment can learn

Ski Vail—Hut to Hut

For an off-the-beaten-path ski experience, try Vail's backcountry hut-to-hut skiing.
The Tenth Mountain Division Hut Association was formed in 1980 to build a backcountry ski hut system in the high mountains between Aspen, Leadville, and Vail.

Now you can reserve the huts for a fee as a take-off for day adventures or to ski from
hut to hut. These shelters are within the White River and San Isabel National Forests,
so stunning vistas are guaranteed. The adventure isn't for everyone, however; the
Forest Service advises that the trails require at least intermediate ability. The Hut
Association also requires that someone in each group be proficient in backcountry
skills, such as avalanche awareness and compass reading.

The huts include woodburning stoves, propane burners, cooking and eating utensils,
kitchen supplies, and mattresses and pillows.

NOTE: With average elevations of 11,000 feet, you need to prepare for high altitude.

Reservations are required; call (970) 925–5775 or write Tenth Mountain Division Hut
Association, 1280 Ute Avenue, Suite 21, Aspen 81611; www.huts.org.

much about the development of skis, bindings, boots, poles, even the first ski suits, knickerbockers, parkas, or the women's fashions of still earlier days when ladies skied in ankle-length black skirts.

The history of Colorado's famous Tenth Mountain Division is well illustrated; an entire room is devoted to the Mountain Troopers and their initial camps and wartime exploits. If the viewer is curious about methods of avalanche control, up-to-date ski racing, or the history of plush, urban, pricey Vail, it's all here in the very center of Vail, with its massive condos next door to the sleek bank, a few steps from the five-star Antlers at Vail complex, and near the ski slopes themselves. The museum features ski videos in a special viewing area. And plaques contain the pictures and biographies of Colorado Ski Hall of Fame members—a somewhat politicized assembly of engineers and entrepreneurs, ski makers, and ski teachers.

Admission is $1.00, and children age twelve and under are free. Open daily from 10:00 A.M. to 5:00 P.M. except Monday; closed during October and May. Colorado Ski Museum, 231 South Frontage Road East, P.O. Box 1976, Vail 81657; (970) 476–1876 or (800) 950–7410; www.skimuseum.net.

Within walking distance of the ski museum—but nicely concealed by a thick grove of fir trees—you'll find the beautifully designed *Town of Vail Public Library.* It was built in 1972 with native Colorado stone and woods and a grass lawn roof. A massive fireplace is lit all year. Picture windows look out into the little forest and onto the footpath that meanders along Gore Creek to Vail Village.

Pam Hopkins, a young local architect, won several design awards for the building. "We wanted light and endless space," she explains. "Yet we aimed for energy efficiency." The library has more than 20,000 volumes, including many mountain books; several hundred magazine subscriptions; an eager reference desk department; plus cassettes and a children's department. The library offers e-books online as well. Most of all, the building feels especially cozy when rain or snow glisten in the needles of the trees outside while you're warm and dry, book in hand. Library hours are 10:00 A.M. to 8:00 P.M. Monday through Thursday, 10:00 A.M. to 6:00 P.M. Friday, and 11:00 A.M. to 6:00 P.M. Saturday and Sunday. For more information write 292 West Meadow, Vail 81657 or call (970) 479–2184; www.vaillibrary.com.

Two hours west of Denver lie some of the state's most impressive mountains—the *Gore Range.* In Vail itself you'll see the Gore Creek, especially in summer. Gore Mountain, Gore Wilderness—who in the world was Gore?

You might call him one of the more interesting visitors who ever roamed through Colorado. The best way to get acquainted with him might be north of

Vail on **Gore Pass,** near Kremmling. Here a bronze plaque is visible beside the highway, at an elevation of 9,000 feet. The words on the bronze may pique your curiosity:

> HERE IN 1854 CROSSED SIR ST. GEORGE GORE. AN IRISH BARONET BENT
> ON SLAUGHTER OF GAME AND GUIDED BY JIM BRIDGER. FOR THREE
> YEARS HE SCOURED COLORADO, MONTANA AND WYOMING ACCOMPA-
> NIED USUALLY BY FORTY MEN, MANY CARTS, WAGONS, HOUNDS, AND
> UNEXAMPLED CAMP LUXURIES.

Lord Gore's party, we learn, dispatched "more than 2,000 buffalo, 1,600 elk and deer, and 100 bears," among others.

Hunting was nothing new in a land where European trappers and fur traders had already searched all of Colorado for beaver. But Lord Gore set a record; besides, no one matched his style. The baronet had brought most of his retinue of hunters and even some porters from Ireland; his safari caravan eventually accumulated 112 horses, twenty-one carts, thirty wagons, and four dozen hunting dogs. He roamed the mountains for many months, shooting grizzly bear, antelope, and other animals and making elegant camp at night, complete with silver service and rare wines.

His Lordship could afford the "unexampled camp luxuries." For one thing, his income exceeded $200,000, which was quite a sum during the mid-1850s. For another, the Irish nobleman had a taste for gourmet cuisine and rare wines—and the cooks and servants to attend his needs. Lord Gore had gone to school in Oxford, and his aristocratic tastes included various mansions in Ireland and houses in East Sussex.

trivia

Shrine Ridge is an easy hike that can be accomplished in two to three hours. You climb through open meadows with abundant wildflowers, then up the steepest part of the trail to the 12,000-foot summit. While atop the mountain, look for "Lord Gore," a man-shaped rock to the northwest.

To reach this spot, take I-70 to Vail Pass, exit 190. Proceed on Road #709 to Shrine Pass Summit. Turn left here and drive to Shrine Mountain Inn, where you can park.

Lord Gore's hunt is still spoken of by schoolchildren in the area. And thanks to the Historical Society of Colorado, future visitors to the region will be reminded of the Irishman and his exploits by means of the bronze plaque.

The summit of Gore Pass and the plaque are 17 miles west of Kremmling and can be reached from Denver via U.S. Highway 40. The Forest Service has provided picnic grounds on the pass. You get to Vail by driving south on Highway 9, then west on I-70.

They Almost Blew It: Vail History

Vail founders never anticipated a success of such magnitude.

Although thousands of mountain troopers and skiers passed through the valley during the 1940s and 1950s, none of them saw the potential of Vail Mountain, since the best slopes were out of sight high above the highway. But Peter Seibert, an ex–Tenth Mountain man and a ski racer, knew a lot about ski areas, and he spent two years hiking, climbing, and skiing all over the Rockies to look for the ideal resort location. One day in 1957, he scaled the Vail Summit with a local prospector who lived in the valley. Upon seeing the bowls and glades and open slopes, Seibert knew he'd found the ideal site.

Seibert and some friends invested their savings. But more money was needed. Unfortunately, at that time Denver's conservative bankers wouldn't gamble on a large new ski area, with Aspen already doing well. All the same, Seibert kept looking for partners. He turned to Michigan, Missouri, Wisconsin, Texas, and other states. He bought a snowcat and brought visitors to his magic mountain. He showed films of his powder bowls all over the country. He invited prospective investors to ski with him. One day, he finally hit a lucky streak. A Michigan oilman-skier recognized the potential and found other wealthy backers who spread Seibert's gospel. They raised $5 million, formed Vail Associates, and successfully tapped the Small Business Administration and the no-longer-reluctant Denver bankers. And they sold real estate to precisely the people who had shaken their heads the hardest.

During the summer of 1962, the bulldozers started to dig in. An excellent Milwaukee architect had drawn up the plans and now supervised the frantic building activity.

When the dust settled, there stood the first lodges, apartments, malls, homes, and lifts of Vail, Colorado.

Mountain flowers! What a variety of life forms! Botanists estimate that there are some 6,000 species in the Rockies alone. Who can doubt it? What a myriad of colors! Lavender, crimson, blue brushstrokes! Bright white, butter yellow, pink! The first sign of spring brings forth a rush of Easter daisies, mountain marigolds, wild sweetpeas, fairy trumpets, pink rockhill phlox, and others in many hues. Wander up in early summer to Colorado's 8,000- or 9,000-foot levels. And lo! Here, almost overnight, you'll see leafy cinquefoils, arnicas, yellow monkey flowers, and the official state flower, the blue Rocky Mountain columbine. (The latter also grows in the foothills.) In July, you'll be welcomed by the star gentians, wood lilies, the mountain aster, and several kinds of larkspur.

You cannot help but admire the hardiness of vegetation at the altitudes of the Rockies. How is it possible that the plants do not die under the battle

Vail Hikes

Missouri Lakes. Hikers are sometimes discouraged by evidence of a water project at the start of this trail. However, after the first mile, the trail cuts into the plush wilderness, the likes of which experienced hikers dream about. Rustic log bridges help you cross Missouri Creek on your way to the crystal-clear lakes.

Anticipate a walk of approximately five hours if you go all the way to the lakes within the Holy Cross Wilderness.

Take I-70, exit 171 to Highway 24. Drive south to Homestake Road #703. Turn right onto #704 and travel to a T in the road. The trailhead is on the left.

For more information call the U.S. Forest Service Rangers Station at (970) 827–5715, or stop by the station, located ½ mile south of exit 171 in Minturn. Visit them at www.econovail.com/hiking.html.

conditions of winter storms? What makes tiny wildflowers get along with less oxygen and more radiation? How do some mountain flowers manage to spite the short summers and harsh climate above timberline? A sense of wonder will fill you at some mountaintop discoveries.

First, smallness helps. The tinier the leaves, the less resistance to the wind. In the tundra, you will discover miniature grasses, sedges, and herbs. You bend down to miniflowers. If you brought a magnifying glass, you'd see details of almost microscopic leaves. There are plants without any stems; others come with stems so short that the swirling air masses can't budge them. At the same time, the roots go deep down into the ground; a 2-foot root is the 2-inch plant's insurance against being ripped out by storms.

Amazing nature! Most mountain flora hold onto the day's warmth at night by closing their petals.

Mountain flowers protect themselves with tiny umbrellas or hairs, fine layers of wool, or waxy leaves that hold moisture. Mountain flowers can also adapt to the cold. In the Rockies, thousands of avalanche lilies push through the snow, thus surprising the traveler with their delicate (and edible) yellow petals.

The growing season is short in Colorado. And nature has wisely arranged for most mountain flowers to be perennials so that they need not struggle each season. Such flora develop slowly but survive for several years. Other wildflowers sprout for a brief period at certain months each year. They thrive and shine under the mysterious direction of sun and season, in concert with the flora elsewhere, waiting and then multiplying.

Swiss botanist Fritz Egli noted the wondrous cycle of those multiplying and then vanishing creations: "Storms sweep up the seeds, blow them away, and wherever they fall—sometimes in the most inauspicious places—a tiny new life tries to take root; just one little life, inconspicuous among millions and millions more. Yet this tiny plant clings, waits, grows, and—bringing forth flower, color, and fruit—to master all the adversities."

Visitors to the Vail area shouldn't miss seeing one of the highest public alpine gardens in North America—the ***Betty Ford Alpine Gardens,*** located at the Gerald Ford Park. The dedication took place in August 1989 in the presence of the former First Lady.

At an elevation of 8,200 feet, tourists encounter a profusion of crocus, heather, forsythia, wild roses, and other perennial mountain plants, shrubs, and trees. A total of some 500 different varieties of alpine and subalpine plants grow in four separate microclimates.

There is no charge to visit the gardens, but donations are accepted. Gardens are open from dawn to dusk. For more information contact Betty Ford Alpine Gardens, 183 Gore Creek Drive, Vail 81657; (970) 476–0103; www.betty fordalpinegardens.org.

trivia

When all was said and done, more than 150,000 native trees, plants, and shrubs had been replanted at the end of the Glenwood Canyon interstate construction in 1992. In addition, engineers had proven themselves up to the challenge of working the road around large old trees instead of chopping them down, and the freshly made rock cuts fit right in with the natural canyon scenery—they had been stained so that they'd appear weathered.

As the vacation season grinds into high gear, park personnel gird themselves for millions of summer motorists, campers, hikers, climbers, backpackers, and other visitors. Every year travelers flock in record numbers to Colorado.

Can anything be done to lessen the impact on the fragile environment? The answer is yes.

As a traveler, you can do much to improve the situation in the Colorado mountains. Begin by not picking wildflowers. (In Switzerland, tourists pay a heavy fine if they're caught gathering edelweiss and some other rare species.)

Continue by not littering. Apparently, one litterer creates another. Many local mountain clubs organize hikes for volunteer crews to pick up trash on or near hiking trails. In Estes Park, the owners of a resort periodically ride up the trails on pack horses with saddlebags to pick up empty cigarette packages and candy wrappers. At the nearby YMCA, mountain guides pick up the empty beer cans of the careless Sunday masses.

The head of a Colorado environmental group says: "Some tourists are poor stewards of the Beautiful Country. They drive spikes into trees, use privies for target practice, shatter the forest stillness with a radio or a TV set. They leave initials in red paint on the rock face."

Hikers can help prevent erosion by not getting off the trail. (The state is blessed with more than 1,000 walking trails, footpaths, and mountain-bike routes.) It's especially important to stay on the paths in the high-altitude "tundra" areas. The flowers and vegetation are fragile. Please, refrain from cutting your initials into trees, a rather common and brutal practice.

If you happen to visit a western ghost town this summer, take nothing but photographs. Forget about carrying off a souvenir piece of an abandoned cabin. Future visitors will be grateful to view the complete ghost town.

The environment credo should also interest people who toss bottle caps into resort streams. Please don't. The cap may get stuck in a fish's throat.

One final good rule: If you carry it in, carry it out. For more information about sound environmental practices, contact Boulder-based Leave No Trace at P.O. Box 997, Boulder 80306; (303) 442–8222 or (800) 332–4100; www.lnt.org.

Lastly, one local conservationist suggests that the state adopt a slogan that warns, "There is only *one* Colorado. Tread gently. Make it last!"

The **Lodge and Spa at Cordillera,** in **Edwards,** 15 miles west of Vail, offers more sports and adventure than most first-class resorts in Colorado. While staying at this remote European castlelike lodge in winter, a guest can enjoy Alaskan dogsled rides, rent contemporary snowshoes and join a professional snowshoe guide, take lessons in cross-country skiing and skating (equipment is for rent), train for cross-country races, and get free bus service to nearby Beaver Creek for downhill skiing. In summer, the Lodge and Spa at Cordillera features guided flower hikes, mountain biking, golfing on an eighteen-hole course, swimming in an Olympic-size pool, sitting in whirlpools or in a genuine Finnish sauna, working out on Stairmasters or Lifecycles in a large gym and weight room, and pampering with massages, body wraps, and facials at the professional spa. All this plus 360-degree mountain views, fly fishing, tennis, seclusion, and privacy on 3,600 wilderness acres. This retreat is further blessed with superb accommodations for eighty-four people, and two restaurants. It's a unique, lively, luxurious setup for a moneyed clientele. (Deluxe rates.) For more information contact Lodge and Spa at Cordillera; (800) 877–3529; www .cordilleralodge.com.

As you continue your journey along I–70 heading west, you'll suddenly find yourself surrounded by spectacular canyon walls. Welcome to **Glenwood Canyon,** known as "Colorado's Grand Canyon." Remarkable in and of itself,

Kayaking the Colorado

For an unforgettable experience, book a two-day novice kayak river trip with the **Boulder Outdoor Center**. The trips take you down the Colorado River as it winds through Glenwood Canyon. Though I was not at all interested in kayaking, I finally succumbed to my spouse's eager desire to try it out several summers ago. Accompanied by accredited instructors, we reveled in seeing the scenery of Glenwood Canyon up close as we learned how to maneuver through class II+ rapids. They even taught us how to roll! Participants must have some previous kayaking experience and be at least twelve years old. Trips run from May through September. Write 2707 Spruce Street, Boulder 80302 or call (303) 444-8420 or (800) 364-9376 for details; www.boc123.com.

with its breathtaking geologic features and lovely scenery, the canyon is rendered even more remarkable by the fact that the interstate highway running through it was constructed with a mind to retaining the canyon's wild and natural beauty. Though it's unfortunate and perhaps even a sad commentary on humankind that such a large interstate was constructed in this incredible setting, it is nonetheless encouraging that those in charge of building the road worked hard to make it as environmentally friendly as possible.

Thus the interstate swoops and bends with the canyon, lifted up and away from the extremely popular **Glenwood Springs Recreation Trail.** Four rest stops along I–70 allow access to the 18-mile trail within the canyon. The trail starts behind the Yampah Spa and Vapor Caves. This paved trail and its rest areas attract not only hikers and sightseers, but also in-line skaters, cyclists, runners, rafters, and kayakers. For more information call (888) 4–GLENWOOD, or contact the Eagle Ranger District at P.O. Box 720, Eagle 81631; (970) 328–6388; www.glenwoodchamber.com.

Pull off of I–70 when you see signs for HANGING LAKE if you want to catch a glimpse of this gem. Hike for 1³⁄₁₀ miles for a peaceful respite after long hours on the interstate, stretching your legs on the steep terrain as you take in the lush green foliage near the stream, the impressive redstone canyon walls, and the gushing power of Deadhorse Creek before you reach the lake itself.

Formed by a geological fault that caused the lake floor to drop down the canyon wall, **Hanging Lake** covers more than an acre and is up to 25 feet deep. Handrails near the top of the path provide welcome help on a steep grade. A boardwalk circles part of the lake, crossing waterfalls as they crash down from the cliff face. The summer mist from the falls is cooling. Autumn adds gilded accents as golden aspen trees mix with pines. Icicles line the lake in winter, and frozen formations stimulate the imagination. Although steep, a hike to Hanging Lake is a great side trip any time of the year.

Glenwood Springs is the gateway to some of Colorado's most dramatic and most photographed peaks, like the Maroon Bells near Snowmass or lone, spectacular Mt. Sopris, which you notice from almost everywhere in the region. The immense **White River National Forest** offers backpackers much wilderness. Anglers rave about the catches of trout (rainbows and browns) in the surrounding rivers—the Roaring Fork, the Frying Pan, and the Colorado. Rivers attract rafters and kayakers as well; guiding services are available in Glenwood Springs. Hiking is plentiful, and hunters flock to the region for elk, deer, grouse, and waterfowl.

trivia

Doc Holliday, the famous— or infamous—cowboy, died in Glenwood Springs in 1887; his gravemarker epitaph declares only this: HE DIED IN BED.

What is one of the most unforgettable sights and experiences in this tourist-happy state? It's the 2-block-long **Glenwood Hot Springs** with happy heads of visitors bobbing in the steam, adults doing their hydrotherapy, small children riding rubber ducks, and—lo!—high mountains on all sides. Surrounded by the Rockies, with views of conifers and meadows, these thermal waters are relaxing. The Ute Indians discovered them and spoke of "miraculous healing powers." The Aspen, Colorado, mining king used these hot springs for relaxation. A famed architect, imported from Vienna, Austria, built the bathhouses here in 1890, and soon assorted American presidents came to visit Glenwood's mineral spa and "Natatorium."

Today the recreational swimming—and walking—part is kept at 85° to 95°F (29° to 32°C); hotter outdoor waters (100° to 104°F, 38° to 40°C) are also available, fed by more than 3½ million gallons. Swimmers relish the almost unlimited space in the pool, while former hospital patients or the temporarily lame—like skiers recuperating from broken legs—enjoy the medical benefits. To be sure, scientists point out that the hot springs contain cornucopia elements, including magnesium, calcium, sulphates, bicarbonates, phosphates, and silica.

Some travelers recline much of the day in deck chairs around the pool— Colorado's version of the *dolce vita*. No Roman bath could match Glenwood's pure air and mountain views, however. For extra luxury, the nearby vapor baths feature massages, plus natural saunas. The pool is open daily, yearround, until 10:00 P.M., opening at 7:30 A.M. in summer and 9:00 A.M. in winter.

Touring Glenwood Springs

Glenwood Springs is 42 miles northwest of Aspen off Highway 82. "Glenwood," as residents call it, sits in the White River National Forest, which is a three-hour drive from Denver. Glenwood's two million acres are renowned for all manner of open-air sports. The attraction includes Flat Tops Wilderness, a huge 117,000-acre plateau north of Glenwood Springs.

Glenwood was named for its hot-spring mineral baths, which are open all year. In the 1880s, silver baron Walter Devereaux decided to convert the springs, which had been used by the Utes, into a health resort for the rich. He built the 2-block-long swimming pool, intended for the guests of the posh adjacent hotel. By the early 1900s, so many wealthy and famous people came to the spa that a rail siding was installed next to the hotel for private railroad cars. Teddy Roosevelt made Glenwood his "Summer White House" in 1901 and hunted bear in the nearby hills.

The mineral baths and vapor caves are open to visitors, with trained personnel to guide and supervise. Locals say the water is a quick cure for visitors' aching muscles and stiff joints after days in the nearby wilderness, on long hikes, or on Aspen's ski slopes.

Cost is $13.50 for anyone age thirteen or older and $8.50 for children three to twelve during the summer; children two and younger are free. Contact the pool at (970) 947–2955.

Luckily, pool guests have a place to stay—in fact, they can see the steaming waters right under their windows. The 107-unit **Hot Springs Lodge** is contemporary, bright, efficient, and ideally located. Rates are not as high as you might expect. For reservations call (800) 537–7946. For more information about the pool or lodgings write to the Hot Springs Lodge and Pool, P.O. Box 308, Glenwood Springs 81602; www.hotspringspool.com.

Glenwood Springs may be one of the state's more interesting communities—historically, economically, scenically—yet it never gets the kind of attention accorded to Aspen (41 miles to the southeast) or overcrowded, overbuilt Vail (59 miles) or Denver (some 158 miles to the east). Both the town and the area are blessed with accommodations for every pocketbook. Economy travelers welcome the numerous campgrounds or inexpensive little cabins flanking the soothing rivers. Large and small motels abound.

You're never far from the parades with floats, carnivals, and other festivities of Glenwood's Strawberry Days, the Fall Art Festival, yearly fishing contests, various rodeos, and the quiet mountain paths under a blue sky.

Sunlight Mountain Resort

Sick of the crowds at the big resorts? Then maybe it's time to try out *Sunlight Mountain Resort.* With more than 460 acres of terrain, plus access to plenty of Nordic trails in the adjacent White River National Forest, this resort offers a great escape. Terrific for families, almost all of the resort's ski runs come right down to the lodge. From Glenwood, head south on Highway 117. For more information contact the resort at (970) 945–7491 or (800) 445–7931; www.sunlightmtn.com. Consider staying at the cozy Sunlight Mountain Inn, located at 10252 County Road 117 in Glenwood Springs. Call (970) 945–5225 or (800) 733–4757; www.sunlightinn.com.

Strawberry Days, now more than one hundred years old, is Glenwood Springs's oldest and most beloved annual event. The festival is thought to be Colorado's oldest civic celebration, dating back to 1898.

Early Glenwood Springs residents loved parties, and nearly everything called for a celebration. Prior to 1898 strawberry picnics celebrated the luscious harvest of berries that farmers grew in nearby fields. The event was a success, growing in attendance and extravagance every year. In 1905 it was estimated that more than 6,000 out-of-town guests plus the residents of Glenwood Springs took part in the festivities.

Today the annual Strawberry Days celebration has been extended by several days and many new activities, including sporting events, kids' events, top-name entertainment, and a marketplace of handcrafted works. Attendance at the fair has risen to an estimated 30,000 people over the peak weekend.

Each year a new theme is chosen for the festival. For example, one theme, "Moon over the Wild Strawberries," had Native American overtones, derived from the Seneca Indian word for the month of June, which translates to mean "Moon When the Wild Strawberries Get Ripe." The celebration usually takes place in mid-June. For more information call (970) 945–6589; www.strawberrydaysfestival.com.

The *Fall Art Festival,* held the fourth week in September, is one of the larger art shows on the Western Slope, attracting more than 400 entries. Professionals and amateurs all compete in their own levels and media. And, of course, almost everything is for sale after the judging. Call (970) 945–2414 for details.

While you're in Glenwood Springs, don't fail to take a leisurely stroll through the stately *Hotel Colorado,* which graces the National Register of Historic Places. The 128-room hotel is one of the oldest in the state. Indeed, it was modeled after Italy's Villa Medici and boasts a Florentine fountain in a landscaped courtyard. The hotel's renovated beige lobby must be one of the most attractive in the western United States. The myriad chandeliers, fireplaces, oil paintings, fountains, and potted palm trees hark back to the days of royalty and the very rich.

The Hotel Colorado was financed by the silver mining of the nearby Aspen region and opened officially on June 10, 1893. The cost was a horrendous $850,000; some sixteen private railroad cars of the industrial barons drew up on a special Glenwood siding. Leading citizens from all over the world registered. European millionaires arrived in droves to stay and dine here. In 1905 President Theodore Roosevelt brought his own appetite; a typical menu encouraged the presidential visitor and his entourage to consume an eight-course repast:

Caviar Canapés	*Spring Lamb*
Consommé Rothschild	*Broiled Squab*
Veal Sweetbreads	*Figs*
Young Turkey	*Roquefort Cheese*

Actually, Roosevelt—an avid bear hunter—made the hotel his Summer White House, complete with direct telegraph connections to Washington and special couriers bringing international news to the hunting head of state.

"The Marvel of Hoteldom" attracted the likes of the Armours of packinghouse fame; the "Unsinkable" Molly Brown, who managed to survive the *Titanic*'s sinking; and President William Howard Taft, who addressed the local populace during his term. World War II transformed the hotel into a naval hospital. In more recent times moneys were spent to update the facilities, to repair leaking roofs and stalled elevators or failing steam heat. Thanks to antiques, several suites are reminiscent of yesteryear's elegant clientele.

trivia

Legend has it that the Teddy Bear was born at the Hotel Colorado. One time when frequent visitor President Teddy Roosevelt had a fruitless day of bear hunting, the hotel's maids sewed a stuffed bear in an effort to cheer him up. When he did succeed in hunting down a real bear, his daughter named the bear "Teddy," a name that stuck.

For more information and reservations contact Hotel Colorado, 526 Pine, Glenwood Springs 81601; (970) 945–6511 or (800) 544–3998; www.hotelco lorado.com.

For more information about the Glenwood Springs area, contact the Glenwood Springs Chamber Resort Association at (888) 4–GLENWOOD or (970) 945–6589; www.glenscape.com. Glenwood Springs is easily reached from Denver by rental car, bus, or train. Motorists use I–70. The distance from Denver is 158 miles.

Even by Colorado standards, the trip to **Redstone** is long and complicated, but it is worth it. The distance only enhances the charms of the little hamlet of Redstone and its historic inn and castle.

You at once see the imposing **Redstone Inn** at the end of the main street. The Tudor clock tower is an unexpected sight in this remote mountain land-scape. The thirty-five rooms seem cozy and unpretentious. Rates are affordable for most people. The lobby and the restaurant are filled with antiques and have a Victorian atmosphere.

Now on the National Register of Historic Places, the small Redstone hostelry was built in 1902 for unmarried coal miners. The building had steam heat and even a barber shop. Later, more than $1 million was invested in hotel facilities. A stay here, at an elevation of 7,200 feet, means pure air and a true escape from the city. In summer horses are for rent and trout fishing is popu-lar. The Crystal River is quiet and lovely. Hikers enjoy the area, as do back-packers. In winter, the inn serves as headquarters for sleigh rides and cross-country skiing. Contact Redstone Inn, 82 Redstone Boulevard, Redstone 81623; (970) 963–2526 or (800) 748–2524; www.redstoneinn.com.

The little hamlet of Redstone is idyllic: just a few houses, some artisan and gift shops, a cafe, and a general store.

You reach Redstone via I–70 west to Glenwood Springs, then Highway 82 south out of Glenwood toward Aspen; turn right at Carbondale on High-way 133—it's 18 miles to Redstone. For more information visit www.redstone colorado.com.

If you continue along Highway 82 south out of Glenwood, it won't be long until you reach the famous town of Aspen. The chairs whir upward over forest spurs and logging roads and enormous ravines that become expert ski runs in winter. From "downtown" Aspen one can see just a small portion of the whole Aspen Mountain; in fact, only a third of it is visible to those who merely stare up from their cars.

trivia

One nugget from the Molly Gibson Mine in Aspen weighed 1,840 pounds. It was 93 percent pure silver.

Aspen called itself Ute City at first because it was in Ute territory. Silver gave the town its big start back in the early 1880s. The first news made the prospectors head up the passes and rush to Aspen—a hard, punish-ing journey, even from nearby Leadville. Some men dropped dead before they could stake their first claim. Western historians still mention the stampede of that winter in 1879. They came on burro, on foot, or on horseback. A man would sometimes keel over and die on the Aspen street. Other prospectors just stuck the body into a snowbank and kept up the frantic search for silver riches. The

Versatile Aspen

Most Colorado ski centers consist of a few condos and a ski hill. By contrast, Aspen has many ski areas and Aspen is a town. At one core area you find a handsome pedestrian mall with flower boxes and benches. Moreover, Aspen's red, Old West brick buildings and the Victorian gingerbread homes are periodically restored. The antique cherry-wood bars shine, as do the contemporary Tiffany lamps and the stained-glass windows. Green plants grace many Aspen stores and cafes. Aspen outranks most North American ski resorts when it comes to the sheer number and variety of restaurants and nightlife possibilities.

There are one hundred-plus spots where one can dine or have lunch. Aspen has bistros, bars, saloons, pubs, subterranean dives, cafeterias, cafes, pastry shops, coffeehouses, and several internationally famous restaurants. It's a cosmopolitan, polyglot, manifold town. Aspen is everything to every skier and, happily, to every nonskier as well; the town seems ideal for couples or families where one member or the other doesn't ski. Several hundred shops invite browsers; amusements and sports of every kind beckon.

best years were from 1885 to 1889, when mines galore—some with fascinating names like the Smuggler or Montezuma—operated above the mountain town. The smelter was booked for weeks, and silver rock would pile up everywhere.

Some miners got rich fast. "The men filled their pockets and fled," wrote one contemporary. The silver barons built the luxurious Victorian **Hotel Jerome** (330 Main Street, 800–331–7213; www.hoteljerome.com) and an opera house. They imported singers and musicians from Europe.

The crash came in 1893, however, and brought lean times. Aspen shriveled from a population of 13,000 to a mere 500. The rebirth followed in the 1930s, with skiing.

Old mining equipment was used as the first tow. After World War II, Chicago industrialist Walter Paepcke became interested in Aspen as a cultural and sports colony. The pace accelerated in the little mountain town. Paepcke made good use of the granitic old opera house, and the guests stayed in the opulent Hotel Jerome, which had been built in 1889. The Aspen Music School flourished.

Some of the townspeople, however, didn't go along with the Chicagoan. When Paepcke offered them free paint for their shacks, not many old-timers took him up on it. They didn't like outsiders and wanted to be left alone. One former prospector complained to the papers that it was a "tragedy to reduce a once-great mining camp to a mere Tenderfoot Playground." Another wrote: "Gallons of printers ink to lure the tourist! And not a drop of ink to tell the world where we stood, back in the eighties shouting to the very top of Castle Peak: 'Here's the greatest ore deposit in North America!'"

In the late 1940s, many Aspen dwellings were peeling. Some stood empty. But the mountain town had uniformity. The residences and streets formed a near-perfect grid pattern. If one studies the town from Aspen Mountain, there was—and still is—a simplicity to it.

The aerial view is about the same even today. Closer inspection, however, reveals some architectural mix. Free enterprise! Aspen, rediscovered as the former mining community, grew into a 10,000-tourist-bed complex, which has meanwhile tripled.

No one seemed to agree on architectural styles, and every year downtown **_Aspen_** looked more citylike. There were the original log cabins and Victorian homes of the early miners. Contractors moved in to build new "mineshaft" condominiums, some of which block mountain views. In the more than fifty years' development, Aspen may have retained some flaws, but it also succeeded beyond all expectations as a resort. The ski facilities, what with four different ski areas and countless lifts, including the rapid _Silver Queen_ gondola, are all extraordinary, as good as anything in the Swiss Alps. Aspen summers are a delight, with classical music, lectures, meetings, trails for hikers and bikers, rivers for anglers, areas for kiters, and an expanded airport for private pilots. Gourmets flock to the mostly overpriced Aspen restaurants; finicky guests check into ultraexpensive new hotels. And on Red Mountain, where the movie stars live, the parties go on every night.

Fishing near Aspen, Colorado

Aspen Highlands

Few people know that at one point in mining history—circa 1879 to 1882—Aspen had a nearby competitor named Ashcroft. Located in an adjacent valley, Ashcroft actually boasted several hotels, numerous bars, a jail, and even a newspaper. (The Ashcroft silver riches attracted silver millionaire H. A. W. Tabor and his pretty young bride.) By 1883, Aspen was famous for its silver wealth, and fortune hunters arrived by the thousands; the inhabitants of Ashcroft, meanwhile, dwindled to about 100 (from 2,600 in its heyday).

And today? Aspen is a total success as a ski resort and Ashcroft is a ghost town. A half-dozen rickety buildings stand there, bleached by sun and wind, pummeled by snow crystals, silently looking up at Castle Peak.

More than one hundred years after the silver boom and bust, Ashcroft holds some value. The modest **Ashcroft Ski Touring Center** offers thirty miles of cross-country trails. You reach this quiet area by driving west for a ½ mile on Highway 82, and then turning on Castle Creek Road. After 12 miles, you see the cross-country trails.

Call (970) 925–1971 for more information; www.pinecreekcookhouse.com.

Because of the seasonal rush, some little-known accommodations can be recommended. For otherwise hard-to-get lodging, try the ***Limelite Lodge,*** 228 East Cooper Avenue; (970) 925–3025 or (800) 433–0832; www.limelight lodge.com.

The scene is a Saturday morning in ***Ashcroft,*** a remote Colorado ghost town near Aspen. The first sun rays redden the snow. The base of nearby Castle Peak is still mauve. Nothing seems to stir in this winter landscape. Then comes complete daylight, bright, golden, topped by the flawless Colorado sky.

A few human figures assemble down the road from Ashcroft's weather-beaten buildings. Quietly, more people arrive, get together, wait for still others. All carry snowshoes, which will permit an unhurried penetration of this backcountry.

By 9:00 A.M. forty snowshoers stand ready, almost twice as many as the Colorado Mountain Club leader had expected.

Why is old-fashioned ***snowshoeing*** in again? The reasons are easy to understand. For one thing, snowshoeing is just winter hiking. You don't need any lessons; you learn to walk with your webbed contraptions in minutes. Snowshoeing is healthy; that's why you find many doctors devoted to it.

A sports medicine committee of the American Academy of Surgeons made a study of energy output in various sports. According to one of the cardiologists, snowshoeing proved exceptionally good for the heart. The energy expenditure is at a safe level. Besides, you can rest during the trip and survey the scenery. For all ages, this sport means a better workout for heart and lungs, better muscle tone, better-functioning organs, better digestion, and better circulation.

Cardiologists will tell you that leg veins have valves to maintain circulation. Good muscle tone helps squeeze these veins. The valves permit the blood to go one way, back toward the heart. The better the tone of the leg muscles, the better the circulation, and the less work the heart has to do. Vigorous use of the legs is important whether it is walking, bicycling, skiing, snowshoeing, or any other exercise that uses the legs.

trivia

A 130-pound woman burns about 340 calories per hour of snowshoeing.

You can go almost anywhere on snowshoes: up the steep winter meadows of the Continental Divide, across the gentle mounds of eastern Colorado, over frozen Lake Dillon, in the dramatic deep-snow regions above Silverton and Ouray. In a survey made by the Sierra Club (which has an active snowshoe chapter), some members explained their own special motivations: "We don't disturb nature on snowshoes. We don't upset ecology."

That's what makes the sport different from skiing, especially the kind done at resorts. Colorado's snowshoers demand no cutting of trees, no bulldozing of ski boulevards, no base lodges noisy with hard-rock music. Modern ski complexes resemble mechanized cities, with lifts of all kinds, pricey tickets, and long lines of waiting customers. By contrast, snowshoers never have to stand in a queue; they can move whenever they please and stay warm in the process. Most skiing is now a status symbol; fashion is absent from snowshoeing.

Aspen Flights

Since the "Aspens" have everything, how about paragliding? The answer is, yes, paragliding, too.

With no prior experience necessary, you can soar with an experienced certified pilot from near the summit of Aspen Mountain. Scheduled on a daily basis, these summer flights are absolutely unforgettable.

The *Aspen Paragliding School* offers a three-day course of instruction in technique and equipment. All classes are held on Eagle Hill, above Tiehack Cafe.

For information, call (970) 925–7625 or visit serioussports.com/aspenparagliding.

Something Different: Aspen Dogsledding

The free bus connects you with Snowmass. Here is the traditional spot for **Alaskan-style dogsledding at Krabloonik.** It's an expensive but exciting proposition. The same area serves hikers in summer and fall.

For more information call (970) 923–3953 or visit www.krabloonik.com.

You need only be warm. You can therefore dress in your oldest sweater, the most beat-up windbreaker, a plain cap, an ancient faded sports shirt; no one will judge your income from the pants, either. Just make sure you're not wearing cotton, as it is worse than useless when wet. Any kind of waterproof boot will do, including the kind used for hiking. All this drives down the cost.

Snowshoe equipment is astonishingly reasonable. In a major city like Denver, for instance, you can rent a good pair of shoes with harness. What's the charge for the weekend? Fifteen dollars per day for adult sizes. At an average retail store, you can buy a pair of new snowshoes for a reasonable price.

It's a fairly simple matter to choose a pair of snowshoes. The shape and material may vary, but all the shoes consist of a frame connected to some lacing. The binding is uncomplicated.

Unless you're in first-rate shape, the first trip will result in some muscle pains. Snowshoes can weigh several pounds, and every step means a workout for your legs. As you start out, the shoes feel awkward, and it will take fifteen minutes until you get used to the wide stance required for walking. (If you step normally, your own legs will be in the way.)

You'll eventually learn to raise your feet as little as possible, and after a half mile you won't step on top of your own shoes. But unlike skiing, where you must become familiar with the technique, snowshoeing requires mostly good legs. If the snow is right, you can use your leg strength—and body weight—for excellent snowshoe descents.

"The scenic rewards are great," says one enthusiast of the West. "All evidence of man is swept under a deep, sound-absorbing blanket of white. Each pine cone, every spruce branch stand out clearly. Nature is always there."

If you want to try a guided snowshoe tour with a naturalist, look no further than the **Aspen Center for Environmental Studies (ACES).** During the winter, a variety of Snowshoe Tours leave daily at 10:00 A.M. and 1:00 P.M. and include a lift ride, snowshoes, instruction, a guide, and a snack. Along with

Naturalist Nights

Interesting and educational, Naturalist Nights take place every Thursday evening at Aspen Center for Environmental Studies (ACES) from 7:00 to 8:30 P.M., January through March. Naturalist Nights cover a variety of topics, such as "Survival in the Avalanche Zone," "Wolves in the West," and "Birds of the Winter Forest." Admission is $5.00 for adults and $2.00 for children and teenagers seven to seventeen; children seven and younger may attend at no charge.

viewing stunning scenery in a peaceful alpine setting, tour participants learn about the various kinds of plants and animals that dwell above 10,000 feet. No experience is necessary, but warm clothes and boots are a must. Prices are $45 for adults, $29 for children and teenagers seven to seventeen and senior citizens older than sixty-five. Children younger than seven are not allowed on Snowshoe Tours. Call ACES for more information at (970) 925–5756, or write 100 Puppy Smith Street, Aspen 81611; www.aspennature.org.

If snowshoeing doesn't suit your fancy, consider trying out **Buttermilk.** Buttermilk? One of the local farmers liked to drink it, hence the name. Buttermilk provides Aspen's easiest skiing. The hills here are gentle—a boon for the novice, and ideal for the lower-intermediate. Buttermilk's undulating terrain caters to older skiers as well. Even the nonathletic can have a ball on these tame slopes. On the other side of the same area, a few trails appeal to hardier

Snowmass Summers

Snowmass summers are mellow. The rocks are warm and the moss is dry, and there is the promise of anemones, bluebells, gentian, and Indian paintbrush. The hikers move upward through the meadows. In a nearby ranch building, an arts-and-crafts school will be in session. Aspen's music festival is only twenty minutes away.

In summer, Snowmass is a center for picnickers, kayakers, jeepsters, and rock searchers. The climbers will be there, setting out for the Maroon Bells. Soon, the fishermen arrive, resplendent with nets and tackles and flies. They're ready to angle rainbow trout from many creeks. All summer, there are tenderfoot horseback riders, too. Pale city faces shielded by bold cowboy hats, they climb into the saddle and trot upward, their bodies aching for days afterward.

Then come the hunters, stalking deer in the timbered areas and in the mountain cirques.

Taking It Slow in Aspen

Cross-country skiing is better than average in the Aspen area. There are many options. A good place for beginners is at the **Aspen Cross Country Center.** Trails link a nearby golf course to the Nordic Council trail system (which is free). The center is off of Highway 82 between Aspen and Buttermilk. Write 39551 West Highway 82, Aspen 81611, or call (970) 544–9426; www.ute.mountaineer.com/aspen_xxcl.html.

Another possibility is the **Snowmass Lodge & Club** touring center. This facility, too, connects with the free trail system and offers a rental shop and refreshments as well. It's just off the golf course in Snowmass. For more information call (970) 923–5600 or write P.O. Box G-2, Snowmass Village 81615; www.snowmassclub.com.

For a scenic tour, try **Ashcroft Ski Touring.** The terrain has perfect tracks for diagonal-stride skiing an skating. It also features the Pine Creek Cookhouse. Call (970) 925–1971 for more information; www.pinecreekcookhouse.com.

types. ***Crazy Train,*** complete with a superpipe and more than thirty trails, is the world's largest terrain park, stretching for 2 miles.

Two cafeterias—one on the summit, facing spectacular Pyramid Peak, and one at the bottom—provide perfect places for people who want to rest.

For more information on Buttermilk skiing, contact Aspen Skiing Company, P.O. Box 1248, Aspen 81612; (970) 925–1220 or toll-free (800) 525–6200; www.aspensnowmass.com.

In another world, the rapid ski lift purrs you upward to 9,000 feet, 10,000, 11,000. At 11,500 you slide off your perch and cross the clearing to a vantage point. You have done it before. But each time you catch your breath. The sight is all grandeur. The white surface ripples downward to your left and right, agleam in the morning sun. What vastness! Your skis stir impatiently. Is this descent 3 miles long? Four? More? You can tell from the tiny dots at the bottom—skiers!— that the distance is plenty enough to let you ski to your heart's content.

Suddenly, temptation gets the better of you, and you push yourself off in a flash of poles and shoot down the bowls.

Aspen, Colorado. It could also be Vail. Or Loveland Basin or Winter Park. Width and breadth are a western trademark.

Skiing remains one of Colorado's major attractions: Colorado has more resorts and ski areas than most other states, east or west.

A skilled skier aims with precision; he or she can zip around a standing novice, can pick his or her way around trees, can jump a knoll without falling. If you become good at it, you can ski as fast or as slow as you please and still

Skier's Locomotion up Aspen Mountain

When the Aspen Skiing Corp. (now the Aspen Skiing Company) opened its first lifts on Aspen Mountain in 1947, it eliminated one of skiing's biggest drawbacks: climbing the hill.

Skiing fifty years ago was for the truly committed, because if you wanted to enjoy the slopes in winter, you had to hoof it. If skiers were lucky, they could catch a ride with miners up the back side of Aspen Mountain.

A year later, you could ascend Aspen Mountain in a single chair. The trip took more than an hour and you could get a free ticket by helping to "pack" the slopes in the morning. As many as 100 volunteers worked the slopes at the same time.

stop at a moment's notice. (That's the secret, of course—the ability to come to a halt.)

Let no one tell you differently: The snow is much, much better in Colorado's Rockies. It is light, fluffy, easy-to-ski snow, the kind that obeys you. (By contrast, eastern snow means a constant struggle: You must battle ice and more ice.) Eastern landscapes are pleasing to the eyes: gentle, wooded hills; white church spires; rolling terrain. Colorado's western landscapes are grandiose. You feel a powerful impact when you look down into the valleys—far, far down—from the Crested Butte sundeck.

Rifle Falls State Park

Before you head too much farther west, consider making a side trip to *Rifle Falls State Park.* Though small, this unique gem of a state park offers visitors the unlikely opportunity to get downright tropical—or close to it! The triple waterfall plummets down 80 feet past limestone cliffs, keeping the lush vegetation moist. Dark, cool caves beckon to curious explorers, and interpretive signs help explain the phenomena. With its $5.00 per car entry fee, the park makes for a worthwhile side trip and a terrific place to have a family picnic.

From Aspen, take Highway 82 north about 41 miles. In Glenwood Springs turn left onto 6th Street then left onto North River Drive, following signs to I-70 west.

Take I-70 west about 25½ miles to the Rifle exit. Go north on Highway 13 for 3 miles. Turn right on Highway 325 and drive 9⁹⁄₁₀ miles. Call (970) 625–1607 or write Rifle Falls State Park, 0050 County Road 219, Rifle 81650; parks.state.co.us/rifle_falls.

The state's ski meccas are justly famous. None of Colorado's ski resorts look alike; each has its special character made up of a dozen variables. Century-old mining towns like Breckenridge and Crested Butte have been revived. Aspen is immense and complex. Vail is a giant in every way, an American St. Moritz. Winter Park serves vacationers during the week and young Denverites on weekends. Loveland Basin and Keystone yield good winter days, made up in unequal portions by sun-stroked faces, pure air, and a snowscape that tugs and pulls.

If you come to this state anytime between late November and April, you should try to ski, even if you've never done it before.

For more information contact Colorado Ski Country USA, 1507 Blake Street, Denver 80202; (303) 837–0793; www.skicolorado.org.

Peach Harvests

Noon at **Palisade,** Colorado. The golden peach of the sun has already climbed to the top of the trees, which stand out against a poster-blue sky. You've been in the **Clark Family Peach Orchards** since seven that morning, up and down the ladders. The guys in Denver's health clubs (pumping iron indoors) should envy you out there in the fresh country air. You've gulped big amounts of it, breathing deeply. No pollution. Your nostrils take in the Elberta peach bouquet.

You reach rhythmically for the warm, ripe fruit, which you plop into a sack hanging from your shoulders. When it's full, it weighs forty or fifty pounds, enough for the waiting baskets.

Your arms must stretch, your trunk must rotate, you keep bending. Your legs withstand the extra load; you rejoice in the climbing and descending from and to terra firma. In fact, you've gotten your second wind. Despite the heat, you accelerate before lunchtime. The bushels add up. The mood in the orchards is relaxed.

The pleasures of working a peach harvest should not be underestimated. When other people must slave in office cubicles in dirty cities, some folks are outdoors, in the clean, sweet-smelling orchards, getting paid for being in touch with trees and leaves and fruit. This is a pretty world for summer sport, with the colors lingering behind your eyelids for a long time.

At Palisade, on Colorado's Western Slope, you're into Elbertas. A collegian from Colorado Springs who has come to Palisade ever since he was a high schooler feels nostalgic about it. He says, "Peach time reminds me of home-made ice cream, or a secret treasure in the lunch box, a tantalizing centerpiece, or even a long drive back from the orchards amid bushels of tree-ripened Elbertas, munching on the way and saving the pits to plant."

Suddenly, it's late August, and the hundreds of growers in Palisade (which is 238 miles west of Denver) must round up thousands of harvesters to empty some 500,000 trees. The need can be so great at this juncture that the orchardists enlist the help of relatives, transients, hoboes (who arrive on freight trains), high school kids (nearby schools close for the occasion), laborers from Mexico, and university students, as well as yearly regulars headed by crew chiefs, who come to western Colorado for those two weeks.

trivia

Palisade is also known for its vineyards, which are some of the best in the United States. For a flavorful outing, try out one of the free winery tours and tastings. Check out www.palisadecoc.com for details.

In Colorado alone the bounty amounts to some 250,000 bushels. Because much of the harvesting is still done by hand, it takes an army of people to harvest, sort, and crate the peaches. This creates an incredible number of temporary jobs.

Negative aspects? Pay is minimal, by the bushel. Unless you're in good physical shape, you'll find it hard to scale ladders all day, to stretch your limbs until they ache. The string of your filled harvest sack bites without mercy into your shoulders or neck. You keep lugging forty-eight-pound bushels.

trivia

Remember that, in Colorado, state law says bicycles are considered vehicles and must obey the same traffic laws as automobiles. Ride single file on the right in the same direction as traffic. Always signal when stopping or turning. When you need to catch your breath, move off the road. It's also good advice to wear a helmet and protective glasses.

The work guarantees to make almost anyone lose weight. But you can't compare it to a tennis game in a breeze. In fact, some orchards—especially in those sun-baked, parched, wrinkled Colorado plateaus—get extremely hot. The canopy of trees is pierced by the sun's rays. Count on sweating a lot. You're only cool at 7:00 A.M. when you start, and in some parts of the country at 6:00 P.M. when you finish. (The Palisade Chamber of Commerce crows about the annual average of 78 percent sunny days.)

Some comers also forget about the peach fuzz. You won't feel it for a few hours, but after a day it stings. (Some people are allergic to the fuzz and break out in hives.) Talcum can help the average harvester. But it remains a problem.

Benefits? You can easily make friends, learn about other harvests, and get tips on where to split to next. In Palisade, the Orchard Cafe is full of beer drinkers at night, hatching plots for the balance of the year and the coming seasons. Colorado peach harvesting is a trip that usually leads to another trip.

From Denver, drive west on I–70 toward Grand Junction until you see the Palisade turnoff. Contact Clark Family Orchards at 3887 G Road, Palisade 81526; (970) 464–5385. Another useful contact is the Palisade Chamber of Commerce, 319 Main Street, Palisade 81526; (970) 464–7458; www.palisadecoc.com. Click on "Fruit Industry" for a full list of growers and contact information.

If picking peaches sounds too tough for your tastes, perhaps you'd have more fun simply watching how fruit was harvested 100 years ago. You can do just that at the *Museum of Western Colorado's Cross Orchards Living History Museum.* Located in Grand Junction, the farm is a site listed on the National Register of Historic Places. And a tour of the facility—especially with children—can be memorable. Here are ancient tractors and other weather-beaten farm machinery, plus old tools. Here you can see the first gas pumps (offering gasoline at fourteen cents a gallon). Costumed Cross Orchards staff members and volunteers demonstrate weaving, candle making, and blacksmithing circa 1896. A narrow-gauge railroad is still in place, and your kids are allowed to climb into the caboose.

trivia

Despite receiving only 11 inches of rainfall annually, the area encompassed by the Colorado National Monument was continuously inhabited for thousands of years until 1881. That year, the area's most recent inhabitants, the utes, were moved by the U.S. military to a Utah reservation. Past inhabitants left evidence of their existence through rock art and other artifacts.

The former Cross apple orchards can be visited from mid-April through mid-October. Hours are 9:00 A.M. to 4:00 P.M. Tuesday through Saturday. Cost is $4.00 for adults, $3.00 for seniors sixty-five and older, $2.50 for children five to twelve, and $10.00 for a family group. The address is 3073 Patterson (F) Road, Grand Junction 81504; the phone number is (970) 434–9814; www.wcmuseum.org/crossorchards.htm.

Before you leave this part of Colorado, be sure to stop at the *Colorado National Monument,* known for its steep plateaus, sheer drop-offs, and craggy rock spires. If you're into cycling, a great way to experience the grandeur of this place is to ride the Rim Rock Bike Route. This 33-mile loop follows paved roads through the stark and beautiful scenery, with some challenging climbing—2,300 feet of it!

The view when you reach the top of the plateau is well worth the effort. From your open-air perch you'll absorb more of the Colorado scenery and atmosphere than those who pass you in automobiles. Use extra caution when passing through the short tunnels on this scenic ride. Take a few minutes to stop at the visitor center before your final descent into the town of Fruita. From there, Grand Junction is just a few miles away along the Colorado River. Expect the ride to take about three hours.

To reach the Colorado National Monument, follow Monument Road out of downtown Grand Junction, which will take you to the entry gate. Pick up a map there. Fees are $3.00 per person or $5.00 per vehicle. For more information call (970) 858–3617 or write Colorado National Monument, Fruita 81521; www.nps.gov/colm.

Places to Stay in the Western Mountains

The rating scale for hotels is based on double occupancy and is as follows:
Inexpensive:
Less than $75 per night
Moderate:
 $75 to $100 per night
Expensive:
$100 to $150 per night
Deluxe:
More than $150 per night

ASPEN

Aspen Mountain Lodge,
311 West Main Street;
(970) 925–7650 or
(800) 362–7736
Moderate to deluxe

Boomerang Lodge,
500 West Hopkins;
(970) 925–3416
Expensive to deluxe

Limelite Lodge,
228 East Cooper Avenue;
(800) 433–0832
Inexpensive to deluxe

BRECKENRIDGE

Bed & Breakfasts on North Main Street,
303 North Main Street;
(970) 453–2975 or
(800) 795–2975
Moderate to deluxe

Evans House,
102 South French Street;
(970) 453–5509
Inexpensive to expensive

Hunt Placer Inn,
275 Ski Hill Road;
(970) 453–7573 or
(800) 472–1430
Expensive to deluxe

River Mountain Lodge,
100 South Park Avenue;
(970) 453–4711 or
(800) 627–3766
Expensive to deluxe

Swan Mountain Inn,
16172 Colorado 9
at Swan Mountain Road;
(970) 453–7903 or
(800) 578–3687
Inexpensive to deluxe

DILLON

Best Western Inn,
652 Lake Dillon Drive;
(970) 468–2341
Moderate to expensive

Dillon Inn,
708 Anemone Trail;
(970) 262–0801
Moderate

Four Points by Sheraton
(Summit County),
560 Silverthorne Lane,
Silverthorne;
(970) 468–6200
Moderate to deluxe

Silver Inn,
691 Blue River Parkway;
(970) 513–0104 or
(888) 513–0104
Inexpensive to moderate

Ski Tip Lodge
(one of Colorado's first lodges; great atmosphere; a little cramped; make reservations far in advance),
764 Montezuma Road
Keystone;
(970) 496–4950 or
(800) 742–0905
Moderate to deluxe

GEORGETOWN

Alpine Hideaway Bed & Breakfast
(has good views of Georgetown),
2045 Blue Bird Drive;
(800) 490–9011
Expensive to deluxe

SELECTED WESTERN MOUNTAINS
GENERAL INFORMATION RESOURCES

ASPEN

Aspen Chamber Resort Association,
425 Rio Grande Place;
(970) 925–1940
www.aspenchamber.org

BRECKENRIDGE

Breckenridge Resort Chamber,
P.O. Box 1909, 80424;
(888) 251–2417
www.gobreck.com

GEORGETOWN

**Downtown Georgetown
Community Center,**
P.O. Box 834, 80444;
(303) 569–2888 or (800) 472–8230
www.georgetowncolorado.com

GLENWOOD SPRINGS

**Glenwood Springs Chamber
Resort Association,**
1102 Grand Avenue;
(888) 4–GLENWOOD
www.glenwoodchamber.com

IDAHO SPRINGS

**Idaho Springs Chamber
of Commerce,**
P.O. Box 97, 80452;
(303) 567–4382
www.idahospringschamber.com

PALISADE

Palisade Chamber of Commerce,
319 Main Street;
(970) 464–7458
www.palisadecoc.com

VAIL

**Vail Valley Chamber
and Tourism Bureau,**
100 East Meadow Drive;
(970) 949–5189 or (800) 525–3875
www.visitvailvalley.com

Georgetown Motor Inn
(well-established, peaceful
motor inn; a modest
restaurant on premises),
1100 Rose;
(303) 569–3201 or
(800) 884–3201
Inexpensive to moderate

Hardy House Inn
(located in historic district),
605 Brownell Street;
(303) 569–3388
Inexpensive to expensive

**Mad Creek Bed
& Breakfast,**
167 West Park Avenue,
Empire
(303) 569–2003 or
(888) 266–1498
Inexpensive to moderate

GLENWOOD SPRINGS

Hot Springs Lodge
(across from Glenwood pool),
415 Sixth Street;
(800) 537–7946
Moderate to expensive

Hotel Colorado
(historic hotel; well-restored),
526 Pine;
(970) 945–6511 or
(800) 544–3998
Moderate to expensive

Redstone Inn,
82 Redstone Boulevard,
Redstone;
(800) 748–2524
Inexpensive to expensive

GRANT

The Tumbling River Ranch
(large swimming pool;
outstanding stables; a stay
here guarantees a quality
experience);
P.O. Box 30;
(303) 838–5981 or
(800) 654–8770
Deluxe

IDAHO SPRINGS

H & H Motor Lodge
(simple, clean motel),
2445 Colorado Boulevard;
(303) 567–2838 or
(800) 445–2893
www.hhlodge.com
Inexpensive to moderate

Heritage Inn
(quiet motel; within walking
distance of cafes),
2622 Colorado Boulevard;
(303) 567–4473
www.theheritageinn.com
Inexpensive to expensive

Places to Eat in the Western Mountains

The rating scale for
restaurants is as follows:
Inexpensive:
Most entrees less than $10
Moderate:
Most entrees $10 to $15
Expensive:
Most entrees $15 to $20
Deluxe:
Most entrees more than $20

ASPEN

Cantina
(Mexican, American),
411 East Main Street;
(970) 925–3663
Moderate to expensive

Paradise Bakery & Cafe
(delicious muffins, home-
made ice cream),
500 West Main Street;
(970) 920–1444
Inexpensive

Takah Sushi,
420 East Hyman Avenue;
(970) 925–8588
www.takahsushi.com
Deluxe

Ute City Bar and Grill
(centrally located),
501 East Hyman Avenue;
(970) 920–4699
Moderate to expensive

Wienerstube
(continental; a small
restaurant),
633 East Hyman Avenue;
(970) 925–3357
Moderate to expensive

BRECKENRIDGE

Breckenridge Brewery
(ribs, fish & chips, fajitas),
600 South Main Street;
(970) 453–1550;
www.breckenridge
brewery.com
Moderate

Cafe Alpine
(continental),
106 East Adams;
(970) 453–8218
www.cafealpine.com
Deluxe

Poirrier's Cajun Cafe,
224 South Main Street;
(970) 453–1877
Expensive to deluxe

St. Bernard Inn
(steak, seafood; extremely
busy in season),
103 South Main Street;
(970) 453–2572
Moderate to expensive

DILLON

Ristorante Al Lago
(higher than average prices;
veal, seafood, linguini),
240 Lake Dillon Drive;
(970) 468–6111
Expensive

**Silverheels at the
Ore House**
(Spanish tapas and
southwestern specialties),
601 Main Street (Frisco);
(970) 668–0345
Moderate to expensive

GEORGETOWN

The Happy Cooker
(unpretentious, homestyle
American restaurant;
outdoors in summer),
412 Sixth Street;
(303) 569–3166
Inexpensive to moderate

GLENWOOD SPRINGS

Daily Bread Cafe
(sandwiches, salads, soups),
729 Grand Avenue;
(970) 945–6253
Inexpensive to moderate

Dos Hombres (Mexican),
51783 Highway 6;
(970) 928–0490
Moderate

Florindo's (Italian),
721 Grand Avenue;
(970) 945–1245
Moderate to expensive

Los Desperados (Mexican),
55 Mel Rey Road;
(970) 945–6878
Moderate

Mancinelli's Pizza,
172 West Sixth Street;
(970) 928–9594
Inexpensive

River's (seafood, wild game),
2525 South Grand Avenue;
(970) 928–8813
www/theriversrestaurant.com
Moderate to expensive

IDAHO SPRINGS

BeauJo's
(famous homemade pizza),
1517 Miner Street;
(303) 567–4376
www.beaujos.com
Moderate

**The Buffalo Restaurant
and Bar**
(historical; pizza, barbecue
and Mexican; not exactly a
gourmet restaurant, but
adequate),
1617 Miner Street;
(303) 567–2729
www.buffalorestaur
ant.citysearch.com
Inexpensive to moderate

VAIL

Half Moon Saloon
(Mexican, American,
vegetarian options),
2161 North Frontage
Road West;
(970) 476–4314
Moderate

Left Bank (French),
183 Gore Creek Drive;
(970) 476–3696
Expensive

Pazzo's Pizzeria
(calzones, pizza),
122 East Meadow Drive;
(970) 476–9026
Moderate

Sweet Basil
(award-winning American
cuisine),
193 East Gore Creek Drive;
(970) 476–0125
Expensive to deluxe

The Tyrolean
(wild game, veal; terrific,
Austrian food),
400 East Meadow Drive;
(970) 476–2204
Deluxe

OTHER ATTRACTIONS WORTH SEEING IN THE WESTERN MOUNTAINS

ASPEN

**Aspen Historical Society
Wheeler/Stallard Musem,**
(970) 925–3721
www.aspenhistory.org/wsh.html

Independence Pass
(Highway 82, closed in winter)
www.independencepass.org

DILLON

Copper Mountain Resort Ski Area,
(866) 841–2481
www.coppercolorado.com

GEORGETOWN

Loveland Ski Area,
(800) 736–3754
www.skiloveland.com

GLENWOOD

White River National Forest,
(970) 945–2521
www.fs.fed.us/r2/whiteriver/

IDAHO SPRINGS

**Idaho Springs National
Historic District,**
(303) 567–4709
www.idahospringschamber.com/
f_activity.html

Southern Colorado

Colorado Springs and Beyond

Contrary to rumors, mountain driving is not especially dangerous or tricky. According to the Colorado State Patrol, most accidents actually happen in the flat, straight stretches at high speeds.

But the stranger to winter is better off knowing a few special driving precautions and tricks. Hence, some thoughts are in order:

- When renting a car in winter, insist on special snow tires, even if the pavement is dry. Also, it's better to carry tire chains unnecessarily than to be caught without them; they are essential in blizzards. Front-wheel drive is preferable for better traction.
- Before starting out on any extended trip in wintertime, the following safety equipment should be checked: brakes, headlights and taillights, exhaust system, windshield wipers, defrosters, heaters, and tools. Toss in a spare blanket, high-energy food that is not perishable, flares, gloves, a hat . . .
- Starting slowly on snow provides better traction and prevents spinning of wheels or skidding sideways into parked cars or

other vehicles or objects. On a slick surface, start in second gear; this keeps the car's wheels from spinning.

- When driving in a fog or snowstorm, you get better visibility by using the lower headlight beam. The upper headlight beam tends to reflect back off the fog and blind you.
- Whenever visibility becomes so poor, due to fog or snow, that it is impossible to see more than a few feet ahead, it is best to pull off the road. Clean the windshield or wait until the weather eases up.
- Car heaters draw in fresh air from the outside. Vehicles should never be parked directly behind another car that has the motor running.
- When roads are wet and the temperature drops to 32°F or below, the surface will become icy. Extreme caution is indicated. A single driver can start a chain of mass collisions on ice.
- Get the feel of the road when pavements are slippery by trying brakes occasionally while driving slowly and away from traffic.
- As the temperature rises, ice (and, to a lesser degree, snow) becomes much slicker. For example, at 20 miles per hour when the temperature is 32°F, stopping distance on ice without tire chains or snow tires is 250 feet. When

AUTHOR'S FAVORITES IN SOUTHERN COLORADO

Camp Hale,
(970) 827–5715 or (970) 827–9343
www.camphale.org

Garden of the Gods,
(719) 634–6666
www.gardenofgods.com

Great Sand Dunes National Monument and Preserve,
(719) 378–2312
www.nps.gov/grsa

Manitou and Pikes Peak Railway,
(719) 685–5401
www.cograilway.com

Mesa Verde National Park,
(970) 529–4465
www.nps.gov/meve

Mollie Kathleen Gold Mine,
(719) 689–2466 or (888) 291–5689
(then enter pin number 9101)
www.goldminetours.com

Royal Gorge Bridge and Park,
(719) 275–7507 or (888) 333–5597
www.royalgorgebridge.com

Seven Falls,
(719) 632–0765
www.sevenfalls.com

Shelf Road,
(719) 269–8500
www.co.blm.gov/recweb/rectouring.htm

The Spa at Pagosa Springs,
(970) 264–5910 or (800) 832–5523
www.coloradodirectory.com/sparesort

the temperature is at zero, stopping distance is 110 feet. The difference of 140 feet might well cause a serious accident.

- By stopping slowly, the driver can prevent skidding and come to a safer halt. If your vehicle starts to skid or the wheels lock, release the brake pressure. Pump the brakes; that is, apply the brakes lightly and intermittently. This is especially important with old-model cars. A minimum of pressure should be used. Steady, even braking does the trick. Or do you have ABS or disc brakes? If so, just increase the pressure steadily until your car slows down.
- Keep your windshield and windows clear, making sure you can see danger in time to avoid trouble. Windshield-wiper blades should not be too worn; they should be up to the task of removing rain or snow without streaking. Also, the defroster should function efficiently. Ensure good visibility in the rear by removing the snow and ice from the back window when necessary.
- Occasionally a patch of ice will remain on a curve or other shaded spot after the rest of the road has been cleared. Be on the lookout for these ice patches.
- A thorough check of the exhaust system should be made at regular intervals; possible leaks could cause a tragedy. (Carbon monoxide poisoning is a deadly driving hazard during wintertime.) It is a good idea to leave at least one window slightly open when driving in cold weather.
- Weather and road conditions in Colorado's mountains are subject to abrupt changes. It is possible to get a report that a certain area is clear, yet you arrive there two or three hours later to find a snowstorm in progress or the highways icy and snow covered. The reverse is also true, and adverse weather conditions often clear up in a short time.

The *Devil's Head Lookout Trail,* in the Rampart Range west of the little community of Sedalia (south of Denver), is one of the state's most scenic trails. It got its name from the red rock formations that stick out like two horns. You walk up through deep pine forests interspersed with aspen, past giant red cliffs. The trail's length—just 1⅜ miles—doesn't sound like much; it climbs steeply, though, and includes a 1,000-foot vertical elevation gain. (The summit is at 9,747 feet, the parking lot at 8,800 feet.)

trivia

The Devil's Head Lookout Tower at the end of the Devil's Head Lookout Trail rests on the highest point in the Rampart Range. It is the last operational lookout on the Front Range.

Along the way, you get views of the "fourteeners" (peaks over 14,000 feet high) and the Great Plains. Benches for the tired line the uphill paths. Motorized vehicles are outlawed in the ascent to Devil's Head.

TOP ANNUAL EVENTS IN SOUTHERN COLORADO

Pagosa Springs Winter Fest;
second weekend in February;
(800) 252–2204
www.pagosa-springs.com

Music and Blossom Festival,
Cañon City; mid-March;
(719) 275–7200
www.canoncitychamber.com

Royal Gorge Rodeo,
Cañon City; May;
(719) 275–0118
www.horsestop.net/royalgorgerodeo.htm

Donkey Derby,
Cripple Creek; late June;
(877) 858–GOLD
www.cripple-creek.co.us

Colorado Renaissance Festival,
Larkspur; June and July;
(303) 688–6010
www.coloradorenaissance.com

**Cattlemen's Days Rodeo
and County Fair,**
Gunnison; mid-July;
(800) 323–2453
www.gunnisoncounty.com

Boom Days and Burro Race,
Leadville; first full weekend of August;
(719) 486–2887
www.leadville.com/boomdays

Pikes Peak or Bust Rodeo,
Colorado Springs; mid-August;
(719) 635–3547
www.coloradospringsrodeo.com

Colorado State Fair,
Pueblo Fairgrounds;
late August–early September;
(719) 561–8484 or (800) 876–4567
www.coloradosfair.com

Colorado Springs Balloon Classic;
Labor Day weekend;
(719) 471–4833
www.balloonclassic.com

Durango Cowboy Poetry Gathering,
Durango; first week of October;
(800) 525–8855
www.durango.org

Driving directions? From Denver, take Santa Fe (U.S. Highway 85) south to Sedalia (13 miles); turn west toward Deckers (Highway 67) for 10 miles and make another left turn onto the Rampart Range Road (Highway 5); go another 8.5 miles until you see the DEVIL'S HEAD sign. For more information contact South Platte Ranger District, 19316 Goddard Ranch Court, Morrison 80465; (303) 275–5610; www.fs.fed.us/r2/psicc/spl/devils_head.shtml.

En route from Denver to Colorado Springs via the interstate, you may see a modest sign that says LARKSPUR. Few travelers have ever heard of it. Even some Denverites are unfamiliar with this hamlet.

Yet, on weekends from mid-June through July, tiny *Larkspur* comes alive with a bang. Cannon shots can be heard from afar. When your car draws closer to the hillside, the cannons are followed by medieval trumpets, played in unison.

For more than twenty years, the zany, lively *Colorado Renaissance Festival* has entertained summer visitors in its offbeat location above Larkspur on a wooded Colorado hillside, part theater, part learning experience, part petting zoo for children, part commerce. The Renaissance theme begins when you enter the walled compound and you're greeted as "My Lord" or "My Lady." Artisans galore demonstrate their craft: blacksmiths hammer away, glassblowers regale onlookers with their art, potters have brought their wheels, leather workers show their stuff. Bands of costumed musicians wander up the mountainside. Harpists, flutists, bagpipers, and minstrel singers materialize and harmonize.

Several times a day, "King Henry" and his "Court" introduce you to knights jousting on horseback at a gallop, doing tricks with their lances. The stages are busy with storytellers and merrymakers; the pubs dispense barrels of beer and huge turkey legs. Processions of celebrities—Shakespeare, Anne Boleyn— march among the visitors while, a few yards away, you can be a medieval archer or knife thrower or dart artist. Encounter the unexpected: Youngsters ride real camels and elephants; a few steps away, jugglers and puppet masters dazzle the onlookers. A good time is had by everyone.

All this against the backdrop of—and amid—Colorado's mountains. No charge for parking weekends June through July. To reach Larkspur, take exit 172 from Interstate 25 and follow the signs. Open 10:00 A.M. to 6:30 P.M. Saturday and Sunday. Admission costs $15.95 for adults and teenagers thirteen and older and $8.00 for children five to twelve; children four and younger free. Discount tickets can be purchased at any King Soopers (a local grocery store chain). For more information contact the festival at 409F South Wilcox Street, Castle Rock 80104; (303) 688–6010; www.coloradorenaissance.com.

A ten-minute drive south of Larkspur, on the same little Country Road 105, and you will suddenly come face-to-face with *Palmer Lake.* Almost no travel guide mentions it. Most people bypass it via speedy I–25. Palmer Lake used to be busy and important; now it's almost forgotten. A few lost souls are fishing here. Others walk around the idyllic lake on a footpath or take their young children to the small playground. Mountains rise on all sides. Traffic is minimal. It's a fine place to relax. For more information contact the Town Offices at 42 Valley Crescent, Palmer Lake 80133; (719) 481–2953; www.ci.palmer-lake.co.us.

For those who like to hike or bike, the 15-mile *Santa Fe Regional Trail,* one of the largest continuous trails in El Paso County, begins at *Palmer Lake Recreation Area.* It goes through the town of Monument to the south, ending at the southern boundary of the *United States Air Force Academy.* For more information call (719) 520–6375; www.adm.elpasoco.com/parks.

The Air Force Academy is one of Colorado's most visited landmarks. Whether you hike, bike, or drive, you should consider a stop at the academy's visitor center, located at exit 150B off I–25. A nature trail and the attractive **Cadet Chapel** appeal to the curious passerby. Eyes are invariably drawn upward by the chapel's seventeen silver-hued spires that sweep to heights of more than 150 feet. Completed in 1963, the chapel, considered to be the architectural centerpiece of the academy's campus, holds Protestant, Catholic, and Jewish services. It is open Monday through Saturday, 9:00 A.M. to 5:00 P.M.; Sunday from 10:00 A.M. to 5:00 P.M. Sunday services are open to all; call (719) 333–2636 for times.

When visiting the academy, request a map at the gate. The visitor center is open from 9:00 A.M. to 5:00 P.M. daily in winter, and until 6:00 P.M. in summer. For more information call (719) 333–2025; www.usafa.af.mil/hc.

trivia

The Air Force Academy's Cadet Chapel received a 1996 American Institute of Architects' award. The chapel conducts services for Protestant, Catholic, and Jewish worshippers.

Not far from the U.S. Air Force Academy, you'll discover your next stop— the **ProRodeo Hall of Fame and Museum of the American Cowboy,** which presents the West's unique cowboy heritage in a facility that is both entertaining and educational. The cowboy played a vital role in opening the West to the expansion of the nineteenth century, and his reputation for courage and individualism has become part of our national folklore and has shaped the American character.

Families with children will enjoy the outdoor corral with its live animals. Inside, dioramas and exhibits of well-displayed saddles, boots, buckles, spurs, ropes, chaps, branding equipment, and other paraphernalia await examination, all telling the story of rodeo's history in this country. Rodeo as a sport comes alive through the mementos of America's major rodeo champions.

The visitor can learn about such colorful rodeo champs as bull rider Warren G. "Freckles" Brown, reputed to be the oldest man in ProRodeo history to win a riding event. His long career was interrupted by a broken neck, as well as by World War II. With typical spirit during wartime parachute jumps into China, Brown put on a rodeo using army mules and native cattle and declared himself the Orient's all-around champion of 1942.

Over the years, rules and equipment were standardized, judging was streamlined, prize money increased, and the freewheeling entertainment of the 1800s evolved into the modern sport of professional rodeo.

Here the visitor can learn the fine points of saddle bronc riding and how to judge a rider's performance—and can get the jolting sensation, through film with stereo sound, of what it's like to ride a bucking Brahma bull. Other films trace the historical development of rodeo.

The ProRodeo Hall of Fame is located just north of Colorado Springs on I–25 at exit 147. Hours are 9:00 A.M. to 5:00 P.M. daily except for major holidays. A modest fee is charged to help defray expenses of the nonprofit museum. Call (719) 528–4764 or write 101 ProRodeo Drive, Colorado Springs 80919; www.prorodeo.com.

The wonders of nature blend together at the *Garden of the Gods* in Colorado Springs to create one of the most varied natural settings in Colorado. Established as a free city park in 1909, the almost 1,370 acres are filled with silent and spectacular red sandstone rock formations, including Gateway Rocks, Cathedral Spires, and the Balanced Rock.

trivia

The Garden of the Gods was once sacred ground to Native Americans.

Grasslands meet mountain forests to provide contrasts of scenic beauty. A common resident of the park is the great horned owl, whose keen, light-gathering eyes and superior hearing make it an effective nighttime hunter.

Hike, picnic, and horseback ride to fully appreciate the park's natural beauty. But most of all, bring your camera and photograph these wonders (especially at sunset or sunrise when the low sun accents the naturally colorful red stone).

The park itself is open daily from November 1 through April 30 from 5:00 A.M. to 9:00 P.M. and May 1 through October 31 from 5:00 A.M. to 11:00 P.M. The visitor center is open daily from 9:00 A.M. to 5:00 P.M. The center offers free color maps of the park and free entrance to the *Museum of Natural and Cultural History.* Arrive via exit 146 off I–25. Go west on Garden of the Gods Road, and then south on North Thirtieth Street. The Visitor Center will be on your left at Gateway Road. For more information: Garden of the Gods Visitor and Nature Center, 1805 North Thirtieth Street, Colorado Springs 80904; (719) 634–6666; www.gardenofgods.com.

If you want to vacation in the lap of luxury, consider the five-star *Broadmoor,* which has 14,110-foot Pikes Peak for a backdrop. The Broadmoor actually began in the 1850s with a Silesian count. He hoped to create another Monte Carlo against the backdrop of Colorado's mountainscape. Eventually, two Philadelphians, Charles Tutt and Spencer Penrose, took over. They'd gotten rich in Cripple Creek mining and real estate; as world travelers, they knew what they wanted—a regal, Renaissance-style hotel.

The Broadmoor's doors opened on June 29, 1918; among several notables, the first to register was John D. Rockefeller Jr. Since that day, there has been a stream of industrialists, diplomats, movie moguls, film stars, and titled ladies

A Tour of NORAD

Cheyenne Mountain houses the bomb-proof headquarters of the *North American Aerospace Defense Command,* (NORAD). Here, some 100 computers and more than a million miles of communications lines monitor the horizon for enemy missile attacks. More than 1,700 people populate a small city deep inside this hollowed-out mountain, where the fifteen buildings are supported by 1,319 steel springs weighing 1,000 pounds each. Rock reservoirs hold 6 million gallons of water, and steel blast doors protect the complex. (In case of nuclear attack, these 25,000-pound gates can be closed in 30 seconds.)

NOTE: At press time, public presentations for adults and children twelve and older have been put on hold due to increased security concerns. For more information write to NORAD Attn: Major David H. Patterson, Chief, Commander's Action Group, 1 NORAD Road, Suite 101–213, Cheyenne Mountain AFS, 80914 or call (719) 474–2238; www.norad.mil.

and gentlemen. They mingle nicely nowadays with anyone who can afford this pricey, year-round retreat. It is the largest, plushest, and most elegant in Colorado, offering every conceivable amenity.

The (deluxe) Broadmoor isn't for economy travelers; bring lots of traveler's checks or your best credit card. For more information call (800) 634–7711; www.broadmoor.com.

Seven Falls is ten driving minutes west of the Broadmoor resort. "The Grandest Mile of Scenery in Colorado" lives up to its slogan: A 1,000-foot-high granite canyon leads to seven waterfalls flanked by healthy forests of juniper, blue spruce, Douglas fir, and ponderosa pine. Not far from the dramatic, perpendicular "pillars of Hercules," you can climb several hundred steep steps to platforms from which you view these scenic wonders.

Cheyenne Mountain Zoo

Above the Broadmoor resort, you can visit the *Cheyenne Mountain Zoo.* The giraffes, bears, elk, deer, penguins, and other creatures are kept in their natural environment. To reach the zoo, from I-25 go south on Nevada Avenue. Turn right on Lake Avenue. Turn onto Mirada Road and follow signs. Admission is $12.00 for adults, $10.00 for seniors sixty-five and older and $6.00 for children three to eleven; children two and younger free. For more information call (719) 633–9925 or visit www.cmzoo.org.

You get to Seven Falls via Cheyenne Boulevard and Mesa (exit 140B off I–25). Hours vary from 8:30 A.M. to 10:30 P.M. in midsummer to 9:00 A.M. to 4:15 P.M. in winter; call for details. Admission costs $8.25 for adults and $5.25 for children ages six to fifteen. For more information write to Seven Falls Company, P.O. Box 118, Colorado Springs 80901 or call (719) 632–0765; www.sevenfalls.com.

The year was 1806; the discoverer of Colorado Springs's "Great Mountain" was Lieutenant Zebulon Montgomery Pike. Neither he nor any of his party got even close to the summit, due to bad weather and perhaps a lack of planning. At that time, it certainly wasn't conceivable that one of America's most unusual railroads ever constructed would carry thousands of persons to its summit.

Today a visit to Colorado Springs can be enhanced by a trip on the country's highest railroad to the summit of famous Pikes Peak. The ***Manitou and Pikes Peak Cog Railway,*** which is 46,158 feet long, climbs from an elevation of 6,571 feet at the Manitou Springs station to one of 14,110 feet at the summit. This is a vertical gain of 7,539 feet, or an average of 846 feet per mile. Actually, the distance is longer than any covered by the famous cogwheel rails in Switzerland.

trivia

Some of the bristlecone pine trees along the Manitou and Pikes Peak Cog Railway are estimated to be almost 2,000 years old, making them among the oldest living things on earth.

Along the entire route you'll be treated to a continuous panorama of scenery. At the 11,578-foot level, the trains emerge from a sea of quaking aspen into the windswept stretches of timberline and climb into the Saddle, where you get an unparalleled view of Manitou Springs and of the Garden of the Gods in the valley below. You also see the vast expanses of the Great Plains stretch toward the horizon.

The Manitou and Pikes Peak Cog Railway

Some Little-Known Facts about Manitou Springs

It was actually from Manitou Springs's mineral springs that Colorado Springs got its name.

"Manitou" is a Native American word for "Great Spirit."

Native Americans attributed supernatural powers to Manitou Springs's waters and temporarily reserved the surrounding area as a sanctuary.

On clear days, it is actually possible to spot Denver 75 miles to the north of Colorado Springs and the dramatic Sangre de Cristo Mountains in southern Colorado. The view of the west is astounding; mile upon mile of snowcapped giants rise into the blue Colorado sky.

Be sure to leave time to peruse the offerings at Steamer Stop Shop (clothing and curios) at the Manitou Springs Station. You can purchase a box lunch to eat while on the train ($8.00 per lunch). The Cog Railway runs from April through December. Tickets run about $25 for adults, $13 for children three to eleven, and children younger than three ride free if held on a lap throughout the ride. Reservations are highly recommended. The round-trip takes three hours and ten minutes; call for departure times. Take exit 141 (U.S. Highway 24) off I–25. Head west on US 24 for 4 miles to the Manitou Springs exit. Go west on Manitou Avenue for 1½ miles. Turn left on Ruxton Avenue. The station is ¾ mile up. For more information call (719) 685–5401, or visit www.cograilway.com.

Back in 1891, the ***Cripple Creek*** gold strike proved to be the last major gold rush in North America. Within a few years, those mines in the mountains west of Colorado Springs yielded almost a billion dollars' worth of the valuable mineral. By 1900 Cripple Creek grew to some 50,000 inhabitants. The miners could patronize seventy-five saloons, forty grocery stores, seventeen churches, and eight newspapers. Every day a dozen passenger trains steamed into the depot. Eventually, 500 gold mines operated in the area. Some 8,000 men brought on a gambling, carousing, and whoring boom.

trivia

Mining experts considered Cripple Creek worthless despite frequent reports of gold; still, novice prospectors, mining with pitchforks, eventually developed the "300-million-dollar cow pasture."

Some Little-Known Facts about Cripple Creek

In its heyday, the Cripple Creek area produced $25 million in gold in one year.

Famous Cripple Creek workers included Jack Johnson and Jack Dempsey. Dempsey once fought a bloody, drawn-out battle here in Cripple Creek . . . for fifty dollars.

Speakeasy hostess "Texas" Guinan started in Cripple Creek. Perhaps this is one of the reasons why the city is now best known for its Las Vegas–style gambling.

Ironically, the man who discovered the first gold vein sold his claim for $500 and proceeded to drink it all away. Colorado Springs owes part of its existence to the prospectors. In time, celebrities came and went. Adventurer Lowell Thomas was born in nearby Victor, now nearly a ghost town. Groucho Marx once drove a grocery wagon in Cripple Creek. Jack Dempsey, for a brief bout a miner, trained and boxed in the region. Financier Bernard Baruch worked as a telegrapher here. Teddy Roosevelt, after a Cripple Creek visit, told the world that "the scenery bankrupts the English language." The politicians arrived in droves to see for themselves.

By and by, gold prices dropped. Production began to slip. The miners scattered. By 1920 fewer than 5,000 people lived here.

And today? Cripple Creek attracts hordes of summer tourists. They come for the narrow-gauge train rides. They pan for gold on Main Street. They play at the slot machines. They attend one of the summer performances put on by the *Cripple Creek Players* at the newly renovated *Historic Butte Opera House.* This building, originally constructed in 1896, has had many uses throughout its history. Before its renovation in the late 1990s, the building served as home to the Cripple Creek Fire Department. Extensive renovations by the city of Cripple Creek served to restore the theater's splendor. The Historic Butte Opera House now seats 174 people and boasts a 1,350-square-foot stage, state-of-the-art sound equipment and movie projectors, and a snack bar. For more information and performance dates, contact the Cripple Creek Players at (719) 689–2513 or (800) 500–2513; www.cripplecreekplayers.com.

trivia

The Cripple Creek Mining District, made up of roughly 25 towns in the Cripple Creek area, was once known as "The World's Greatest Gold Camp."

The old railroad depot has become the *Cripple Creek District Museum,* along with an old assay office and the Colorado Trading and Transfer Company building, constructed in 1893. These three buildings are crammed with mementos of the mining age. Superbly kept up, the museum is well worth a visit. Hours are 10:00 A.M. to 5:00 P.M. daily Memorial Day through September; weekends for the rest of the year. Call (719) 689–2634 or (719) 689–9540; www.cripple-creek.org. The museum is on Bennett Avenue in Cripple Creek.

The local folks are calm and friendly despite the tourist hubbub. Cripple Creek jumps with visitors all summer. They flock to the redbrick souvenir and antiques shops, where a 1929 beer bottle or a 1950s glass pitcher sells as if it were a rare treasure. You can watch the donkeys on Bennett Avenue, buy cowboy boots in a real western store, and eat home-cooked food in little cafes.

Not many travelers venture on foot beyond the central core of this community. Yet visual rewards await those who make the most of Cripple Creek's lovely location. It is nestled among the Colorado hillsides that climb from town in every direction. Nature awaits the walker who leaves the redbrick confines and heads for the slopes of conifers and aspen trees. The mountains here are studded with old abandoned mines, which you reach by hiking up the unused roads past rusting machinery, past the old wooden mine trestles, past the piles of forgotten ore.

The *Mollie Kathleen Gold Mine* still attracts visitors, who can tour the 1,000-foot deep historic mine. Back in 1891, Mollie Kathleen Gortner moved to the area with her family, including her husband, an attorney by the name of Henry. On an excursion by herself to see a herd of elk (she'd never seen them before), Mollie Kathleen came upon an outcropping of quartz that was veined with gold. Upon attempting to file her claim in town, she was informed that as a woman, she had no right to do so. Not to be deterred, Mollie Kathleen seized the papers and signed them anyway, declaring that the issue could be taken

Take a Ride on the Railroad

For an unusual perspective, try viewing the area from a car on the *Cripple Creek and Victor Narrow-Gauge Railroad.* It takes about forty-five minutes to complete the 4-mile ride behind a coal-burning steam locomotive. You travel past the area's abandoned mines. The railroad is open from mid-May through the second week of October. Call (719) 689–2640 for departure times. The fare is $9.00 for adults andd teenagers thirteen and older, $8.00 for senior citizens sixty-five and older, and $5.00 for children three to twelve; children two and younger ride free; www.cripplecreekrailroad.com.

up with her husband if there was a problem. Thus Mollie Kathleen Gortner became the first woman in the area to stake a gold claim. Her mine continued to produce gold uninterrupted for the next seventy years, with the exception of a period of time during World War II when all gold production ceased due to a nationwide ban. Today the gold that came out of the mine would be worth more than $100 million.

trivia

Cripple Creek's Mollie Kathleen Gold Mine, the longest continually operating gold mine tour in the world, boasts the only 1000-foot vertical-shaft gold mine tour in the United States.

Appropriate for all ages (there are no steps or ladders to climb), the forty-minute tours of the Mollie Kathleen Gold Mine depart at frequent intervals during the peak season. The mine is open for tours daily from early April through early November. During the off-season, tours take place on some Fridays, Saturdays, and Sundays. Call ahead. Rates are $11.00 for adults and $5.00 for children three to eleven; children two and younger tour free. For more information call (719) 689–2466 or (888) 291–5689–9101. When using the toll-free phone number, you must enter a PIN number (9101); www.goldminetours.com.

Cripple Creek deserves more than a few hasty hours. At least one overnight stay makes sense. Slot machines and other gaming devices have come to this community. Many visitors hope to strike it rich at the town's plethora of casinos, but the richness of Cripple Creek's history should not be neglected!

Cripple Creek is 45 miles west of Colorado Springs. From there it can be reached via US 24 west, then Highway 67. For more information write the Cripple Creek Welcome Center, P.O. Box 430, Cripple Creek 80813; call (877) 858–4653 or (719) 689–3315; or visit www.cripple-creek.co.us.

Driving farther south, you may want to stop in **Pueblo,** a quiet, hospitable community of 105,000 souls who, in recent years, have gone historic.

trivia

More than half of Colorado's goods are made in Pueblo.

The citizenry is especially proud of the *Historic Arkansas Riverwalk of Pueblo (HARP) Authority.* The twenty-six acres of HARP serve as a demonstration of just how beautiful an urban waterfront can be. Pedestrian walkways and bike paths crisscross the area. A lakeside promenade for waterfowl and other wildlife exists alongside Lake Elizabeth, and the original stone wall from the Arkansas River remains intact, in keeping with HARP's historical theme. For more information call (719) 595–0242, or visit www.pueblo harp.com/aboutHARP.htm.

Pueblo's El Pueblo History Museum

Designed to be the gateway to HARP, the new *El Pueblo History Museum* includes a permanent gallery covering the history of Pueblo along with an atrium gallery and a children's gallery. An additional temporary exhibit gallery displays western history–themed exhibits. In addition, the museum serves as a central location for tourist information. Please contact the museum at (719) 583–0453 for details or visit www.coloradohistory.org/hist_sites/pueblo/pueblo.htm. The museum is located at 301 North Union Street in Pueblo.

Pueblo, located some 40 miles south of Colorado Springs, hosts the yearly *Colorado State Fair & Exposition,* one of the biggest events in the state. Every summer, the fair promises to be an action-packed seventeen-day experience for all who visit, whether youth or adults, singles, or families.

The Colorado State Fair is unique. Witness the variety of activities planned, from PRCA championship rodeo to the largest carnival and midway in the state. There are hundreds of lambs, steers, hogs, horses, and other animals to see and touch, a popular children's barnyard, parks with all types of free entertainment, along with scores of exhibits and creative arts, and evening performances by some of the nation's top entertainers.

General admission to the state fair is $7.00 Friday through Sunday and $5.00 Monday through Thursday; children six and younger get in free. Hours run 2:00 P.M. to midnight Monday through Friday and 10:00 A.M. to 11:00 P.M. Saturday and Sunday. From I–25, take exit 97A west (Central Avenue). This will take you to Northern Avenue. Follow Northern west; the state fairgrounds will be on your right. Call (719) 561–8484 or (800) 876–4567 for details, or visit www.coloradosfair.com.

trivia

Originally, Pueblo was a crossroads for travelers, including Spaniards, fur traders, and Native Americans.

In a nearby residential district, there awaits one of Colorado's most stately bed-and-breakfasts; this mansion is known as the *Abriendo Inn.* This distinguished small hostelry couldn't have a better location, not far from the community college and the historic Union Avenue. The inn has only ten rooms, each a little different, but all with period furniture, old-fashioned lace curtains, canopied or brass beds, fresh flowers, oak antiques, and original art. Intriguingly, each room comes with appropriate magazines like *Victorian Homes, Country Living,* and *Architectural Digest.* The owner, Kerrelyn McCafferty Trent, happens to be an interior designer and noted

trivia

In December 1999, the city of Pueblo was astonished to find seventeen trees on its Historic Arkansas Riverwalk destroyed within a matter of days. The culprit? A Colorado beaver whom officials affectionately deemed "Bandit" before they relocated the creature to a place a little farther out of town.

gourmet whose staff serves up free evening snacks and unexpected breakfast inventions. The aristocratic atmosphere makes one think of an embassy; in fact, the inn is so perfect that it's slightly intimidating. (The grandeur is inexpensive, however; a night at the Abriendo Inn costs about one-half of Grand Hotel accommodations.) For more information call (719) 544–2703, or visit www.abriendoinn.com.

For more information on visiting the Pueblo area, contact the Greater Pueblo Chamber of Commerce, P.O. Box 697, Pueblo 81002; (800) 233–3446; www.pueblo.org.

From Pueblo, head west on U.S. Highway 50 to Cañon City and its nearby attractions, including **Shelf Road.** Shelf Road makes up part of the **Gold Belt Tour,** a designated Colorado Scenic Byway. From stunning limestone cliffs that attract rock climbers from all over the world to the sheer drop-offs on the side of the road (hence the name) into lush green valleys, the views and the isolation encountered along Shelf Road are idyllic. Abundant wildlife viewing potential rounds out the area's special charm—past sightings include mule deer, foxes, hawks, American black bears, and owls.

Bear-ly Noticed

We were driving along the Shelf Road one bright and sunny Colorado morning on our way to rock climb. My eyes lazily roved over the lush greenery of Helena Canyon several hundred feet below while I silently wondered at its isolation and wildness, despite the private road that cuts through a portion of it. Suddenly my attention was drawn to a black lumbering shape, ambling along that very road.

"A bear!" I exclaimed, filled with excitement.

My spouse slammed on the brakes and we hopped out of the car, looking down the sheer canyon walls at the bear hundreds of feet below us, yet still clearly visible. The bear, an American Black Bear, continued to snuffle its way along as we watched, until a change in the wind must have brought our scent to its attention: it raised its head, stared straight at us, and took off running in the other direction. I was filled with both amazement at the gift of watching such a being in its natural setting and an odd sense of sadness that my very presence, hundreds of yards away from this creature, could so frighten it.

Bureau of Land Management and U.S. Forest Service

The Bureau of Land Management (BLM) administers millions of acres of public lands around the country, including 8.4 million acres in Colorado, while the U.S. Forest Service (USFS) manages 14.3 million acres in the state. State offices for both organizations can direct you to specific regional and local offices, many of which are listed throughout this book as well. For more information, look on the USFS Web site—www.fs.fed.us/r2—or contact the USFS Rocky Mountain Regional Office at (303) 275–5350. For information about BLM lands in Colorado, visit www.co.blm.gov/index.htm or contact the BLM Colorado state office at (303) 239–3600.

Some of the driving is on rough roads (it's not for the faint of heart) and should be avoided in wet or icy weather; furthermore, four-wheel-drive is recommended for portions of Upper Shelf Road. However, any two-wheel-drive vehicle can enjoy some of the sights available along the portion of Shelf Road that leads out of Cañon City. The road becomes narrow once it turns to dirt, so drive carefully and slowly, watching for oncoming traffic. Plan ahead where you are going to turn around; a good place is at mile marker 14. The entire Gold Belt Tour encompasses 131 miles of driving and takes roughly five hours. From Cañon City, venture north on Raynolds, and then head north again on Fields after Raynolds swings west. Nine miles along Fields takes you directly to Shelf Road. For more information call (719) 269–8500; www.co.blm.gov/ccdo/canon.htm.

After a jaunt along Shelf Road, another scenic wonder awaits you at the ***Royal Gorge Bridge and Park.*** The gorge, at 1,200 feet deep, has been compared to the Grand Canyon. With its striking reds, mauves, browns, and yellows, the deep and narrow gauge stopped Lieutenant Zebulon Pike (of Pikes Peak fame) in his tracks back in 1806. He couldn't forge the gorge (and he didn't climb Pikes Peak, either).

In 1929 the Royal Gorge Bridge

trivia

The Royal Gorge Bridge cost more than $10 million to construct.

opened up to traffic after seven months of construction. The bridge is able to support more than two million pounds, so don't worry about your car's weight! Seventy years later, people still flock from all over to drive across this mighty suspension bridge, allegedly the highest of its kind in the world.

The 2,200-foot-long *Aerial Tram* offers another viewing option as it takes visitors for a ride across the fabulous canyon. Painted a fiery red, the thirty-five-passenger tram cabin comes with a guide-conductor who assures timid passengers that the tram will not plunge into the Arkansas River, which rages and roars below. Three braking systems and an extra motor guarantee this. In the terminals, a total of about one hundred tons of concrete and steel anchor the conveyance's enormous cables, providing reassurance with their heftiness. In fact, a helicopter had to string the tram's pilot cable, and more than $350,000 was needed to rig up this tourist attraction.

trivia

The Royal Gorge Bridge and Park averages about 500,000 visitors annually.

After looking at it from above, hop aboard for a five-and-a-half-minute ride on the *Incline Railway* to the bottom of the gorge. The world's steepest conveyance of its kind, the Incline Railway gives you a topsy-turvy view of the gorge as you look back up at the bridge above you. Built by the same crew who built the bridge, the railway opened in 1931 and has been operating ever since.

trivia

Cañon City is the county seat of Fremont County, which has nine state prison facilities and a federal prison complex with four facilities. The state and federal prisons are the largest employers in the area, together accounting for more than 3,000 workers.

Families will appreciate a variety of other attractions including a carousel, a little scale-model open-air train that chugs along around Royal Gorge Park, and a wildlife pavilion. Park admission is $20 for adults and teenagers and $16 for children four to eleven; children three and younger are admitted free. Park hours are 8:30 A.M. to dusk daily. Admission offers unlimited access to all park attractions, although some attractions are seasonal. Call for details. The Royal Gorge Bridge and Park is 12 miles west of Cañon City on US 50. Call (719) 275–7507 or (888) 333–5597; www.royalgorgebridge.com.

The Cañon City Chamber of Commerce is located at 403 Royal Gorge Boulevard; (719) 275–2331 or (800) 876–7922; www.canoncitychamber.com.

Perhaps after Cañon City, your route will take you farther west on US 50 to *Salida.* There are few more outdoorsy places in Colorado. Salida is famous for white-water rafting, kayaking, and jeeping. The local folks are friendly. In fact, the *Tudor Rose Bed & Breakfast* is unashamedly relaxed and western; you're welcome to bring your own horse (stables available; humans can stay in one of the six guest rooms, most of which have spectacular views). The innkeeper can identify the Sangre de Cristos and the Sawach range. As you look around you, the Tudor Rose gets ready for your solid, western breakfast.

For more information on Salida contact the Heart of the Rockies Chamber of Commerce, 406 West Highway 50, Salida 81201; (719) 539–2068 or (877) 772–5432; www.salidachamber.org.

Where the Old West Lives

Camp Hale was nicknamed "Camp Hell" by the Mountain Troopers, who first trained here, 18 miles north of Leadville. From 1942 to 1945, the camp served the famous World War II Tenth Mountain Division. Much of their tough battle preparations took place at the chilly 9,500 feet above sea level, on 6,500 mountain acres, surrounded by 12,000-foot snow giants.

The altitude and the thin air took their toll on young recruits from the Midwest; the new arrivals couldn't sleep at first and felt weak during the day. Smoke from 300 barrack chimneys and railroads hung over the camp, and you could hear a lot of coughing.

Camp Hale days often started at 4:30 A.M. with 15-mile marches through blizzards. Packs weighed eighty pounds or more, and the troopers would be pulled backward. The army skis were often so stiff that they sank into the snow. Some southern and midwestern fellows, recruited at the last minute, termed skis their "torture boards." Each time a novice lifted a leg, his muscles hurt. His arms ached, too, from the unaccustomed efforts. The Camp Hale–based mountain warfare soldiers were made to climb 12,000-foot peaks on skis while the temperature could fall to 20° below zero.

To get these men ready for combat against German *Gebirgsjäger* troops, the U.S. Army made even the basic training as realistic as possible. For a Camp Hale "Infiltration Course," the troopers had to crawl under barbed wire for an hour. Then, suddenly, machine guns with live shells shot directly over their heads. Fifty-pound charges of dynamite blew up right and left. Occasional mistakes would cause actual injuries.

Life at Camp Hale was never monotonous; the Tenth Mountain Division troops were employed to test Arctic snow vehicles and battle-station rescue toboggans. Troopers trained on large snowshoes and learned how to control avalanches. Other men worked with mules and dogs. A Scandinavian explorer was invited to teach the soldiers how to build igloos and other snow caves. Some of the camp's crack skiers and instructors were actually well-known ski racers or ski jumpers; others joined U.S. Olympic ski teams after World War II.

The training of these soldiers became even tougher in February 1944, when the Tenth Mountain men were sent on their first "D-series" maneuvers.

They climbed Colorado's Tennessee Pass and moved for thirty days into the icy wilderness. The snows were so deep that supply vehicles couldn't get through. Loads were so heavy (up to ninety pounds) that only the best troopers could make it. Despite the 35°-below-zero temperatures, no fires were allowed. After devouring K-rations, the food ran out. The struggling Tenth ate almost nothing for three days. When they got back to Hale, the media counted one hundred cases of frostbite. Nearby hospitals filled with pneumonia victims.

In summer soldiers received instruction in advanced rock-climbing techniques; they rappelled down the sheer Colorado cliffs and had to walk on suspended cables and rain-wet logs. Mountaineering knowledge would come in handy. In November 1944, the division left Camp Hale for Italy, where the troopers distinguished themselves in battling the Germans.

And the camp in Colorado? For a time Camp Hale housed German POWs. After the latter went home, the flagpoles, mule barns, and other buildings were forgotten. Suddenly, in 1947, the Pentagon brass decided to send other young soldiers to try the Colorado snows for size. Like the former Camp Hale occupants, these infantrymen pitted themselves against winter cold. When the Korean War broke out in 1950, Camp Hale served the Rangers as a special training ground. A few years later, army helicopters got their battle tests here. By then, ski troopers no longer seemed as necessary as during World War II days, and most of the military skiing moved out of Colorado and north to Alaska. On July 1, 1965, the buglers sounded a last Camp Hale retreat. Afterward, the U.S. Forest Service once more took control of the area.

During the late 1970s the Forest Service invested money and time to build the Camp Hale picnic areas, hiking paths, a wheelchair-accessible trail, and parking spaces at the onetime training camp. In May 1980 many former troopers came to the dedication of the twenty-acre **Camp Hale Memorial Campground.** It is one of the highest such sites in the United States.

Not far away from camp on Tennessee Pass, a fourteen-ton slab of granite reaches 20 feet into the sky. The stone's Roll of Honor lists the 990 comrades who gave their lives for the division. Each year on Memorial Day, hundreds of ex-troopers assemble at Tennessee Pass to remember their companions. Later they get together to talk about the old days, to swap tales, or to introduce their families to one another.

Camp Hale is 180 miles west of Denver via I–70 and Highway 91. For more information call (970) 827–5715 or (970) 827–9343; www.camphale.org.

The Tenth Mountain Division remains alive through its offbeat **Hut Association,** which consists of more than twenty mountain huts; each far-flung Colorado cabin can accommodate from six to twenty hikers, mountain bikers, or cross-country skiers. The shelters are ruggged; you bring your own food and water plus a sleeping bag. The huts are reachable from such major highways as Interstate 70 or from Tennessee Pass and Highway 24, among others. Distances vary. From Vail Pass, for instance, you get to the typical Shrine Mountain hut in 3 miles. All the same, you need to be fit and adequately equipped. (This includes a compass.) The alternative: Hire and pay a guide. Weekends are busiest. In any case, a reservation is essential to secure space at one of the huts. Rates are about one-half of what you'd pay for a cheap ski area motel per night. To be sure, these huts take you into Colorado's backcountry. Contact the Tenth Mountain Division Hut Association, 1280 Ute Avenue, Suite 21, Aspen 81611; (970) 925–5775; www.huts.org.

Now for a story of love and power, of wealth and poverty, of joys and tragedy, of a Colorado mining town whose fortunes flourished and vanished. A story so extraordinary that it became the subject of an opera, a play, and many biographies, some of them bad ones.

The characters were bigger than life. Begin with Horace Austin Warner Tabor, a onetime Vermont stonecutter, and his straitlaced hardworking wife, Augusta. The couple gave up a Kansas homestead to try their luck first in Denver, then under Pikes Peak, then at Oro City. They arrived in **Leadville** with a rickety wagon and an old ox during the 1860s, some years after the first gold had been discovered in California Gulch.

The Tabors established themselves as best as they could—Augusta with a tiny rooming house and a small bakery, Horace with a store and later a part-time job as mayor.

The Tabors' first break came on April 20, 1878. Two destitute miners, new in town, dropped into Horace's shop. Could he help out with some tools and a basket of groceries? The accommodating mayor agreed to help for a third of whatever minerals they might find. A few days later, some hard digging produced a rich silver vein.

trivia

Leadville, at 10,152 feet above sea level, is North America's highest incorporated city.

The Tabors were launched. By summer that first mine—the Little Pittsburgh—lavished $8,000 a week on its owners. Before long there was $100,000 worth of silver per month; this was followed by other Tabor ventures, all successful. In time, Tabor invested in many mines, controlled a good chunk of the local bank, built the Leadville Opera House, and erected mansions in the mining town and in Denver. He owned a lot of real estate and a hotel. By 1879 Leadville had seventeen independent smelters; it took 2,000 lumberjacks to provide enough wood to fire the machinery that processed the silver riches. Thanks to Tabor's new wealth and almost daily discoveries of more ore, the immigrants flooded to Leadville in droves. Celebrities like the "Unsinkable" Molly Brown showed up, as did various Dows, Guggenheims, and Boettchers.

Tabor soon bought an additional mine—the Matchless. He prospered while Leadville grew to a city of 30,000. Oscar Wilde appeared in the famous ***Tabor Opera House.*** The Chicago Symphony Orchestra and the Metropolitan Opera came there, to faraway Colorado. Well-known singers, ballet dancers, actresses, and entertainers arrived to perform.

H. A. W. Tabor became a millionaire many times over. He was a tall man, mustached, kindly, and, as a local historian writes, "outgoing, gregarious, and honest as the falling rain." By contrast, Horace was married to a woman who, although she worked hard, brought Tabor no happiness. She allegedly nagged; she was described as prim and humorless. Colorado's richest man thought he deserved better.

Horace Tabor's luck changed one day in 1882. That evening the fifty-year-old silver magnate saw Elisabeth Doe-McCourt in the restaurant of Leadville's Clarendon Hotel.

"Baby" Doe was twenty-two—a beauty with shining blue eyes and curly, dark blonde hair. Round-faced and charming, she'd been born into an Irish immigrant family of fourteen children. Baby Doe had just emerged from a brief, unhappy marriage with an unsupportive miner in Central City. Recently divorced, she had the good sense to look for a better partner in booming Leadville. She was a respectable young woman. And her search was crowned by success.

What began as a simple flirtation deepened into an abiding love that scandalized people in the Rockies and became the celebrated story of Colorado's opera the *Ballad of Baby Doe,* by Broadway veterans John Latouche and Douglas Moore.

Some Little-Known Facts about Leadville

Leadville is just below the timberline.

Legend says that in the old days, the worth of a barrel of Leadville whiskey was as high at $1,500.

Tents were once pitched on Main Street, and it was boasted that each was "the best hotel in town."

"Unsinkable" Molly Brown made her fortune here; also David May, Charles Boettcher, Charles Dow, and Meyer Guggenheim.

Horace and Baby Doe were snubbed by Denver High Society when Tabor divorced his wife, Augusta, who allegedly received a $500,000 settlement. H. A .W. soon married his new love. The wedding took place in Washington, D.C., in the presence of President Chester Arthur and other dignitaries. Baby Doe received a $90,000 diamond necklace, and she wore a $7,500 gown.

Although young, she actually had greater substance than most of her biographers gave her credit for. She was honest and loyal, helpful to others, and interested in a variety of things. Best of all, she was in love with her much older Colorado husband. Her love was returned.

The Tabors lived the lavish life of luxury to the hilt. Most historians estimate that the Tabors spent some $100 million. Horace Tabor made few worthwhile investments. For a brief time he was elected to the U.S. Senate.

In 1893 disaster struck Leadville. Silver was replaced by paper money. The nation experienced a financial panic. The Tabors were ruined. The mines began to fail. Real estate was sold to satisfy creditors.

The couple moved to Denver, still in love. Thanks to some contacts, Horace got a postmaster's job for a short time. But the financial plunge must have been too much for him. Soon he was ailing. His final hours came on April 10, 1899, at Denver's Windsor Hotel. His wife, Baby Doe, was by his side, holding his hand.

Before Horace Tabor died, he once more spoke about his Matchless Mine in Leadville. It had long played out after yielding some $1 million during its fourteen years of operation. "Hold on to the Matchless," Tabor whispered. "It'll make millions again." His wife nodded.

Baby Doe kept her promise. She moved back to Leadville. Penniless, she lived in a shack beside the mine pit for thirty-six years. She remained faithful to Tabor.

During the winter of 1935, while in her seventies, she shopped at a local grocery for some food. The grocer gave her a ride home in his truck. Baby Doe was dressed in tatters. Her feet were sheathed in sackcloth instead of shoes. The cabin next to the Matchless Mine was squalid, but she kept a rifle in it, protecting her mine.

Leadville's altitude is more than 10,000 feet. It gets cold there on winter nights. Baby Doe Tabor was found in her shack on March 7, 1935. She had frozen to death. No one knows how long the body had been there. Ironically, there were some unopened boxes with new blankets sent by some Leadville sympathizers, which the dying woman had refused to use.

The Tabors are buried side by side in Denver. The *Ballad of Baby Doe* was added to the New York City Opera's repertoire shortly after its 1956 debut in Central City. The role of Baby Doe was among the first that Beverly Sills sang for a company she was to head many years later.

And how about the current Leadville? Thanks to the town's solid mining history, there is a 70,000-square-foot ***National Mining Hall of Fame & Museum***. This museum should be essential for ore seekers, mining school students, and history buffs. Located in a restored Victorian schoolhouse, the facility retraces the entire Leadville history; you can also view old equipment, assorted rocks and crystals, various artifacts, and dioramas.

The Last Chance is a realistic replica of a hard-rock mine tunnel. Stretching more than 120 feet, the "rock" walls have exposed ore veins. Mine-gauge rail tracks are underfoot on the rock-strewn floor. Dripping water adds to the illusion of being underground in a real mine.

Admission costs $6.00 for adults and teenagers twelve and older, $5.00 for seniors sixty-five and older, and $3.00 for children six to eleven; children five and younger are admitted free. Hours in summer (May through October) are 9:00 A.M. to 5:00 P.M. daily; winter hours (November through April) are 10:00 A.M. to 4:00 P.M. Monday through Saturday. For more information call (719) 486–1229; www.leadville.com/miningmuseum.

More than 70 square blocks of Leadville have been designated as a National Historic Landmark District, making it one of the largest such districts in Colorado. You can enjoy this town's history at any time of year by going on a short historic walking tour through this district. Start your free, self-guided tour at ***Ice Palace Park*** in the 100 block of West Tenth. Plenty of parking can be found here. The park commemorates the ill-fated Ice Palace, built nearby in 1896. The palace, constructed of 5,000 tons of ice and 307,000 board feet of lumber, lasted only a few months before going under. From the park, you walk southeast to Harrison Avenue, where most of the tour's attractions await your exploration, including the Heritage Museum, the Hyman Block (where the infamous Doc Holliday shot—but failed to kill—his last victim), and the Tabor Opera House.

A Palace of Ice

The Leadville Ice Palace was the largest such building ever constructed in North America, covering more than five acres. With its spectacular 90-foot towers, heated rooms, enormous ice sculptures, and an ice-skating rink, it was supposed to help the city's floundering economy. Only a few months after opening, the unprofitable palace was forced to close its doors. You can still experience some of the palace's original magic today by staying at the ***Ice Palace Inn Bed & Breakfast,*** built in 1899 using some of the original boards from the Ice Palace. Call (719) 486–8272 or (800) 754–2840 for details, or visit www.icepalaceinn.com.

Leadville Visit

While in Leadville, well-conditioned adventurers won't want to miss a chance to hike Colorado's highest mountain, **Mt. Elbert** (14,433 feet).

Depending on time and ability, hikers can choose one of the Mountain's two main trails:

North Mt. Elbert Trail is a 5-mile hike to the summit. From Sixth Street in Leadville, head south on US 24 for about 4 miles. Go west on Highway 300 for ¾ mile, and then south (left) on Lake County Road 11 for 1¼ miles. Head west (right) on Forest Road 110 for 5 miles, which will take you to the parking area at Halfmoon Campground.

South Mt. Elbert Trail can be serene; it is seldom crowded. It is 5½ miles to the summit with a trailhead near Lakeview Campground. Go south on US 24, and then head west on Highway 82 for about 3½ miles. Go north on Lake County 24 for just over a mile to reach the parking area, just north of the campground.

With a 4,500-foot elevation gain, both trails should be attempted only by hikers who are in good shape and are knowledgeable about safety in hiking.

For more information contact the San Isabel National Forest, Leadville Ranger District, 2015 North Poplar, Leadville 80461; (719) 486–0749; www.fs.fed.us/r2/psicc/leadvile/.

For a map of the tour, visit the Web site www.leadville.com/walktour/ or call the Leadville/Lake County Chamber of Commerce at (800) 933–3901.

To reach Leadville from Denver, take I–70 west, turning off at Highway 91 (exit 195, Copper Mountain).

South and west of Leadville lies ***Crested Butte,*** a sizable, scenic ski center. Thirty minutes north of Gunnison, Colorado, Crested Butte is too far from the big metropolitan cities to attract crowds. (Denver is 235 miles to the northeast.) One local inhabitant explains Crested Butte this way: "In an age plagued by problems of too many people, too many cars and roads and buildings, this kind of country has a special attraction. It seems to have been made *for* people, not *by* them."

Crested Butte aficionados speak of a feeling "that borders on reverence, a joy of simply being here." The ski area and the nearby little mining town of Crested Butte (2 miles away) give off a feeling of relaxation. The atmosphere is pastoral, sometimes even somnolent, informal, tolerant, and rooted in nature.

These mountains are some of the state's most beautiful. They emanate all the power and grace of the Swiss Alps, and you seem to ski in a never-ending symphony of valleys and meadows, of crests and snowfields. Crested Butte is blessed with nicely separated terrain for advanced skiers (only 20 percent of the mountain), intermediates (55 percent), and beginners (25 percent). In addition, experts will find 824 acres of ungroomed terrain known as "Extreme Limits," suitable for expert skiers only. Beginners, too, are well served on this mountain.

One of the area's major assets is a gently sloping, broad, chairlift-served run on the lower mountain more than a mile long. It is excellent for novice skiers, who at many areas are confined to short, makeshift slopes with minimal lift facilities. The upper area holds myriad pleasures for more advanced skiers. One chairlift, for example, serves slopes with an average grade of 44 percent (experts find this steepness challenging, and it will scare the daylights out of average skiers).

The majority of the mountain is for the intermediate skier. This includes a many-trails complex that taps the open ski terrain of Crested Butte's north-side slopes. Here the snow comes earlier, stays longer, and is deeper and lighter than anywhere else on the mountain, with an average 33 percent grade, 1,350 vertical feet. Ideal for intermediate skiing, the Paradise Bowl provides great joy to visitors. Crested Butte's lift situation is adequate, thanks to its fourteen chairlifts.

Colorado's choicest cross-country adventure—indeed, a special pièce de résistance for experts—ties Crested Butte with Aspen, just 28 miles away (guides available).

The ski school has an important and reliable cross-country program for which the surrounding country seems perfectly suited. Some of the area's ski clientele have never seen snow before. The ski school is therefore a patient one. The names of some ski runs give a good clue to the customers—Houston Trail, Kansas Trail. Charters regularly fly in from states like Georgia, and you'll find some midwestern families. It is intriguing to simply sit in front of the base cafeteria and watch the mix of people, especially on weekends.

Crested Butte's ski season runs from mid-December through mid-April. The ski slopes are open from 9:00 A.M. to 4:00 P.M. daily. Prices vary throughout the season. For more information call (800) 810–7669; www.skicb.com.

The town of Crested Butte gets its character from the old mining days, and the streets are full of young and old men with beards who all look alike. On weekends you glimpse sheriffs with badges, and there are some town drunks to be taken care of. Nightlife is limited to saloons with loud banjos and other instruments, beer drinking, and talking to the multitude of ski bums. Many dogs sit in front of the clapboard buildings; dogs of various shapes leap across the pockmarked streets or show up at the lived-in ski area. Food and lodging prices range from moderate to expensive. Accommodations are available in old lodges and well-worn guest houses, plus condos for the rich. There is a glossy hotel.

Fat Tire Week in Crested Butte is a summer party on bike wheels. More than 1,000 people will show up to participate in bicycle polo, races, clinics, and tours that range from mild-mannered rides to the annual Wildflower Rush Race, a NORBA Mountain States Cup event. With more than 300 miles of trails, Crested Butte has a ride to satisfy every cyclist. For more information about this annual June event, contact the Crested Butte–Mt. Crested Butte Chamber of Commerce at (800) 545–4505, or visit www.crestedbuttechamber.com.

Crested Butte was the site of the first mountain biking in Colorado. After a motorcycle gang had ridden their Harley Davidsons over the rough jeep road of Pearl Pass from Aspen, some "Butte" locals decided to one-up the bikers by doing the same route on bicycles.

Since then these bikes have evolved from one-speed clunkers into technological wonders of metal and gears. Crested Butte continues to celebrate this development with the ***Mountain Bike Hall of Fame and Museum,*** 331 Elk Avenue, (800) 454–4505; www.mtnbikehalloffame.com.

Mountain bikes were designed to act like jeeps for going over rough terrain. Tires are big, fat, and knobby for climbing through gravel and maintaining traction on a steep grade. As opposed to racing bikes with skinny tires designed for maximum speed, mountain bikes come with eighteen to twenty-seven gears. This allows you to shift way down to what is called a "granny gear" and, moving at slow speeds, still be able to pedal up and over obstacles. By turning your pedals as quickly as possible—called "spinning"—you ensure that the gears absorb the load, rather than your knees.

Mountain bikes take some getting used to. Riding a trail over rocks and logs and through streams can be a bit intimidating. Be prepared to take a few falls at first.

One way to avoid crashing into obstacles like rocks is to look for a path around them instead of focusing on what is in your path. The technique of keeping your eye on the ball in tennis can be applied to mountain biking. By eyeballing that obstacle in your trail, you will hit it, too. Keep looking up the trail, not just in front of you.

To maintain traction while going down a steep hill, stand up in the pedals and stick your rear end behind the bike seat for more weight on the back tire. Also, brake firmly with the rear brake. Using your front brake alone can abruptly stop the front tire and send you flying over the handlebars in what is called an "endo" (rear end flips over the front). It's a very undignified way to get off a bike, and it can hurt!

Required equipment includes a helmet, eye protection, cycling gloves, and shorts to prevent chafing of inner thighs. Drink from your water bottle frequently to avoid dehydration.

Most of the trails are open for public use. Cyclists are required to yield to hikers and horses. If this means you have to get off your bike and move off the trail, then do it. In many parts of the United States, failure of cyclists to yield has caused some popular trails to be closed to them.

Following on the wheels of Fat Tire Week is the **Crested Butte Wild-flower Festival.** Of course, all mountain towns have wildflowers, but the climate of sheltered valleys seems to provide more floral color here than many other Colorado places. The town also tries to make sure everyone can enjoy these delicate blooms. Days of naturalist walks, tours, photo sessions, painting classes with professional outdoor artists, evening dinners, lunch discussions, horseback tours into the higher meadows, and ski-lift rides to the top of the ski area for a leisurely walk down are some of the offerings. Variable fees for each activity help support the organizers of the event. Posters, books, and varied artwork are on sale. This is a low-key celebration of the natural mountain beauty. Many of the activities are well suited to children or to people who like to move along at a slow pace. For others, the guides will match your speed. Call (970) 349–2571 for more information; www.crestedbuttewildflowerfestival.com.

Crested Butte is a thirty-minute drive north of Gunnison on Highway 135. The Crested Butte–Mt. Crested Butte Chamber of Commerce can be contacted at P.O. Box 1288, Crested Butte 81224; (970) 349–6438 or (800) 545–4505; www.crestedbuttechamber.com.

Heading west from Gunnison on US 50, your travels will take you to the spectacular **Black Canyon of the Gunnison National Park,** which became a national park in 1999. The vision of the sheer, massive rocks is stunning and unforgettable. In the sunlight, the black granite turns mauve. Towers, pillars, and stone blocks scintillate and make humans feel tiny. In all, the Black Canyon of the Gunnison National Park comprises some 30,385 acres. Carved by the river, the canyon is 53 miles long.

trivia

Two thousand miles of trout-fishing streams and Colorado's largest lake are within driving range of Gunnison—excellent fishing!

The canyon's trails are steep. They're shaded by scrub oak; on your descent toward the Gunnison River, you see white daisies, violet asters, mariposa lilies, yarrow, and lupine lilies. Chipmunks and squirrels peer out from the vegetation and the rock cracks. Golden eagles fly overhead.

The Chasm View Nature Trail measures a modest ⅓ mile. The North Vista Trail is more ambitious, at 3 miles, and can be strenuous. A permit is required if you want to hike down all the way to the river. Rock climbing in the canyon is considered hazardous and is only for experienced climbers. (Register at the visitor center.) The national park is open in winter as well, with fewer personnel.

The entrance fee is $8.00 per vehicle or $4.00 per pedestrian (no charge for visitors age sixteen or younger). The North and South Rim stations are open daily, but access is limited in winter. To get to the South Rim take US 50 from Montrose for 15 miles to Highway 347. The visitor center is at the South Rim. The North Rim is 11 miles south of Crawford via U.S. Highway 92 and North Rim Road, which is closed during winter. Contact Park Headquarters, 102 Elk Creek, Gunnison 81230; (970) 641–2337; www.nps.gov/blca.

Accommodations are available nearby in Montrose at the luxurious **Best Western Red Arrow,** 1702 East Main (U.S. Highway 50 East); (970) 249–9641 or (800) 468–9323; www.bestwesterncolorado.com.

Consider the Basques who herd sheep in the western U.S. Rockies and whose homeland is the sometimes foggy Pyrenees, mountains that separate Spain from France. Colorado's Basques are not unhappy with their lot. Bernard De Voto once asked a Basque why he chose to live among sheep. "I seek the quiet heart," the shepherd answered.

The "quiet heart" of solitude can be found by these men among the meadows and knolls of their homeland as well as on the hillsides of Colorado. In the United States, they are concentrated in and around Montrose and Grand Junction. The herders are in tune with their mountains, which make a "mighty big bedroom," as they like to explain.

Most of the younger Basques are single; for them shearing time and the yearly folk festivals—with dancing, weight lifting, and wine drinking—fill a need. Many of these mountain men own their herds and let the unmarried do the herding while they stick to family life. Whether living in the western U.S. Rockies or in the Pyrenees, the Basques hold on to their own difficult-to-learn language. It resembles none other in Europe and still puzzles philologists.

Colorado's Basques wear the berets and the modest working clothes of their ancestors. Their ethnic origins remain unclear; they seem to have been in Europe longer than other groups. Anthropologists theorize that these dark-complected mountain people may have migrated to the Iberian Peninsula from the Caucasus some 2,000 years before Christ. Both the Basque sheepherders and the Basque farmers live modestly and accept their place in the Colorado high country.

Southwestern Colorado

The chute opens and Joe Alexander, champion bareback rider, holds on to the horse's riggings with one hand. The horse rears wildly, resenting the man, hooves in all directions, a bucking, pitching, twisting, snorting, wild-eyed rebel. The cowboy's hat flies high, landing in the dust.

He has been on the horse for five seconds now, and he still hangs on. He leans all the way back, ankles still spurring, his shoulder blades against the

Southwest Colorado Overview

In southwest Colorado, piñons and junipers yield to spruce and aspen as elevations increase north of Durango in the San Juan Range. Surprisingly to many people, the weather here is remarkably mild year-round, despite copious snowfall at high elevations. The mountains are always cooler than the deserts, but usually comfortably so, especially in summer when days are short-sleeves warm, while the heat leaves with the sun and a blanket is de rigeur for sleeping at night.

As is common throughout Colorado, summer is the main tourist season in southwest Colorado, followed by the ski crowd in winter. *Caution:* Skiing through waist-deep, soft powder in the high, dry air on a typical sunny winter day may be addictive. The sun always comes out after a storm, so skiers sans jackets by noon are another common sight.

Colorado's legendary outdoor world has much to do with Colorado's international popularity. The state has 1,143 mountains rising to an altitude of at least 10,000 feet above sea level—and 1,000 are 2 miles high or more. Fifty-four often snow-crowned peaks towering above 14,000 feet give the state more than six times the mountain area of Switzerland. For more information contact the Colorado Fourteeners Initiative at (303) 278–7525, ext. 115; www.coloradofourteeners.org.

animal's spine. The man's outstretched arm hits the horse's bones. It's a human against a beast. Six seconds now. Seven. Eight.

The buzzer sounds. Alexander jumps safely onto the ground. Eight seconds of bareback riding can seem like eight hours. It still takes a strong, bold person to ride at rodeos.

These Wild West riding competitions are an important income source for some Colorado cowboys. After all, the cattle business in the United States has shrunk during the past decades. Much of the profit has been taken out. These days, ranches are fewer, and, although some of the successful ones are in southern Colorado, they're smaller than they used to be.

At one time, hundreds of men were needed to drive 6,000 or more Black Angus, Herefords, Shorthorns, and other breeds of cattle to market. Nowadays trucks often do the job. The old-time cowhand had to feed the stock in winter—a job now often done by helicopters.

In sheer numbers the western cowpuncher has diminished, but a few large Colorado ranches still need these rugged, underpaid men to brand cattle in spring, to put up and repair fences, to rope the creatures, and to look after their health. One ranch manager for a big cattle company thirty minutes south of Denver still rounds up his stock twice a year. In the saddle for long hours, he enjoys the freedom of his 10,000 acres. He dresses the part, too. Cowboy hat, leather vest, leather belts with elaborate buckles, Levis, buckaroo boots. He says he enjoys the heat and getting dirty. Few people know that he has a law degree.

Many ranch hands have learned some veterinary skills; they know a lot about the pharmaceuticals and the vaccinations of the present-day western cattle industry. Likewise, cowboys learn about feeding, and they help with cattle sales. A few hardy cowpunchers still ride with their herds from mountain pasture to mountain pasture all summer long. The riders certainly must look after their horses. And Colorado is the state where it all happens.

This leads back to the rodeo circuit, which has become lucrative for some Colorado cowboys of all ages who can travel to the more than 1,000 competitions that go on during the year in North America. In addition, there are hundreds of nonsanctioned amateur and intercollegiate rodeos, and are even some for kids.

Thirty million American tourists travel to the big spectacles annually. For ten days each July, for instance, many of the Colorado-based cowboys and cattle flock to Calgary, in Canada's province of Alberta, where the purses keep increasing. Altogether some $5 million in prizes go to riders in the United States and Canada; at Wyoming's famous Frontier Days alone, $950,000 in rodeo winnings are split by a cast of 1,500. About 400,000 visitors are entertained here.

The top cowboys often own sizable cattle ranches themselves. The famous ones sometimes fly their own planes.

Rodeo actually began as an exciting pastime of those rough, tough cowhands who rode the range and drove the herds of beef to market. "Ride 'em cowboy" was not much more than a contest of bravery among cowboys of the Old West. From these unassuming beginnings, rodeo has evolved into a big business.

Some Colorado cowboys and cowgirls take care of the horses at dozens of the state's dude ranches. The latter are basically rustic, with western-style furniture against a log-cabin backdrop. The rooms often contain fur-covered sofas, rugged granite fireplaces, elk antlers on the walls, or framed words of cowboy wisdom. The cooking is plain and the food plentiful and included for the help and customer alike. There is a warm feeling about these enclaves, nesting deeply in Colorado's forests, straddling mountaintops, overlooking rivers that rush and splash. The lodges are usually built with the pine or spruce woods and the stone rock of the region. The windows will surely look out upon pretty scenes.

The cowboys at these ranches often prepare breakfast for the guests on a hillside. At one well-known vacation center, the head wrangler teaches riding to first-timers and gives equestrian advice to others. Cowboys usually lead the various outings.

Meet Leslie (Les), a typical Colorado cowboy who owns one characteristic dude ranch west of Denver. Les employs a cook who feeds the guests, a clerk who checks them in, and a lodge manager who looks after details. Les himself is mostly involved with the horses. His life has always evolved around animals.

He hates to wear suits, and he hates to go to the city (where he keeps an apartment all the same). He doesn't like fancy talk, or talk, period. He likes horses and dogs better than people, yet at this moment he leads a group of people—experienced riders all—on another daily excursion, his second one today. He is not outgoing, yet he coddles and protects his "dudes," and no lives are ever jeopardized out here.

Les loves horses more than anything. At dawn, Les had walked over to the red barn and the corral. He'd whistled. His mare, Frosty, came right out. Animal and man were one as Les rode up with the early risers, some of them very slow, typical tourists, at first fearful and uncertain. As always, two other helpers galloped ahead of the group to fry the eggs and get the pancakes ready on the griddle. The coffee boils and sends up whiffs of flavor.

Some cowboys certainly show an adaptable spirit. A few of them, for instance, also take their guests hunting for wild game in the higher mountain ranges. At one horse center, Colorado's famous, luxurious C Lazy U Ranch, two of the cowboys adjusted to the times and to fads: They learned to cross-country ski and now take the guests on ski trips in winter.

Some wranglers don't work at these ranches; they're independent and merely operate their own stables on a busy highway, looking for other work to do in winter.

Inspired by western cowpokes, a whole industry has sprung up in the United States. Much of the fashion in jeans, denim jackets, and cowboy boots harks back to the Old West. (At the dude ranches, meanwhile, the city dwellers arrive garbed in western wear with large western hats.)

Colorado's "cowboy artists," while no longer on horseback or herding cattle, drive jeeps into the wilderness with their easels and paints. Art galleries in Denver sell the artists' output—sceneries with wild buffalo and paintings of wild horses, high mountains, and western prairies.

Cowboy poets enjoy popularity, too. Their output can be read in newspapers; national magazines and even book publishers print their verse.

Poems hang framed on dude ranch walls. The message can be brief and wise, as this little cowboy item from an anonymous author: "Never was there a cowboy who couldn't be throwed, never a bronc who couldn't be rode."

Most of the rhymes are simple, basic, perhaps a little primitive. Example? At one western ranch, a wrangler dug deeply to express the horsey West in a poem:

May Your Horse Never Stumble
May Your Cinch Never Break
May Your Belly Never Grumble
May Your Heart Never Ache.

The poem speaks a universal language.

Still a special person, the Colorado cowboy rides on.

Before you begin your journey into the heart of southwestern Colorado on U.S. Highway 160, turn east and then north on Highway 150 for a stop at the uniquely marvelous **Great Sand Dunes National Park.** Geologists say that sand stretches such as those found here are usually the handiwork of the world's oceans. Didn't the salt water have millions of years to crush, mash, and pulverize the land? The sea pushed, licked, and retreated, eroding rocks into small particles and grinding the earth to fine silt. Moreover, winds blew sand grains from the mountains to the plains. The source of sand is sediments, eroded in time by winds and glaciers and washed into the dunes. More recently, the drying southwesterly winds carried the sands into what became the Great Sand Dunes National Monument before being designated a national park in 2004. Erosive forces and more winds helped fashion sand peaks that crest to heights of 750 feet above the valley floor.

The park looks as if it were flown in from Africa's Kalahari Desert and plunked into the middle of Colorado. White men didn't discover these dunes until 1599, when Spanish explorers first crossed the sands.

The park encompasses 38,662 acres, offering many activities, of which hiking on the dunes seems to be most visitors' first choice. Make sure you wear shoes in the summer—the sand can reach temperatures of 140°F. Save the bare feet for wading across the soft, water-cooled sand creek.

On the other side of the stream, the dunes are incredibly massive, some rising hundreds of feet above the valley floor. Due to shadows, they are deceptively steep. The valley floor is 7,500 feet above sea level, making breathing difficult at first for those not adjusted to the altitude.

But there are few experiences that can compare with being on the dunes. It's like riding the frozen waves of a storm-blown sea. You climb to

trivia

For amateur geologists, most sand at Colorado's Great Sand Dunes is between 0.2 and 0.3 mm in diameter, composed of 51.7 percent volcanic rock fragments, 29.1 percent quartz, 8.9 percent feldspar, 2.5 percent sandstone, 0.7 percent magnetite, 3.4 percent other minerals, and 3.7 percent other rocks.

the top of a ridge, taking in a view of the gold and tan waves stretching for miles to the towering blue mountains, and then descend the trough until you are in a valley completely surrounded by immense hills of sand. These are allegedly America's tallest sand dunes. The highest dune is located opposite the visitor center, and it takes about three hours to climb to the top and return. From the summit you are presented with a sweeping vista that includes a large segment of Colorado's stunning Sangre de Cristo Mountains.

Great Sand Dunes National Park is located on Highway 150 in the south-central part of the state, just 16 miles off US 160, the main east-west highway through southern Colorado. Individuals age seventeen or older pay a $3.00 entry fee. The site is open daily. The visitors center also is open daily, except for winter holidays. Visitor center hours are 9:00 A.M. to 6:00 P.M. from May 30 through September 30, and 9:00 A.M. to 4:30 P.M. during the rest of the year. For more information contact Great Sand Dunes National Park, 11500 Highway 150, Mosca 81146; (719) 378–2312; www.nps.gov/grsa.

Because of the long distance between this and other attractions, you may want to stay in nearby Alamosa at the **Cottonwood Inn Bed-and-Breakfast and Gallery,** 123 San Juan Avenue. Gourmet breakfasts with regional special-ties greet guests each morning as they enjoy their accommodations in the Craftsman-style home or foursquare apartment building. Afternoon brings fresh-baked cookies and perhaps a soak in the eight-person hot tub. Call (719) 589–3882 or (800) 955–2623; www.cottonwoodinn.com. Rates are inexpensive to expensive, depending on the room you stay in and the season.

Farther west, and just south of Wolf Creek Pass on US 160 lies **Pagosa Springs.** Named for the Ute word Pahgosa, meaning "boiling water," Pagosa Springs has a ready supply of natural geothermal energy.

trivia

Pagosa Springs attracts everyone from deer and elk hunters to golfers, tennis players, and plain old vacationers.

Another water wonder near Pagosa is **Treasure Falls.** This is the longest water-fall in the entire San Juan National Forest. To get there, follow US 160 12 miles toward the Wolf Creek summit; enjoy the magnificent alpine scenery en route. A parking area for the falls provides a safe place to leave the car away from the road. A short ¼-mile well-worn trail takes you to Colorado's miniversion of Niagara. For more information write to Pagosa Ranger District, 180 Second Street, P.O. Box 310, Pagosa Springs 81147; (970) 264–2268; www.fs.fed.us/r2/sanjuan.

A *man*-made wonder close to Pagosa is **Chimney Rock.** These stone ruins were home to 2,000 Anasazi Indians more than 1,000 years ago. Still intact, these ruins are well preserved and protected. A locked gate 3 miles from the ruins prevents anyone from exploring without a National Forest Service guide.

Rock house ruins built into the hillside and the round ceremonial underground structures called kivas make the place seem as if the inhabitants just left, cleaning up before they went. Named for its towering twin spires of natural stone, Chimney Rock has been compared to Machu Picchu because it nestles in the high mountains and has grand vistas from almost every vantage point. Scholars have also suggested that during the occupation of Chimney Rock, the inhabitants were all men and that Chimney Rock was a sacred site for prayer and for making powerful medicine. Chimney Rock is located 17 miles west of Pagosa Springs via US 160, and then southwest on Highway 151. Four times daily, the Chimney Rock Interpretive Program tour takes place. Tour costs are $6.00 for adults and teenagers twelve and older and $2.00 for children six to eleven; children five and younger get in free. Fees are paid at the visitor center, which is open from 9:30 A.M. to 4:00 P.M. daily during the season (May 15 through September 30).

trivia

The Pagosa Springs are used for bathing, and some, at 153°F, are used for energy to heat houses and buildings.

Prepaid reservations are required for all special workshops and hikes. Costs run around $20 per person per program. For more information write to Chimney Rock Interpretive Program, P.O. Box 1662, Pagosa Springs 81147; (970) 883–5359 (May 15 through September 30) or (970) 385–1210 (off-season, October 1 through May 14); www.chimneyrockco.org.

On the edge of the Pagosa Springs community there awaits a pleasant resort with accommodations, jeep tours, hikes, and even tennis and mountain biking. A large children's playground and an observation tower beckon, too. For more information write to Fairfield Pagosa, 538 Village Drive, Pagosa Springs 81147; (970) 731–8000; www.efairfield.com/inside/resorts/0017.asp.

For more information about Pagosa Springs write to Pagosa Springs Area Chamber of Commerce, P.O. Box 787, Pagosa Springs 81147; (970) 264–2360 or (800) 252–2204; www.pagosa-springs.com.

Located 18 miles north of **Durango** on U.S. Highway 550, the year-round deluxe **Durango Mountain Resort** remains a secret to many Coloradans. This remote oasis has everything—nature, atmosphere, and amenities. Dramatic triangular rocks line one side, wooded mountains the other. In between lies an undulating eighteen-hole golf course, where elk herds congregate at dawn under stands of ponderosa pine. Condominiums and a stately lodge are nestled atop a 200-foot cliff overlooking this gorgeous mountain scenery. North of

Colorful Locals

In the early days in Durango, there was a rowdy local gang that went by the name of the Stockton–Eskridge gang. These boys and a group of local vigilantes once fought an hour-long gun battle on the main street through town.

In 1885, locals set out on an expedition to New Mexico. What did they want? Why, to "dig up Aztecs." Included in the supplies for the expeditions were five cases of tobacco, three cases of beer, ten gallons of "heavy liquids," four burro-loads of "the stuff that busted Parliament," fuse (seven reels), soap, cigars, one fish line, rubber boots, bread, lard, and a pound of bacon.

Editor "Dave" Day, of the *Durango Herald-Democrat* newspaper in the 1890s, once had forty-two pending libel suits against him.

Ah, the good old days.

Tamarron, some of Colorado's most magnificent alpine scenery is visible, and legendary communities such as Ouray and Silverton await exploration.

Horseback expeditions depart each day from the stables, bringing you into the one-million-acre San Juan National Forest. Guides who are well versed in the history and ecology of the area accompany the riders through the virgin wilderness.

For the adventurous, the Durango Mountain Resort offers myriad outdoor possibilities. For instance, the sports deck can arrange a river-rafting trip. Fishing trips are popular. Durango beckons with a historic narrow-gauge railroad, which winds its way over narrow mountain passes. The resort has its own jeeps for high-country tours, where you can visit old mines and wander among some fifty species of wildflowers.

Accommodations and meals are very expensive. For more information write to Durango Mountain Resort, 40292 Highway 550, Durango 81301; (970) 259–2000 or (800) 678–1000; www.durangomountainresort.com.

Built in 1892, the renovated **Rochester Hotel** in downtown Durango offers fifteen luxurious rooms, all decorated in an Old West motif (inspired by the many Western movies filmed nearby). The hotel is just steps away from the Durango & Silverton railway station and historic Main Avenue.

The local folks claim that a number of famous entertainers have stayed at the Rochester, including Douglas Fairbanks Jr., for instance. For more information write to Rochester Hotel, 726 East Second Avenue, Durango 81301; (970) 385–1920 or (800) 664–1920; www.rochester hotel.com.

Fort Lewis College attracts international students because of its academic standards and natural setting; the school specializes in geology studies.

Durango is said to have the highest per capita number of professional mountain-bike racers in the country.

The bright orange cars of the ***Durango & Silverton Narrow Gauge Railroad*** seem anxious to go, as the engine chugs away waiting for passengers to board. The popular tourist attraction is America's last regularly scheduled narrow-gauge passenger train.

Once serving the miners and ranchers of Silverton and Durango, the train now caters to passengers who want to spend two and a half hours each way thundering through spectacular mountain valleys. The excursion starts in Durango, which Will Rogers described as "out of the way and glad of it." But many people come here to experience a western town in touch with today's world.

Be prepared for some dust and soot. Dress accordingly.

Train reservations are required. The schedule varies according to season but the train runs year-round. Peak-season round-trip costs are $60 for adults and teenagers twelve years and older and $30 for children five to eleven; children four and younger ride free if sitting on an adult's lap. Parlor car seating is $99 and only for those twenty-one or older. Off-season (winter) costs are a bit less. For more information contact Durango & Silverton Narrow Gauge Railroad, 479 Main Avenue, Durango 81301; (970) 247–2733 or (888) 872–4607; www.durangotrain.com.

For more information about Durango write to the Durango Area Chamber Resort Association, 111 South Camino del Rio, P.O. Box 2587, Durango 81302; (800) 525–8855 or (970) 247–0312; www.durango.org.

The admirers of this popular state speak well about Colorado's ***Mesa Verde National Park.*** It is a ten-hour drive southwest of Denver and is about

Ridgway

Sooner or later, a trip will find you in southwestern Colorado, ready to downhill ski in spectacular Telluride or seeking some peace in Ridgway. Stay at *Chipeta Sun Lodge and Spa* in sleepy Ridgway. It features unique architecture and a staff eager to please. Fountains, hot tubs, and a two-story garden solarium, in which breakfast is served every day, are just some of the attractions there. The Sun Lodge is pure adobe, with southwestern decor, solar heating, and the clean air at 6,995 feet, as well as views of the San Juan mountain range. Explore the nearby kiva.

Ridgway is located north of Durango via US 550 to Highway 62. For more information write to Chipeta Sun Lodge and Spa, 304 South Lena, Ridgway 81432; (970) 626–3737 or (800) 633°5868; www.chipeta.com.

Telluride

Telluride is renowned for its breathtaking alpine beauty, but many people don't realize that Telluride lies in the center of the greatest diversity of geology and archaeology in the nation. This area, known as the Grand Circle, encompasses four states, numerous state and national parks, and a variety of topography from the Rocky Mountains to the Painted Desert.

an hour and a half west of Durango on US 160, midway between Mancos and Cortez. About 500,000 visitors come here each year.

Mesa Verde yields an extraordinary educational experience. A very small area here provides you with much that is of archaeological interest. Before you drive the distance, however, you should keep in mind that Mesa Verde differs substantially from other parks. There is no fishing here; nor is there boating, swimming, or rock climbing. Your pets have to be on a leash and are not allowed in the ruins. And you can see the historic, wondrous cliff dwellings only in the company of park rangers.

The 21-mile road from the park entrance curves and swings and rotates upward; its width doesn't approximate that of an interstate highway. You may have trouble if you come in a truck or try to pull a large camper.

A visit to Mesa Verde National Park should be planned with care. Earmark one or two days for the park itself and try to arrive early in the day or during the off-season. The historical scene and the colors come through especially well if you can visit Mesa Verde at dawn. The moment you see the sudden, flat-topped plateau, the cliff dwellings of a prehistoric civilization, you'll be happy that you braved the distance. No other national park can equal this one.

Begin with a visit to the park's ***Chapin Mesa Archeological Museum*** for clues to the mysterious Basket Weavers. These Indians left behind an amazing array of agricultural tools, pottery, and baskets. The tribes arrived in the area around A.D. 450 and abandoned the site in 1276. It took another 500 years for Spanish explorers to discover the old, russet blocks of stone, the turrets and primitive apartments known as cliff dwellings hanging under a canopy of glorious rock. You will never forget the Balcony House and Cliff Palace.

At its height, the Mesa Verde Plateau supported 50,000 Indians. By the close of the thirteenth century, it was completely deserted. What happened to the Anasazi—the most famous builders of southwestern cliff dwellings and the ancestors of today's Pueblo Indians—is not known. Archaeologists theorize that a thirty-year drought starting in 1246, combined with soil that had been depleted by constant use, caused successive crop failures and that the Anasazi moved farther south into New Mexico and Arizona.

Cliff Palace,
Mesa Verde National Park

The National Park Service does a good job of looking after Mesa Verde's 80-square-mile area of ponderosa pine, spruce trees, and juniper, all laced by a few paths. Not a billboard or soft-drink sign in sight.

When visiting Mesa Verde you're not too far from the Four Corners area of Colorado, Utah, New Mexico, and Arizona. This is butte country. The sky is even bluer here in the southwestern corner of the state. The plains seem to stretch wider than in the northern corners. The Colorado peaks resemble those of the Alps, with jutting slopes and deeply carved valleys. (Bring a warm change of clothes.)

After the Mesa Verde experience, your own state or province will never be the same again. Park entry fee is $10 per vehicle. The Chapin Mesa Archeological Museum is open daily at 8:00 A.M., closing at 6:30 P.M. in summer and fall and at 5:00 P.M. in winter and spring. Call (970) 529–4631 for details. The Far View Visitor Center is open from mid-April through mid-October from 8:00 A.M. to 5:00 P.M. Call (970) 529–5036. Mesa Verde National Park is open daily year-round; www.nps.gov/meve.

A 50-mile drive from the historic canyons of Mesa Verde will take you to another area of Indian ruins. This is little-known ***Hovenweep National Monument,*** west of Cortez, Colorado, reached by traveling gravel and rough black-top roads. You will escape the crowds when you visit these ruins.

Here the terrain is high desert plateau. Sagebrush and scattered juniper trees dot the horizon. It seems desolate, almost barren. But there was life here. A canyon opens in the plateau, and scattered cottonwood trees indicate the presence of water. A spring still flows into a small depression in the shadow of the canyon wall. This water was the center of the community 700 years ago. The towers of Hovenweep are thought to be watch towers and fortifications to protect this precious liquid resource.

With artistic skill that would rival a stonemason's today, ancient Pueblo Indians built these towers in several configurations. Round, square, and oval structures dot the canyon edge. Each rock was trimmed to fit exactly with its neighbor, and the lines of the buildings are straight and almost smooth. Small peepholes and keyhole entrances could have provided views of a possible enemy approaching or just been a way to keep an eye on the rest of the community. Standing at the structure called Hovenweep Castle, you can look east and see a tower on almost every promontory of the canyon. Hiking and interpretive trails link most of these. Allow at least a half-day to explore the exposed ruins.

The ranger station is open year-round and operates a bookstore and a small museum. Don't count on buying lunch here, because Hovenweep has no food concession. A quiet little campground with picnic tables and water beckons, however. A $3.00 entry fee per person or $6.00 per vehicle is charged. Call for directions; the only paved entrance is from Utah. Hovenweep is open year-round from 8:00 A.M. to 4:00 P.M. (except Christmas Day). For more information call (970) 562–4282; www.nps.gov/hove.

The **Ute Indians** are the oldest continuous residents of Colorado of the seven original tribes who still live in the southwestern part of the state today. For those with an interest in Native American culture, the city of Durango is the gateway to both the **Southern Ute** and **Ute Mountain Ute Indian Reservations.**

Nearly a century ago these Indians accepted government allotments and settled on a strip of land along the Colorado–New Mexico border, near the present town of **Ignacio** (population 800). Eventually, these Utes became known as the Southern Ute Indian tribe. Claiming more than 1,000 members, the Utes have their headquarters in Ignacio.

Here they have built an Indian Country vacation complex, complete with a thirty-eight-room motel, indoor/outdoor pool, museum, and a fine arts-and-crafts shop. The tribe lives on a reservation.

In some ways the present-day Utes can hardly be distinguished from any other Americans. Sounds of televisions, radios, and VCRs fill their modern-day urban homes. Basketball and swimming are popular reservation sports.

The ancestral home of these Native Americans once spanned most of the present state of Colorado. Although reigning over a large empire, they lacked a common Ute political organization. Instead, they formed independent bands that followed their own chiefs. The most famous groups included the Uncompahgre or Tabeguache, whose central home was the area around the present sites of Gunnison and Montrose, Colorado; the White River and Yampa bands of northwestern Colorado; the Mouache, who roamed along the front range of the Rockies in Colorado; the Capotes, who lived in the San Luis Valley of Colorado; and the Weminuche, who lived in the San Juan Basin in southwestern Colorado.

While hunting and roaming their enormous territory, the Utes often fought against other tribes, yet they remained on generally good terms with white men who trapped, traded, and prospected for gold on Indian lands.

As Anglo settlers streamed onto Colorado's eastern slope, the government, fearing trouble between Anglos and Utes, tried to persuade the Utes to move to the west of the Continental Divide. Finding it difficult to negotiate with so many chiefs, the government designated an Uncompahgre leader, Ouray—his name means "arrow"—as the Ute tribal spokesman. Chief Ouray wanted to preserve his home and Ute territory; he resisted departure from the San Luis Valley and surrounding areas. Finally, under the treaty of 1868, the Native Americans agreed to move westward.

Subsequent treaties and promises made and broken resulted in combative Indians. Trouble erupted when Utes attacked and killed U.S. soldiers in the Meeker and Thornburgh massacres, and they were later driven off their lands.

These days all is peaceful in southern Colorado, though, and the Native Americans welcome tourists, especially since legalized gambling is allowed on the reservation. Glitzy casinos offer several types of gaming and bingo.

For more information contact the Southern Ute Indian Tribe, P.O. Box 737, Ignacio 81137; (970) 563–0100; www.southern-ute.nsn.us.

Places to Stay in Southern Colorado

The rating scale for hotels is based on double occupancy and is as follows:
Inexpensive:
Less than $75 per night
Moderate:
$75 to $100 per night
Expensive:
$100 to $150 per night
Deluxe:
More than $150 per night

CAÑON CITY/
ROYAL GORGE

Best Western Royal Gorge Inn,
1925 Fremont Drive;
(719) 275–3377 or
(800) 231–7317
www.bestwestern.com
Inexpensive to moderate

Cañon Inn,
3075 East US 50;
(719) 275–8676 or
(800) 525–7727
www.canoninn.com
Inexpensive to moderate

Days Inn,
217 North Reynolds Avenue;
(719) 269–1100
www.daysinn.com
Inexpensive

COLORADO SPRINGS

Antlers Adam's Mark,
4 South Cascade Avenue,
at Pikes Peak Avenue and
Cascade Avenue;
(719) 473–5600
www.antlers.com
Expensive to deluxe

The Broadmoor Resort,
1 Lake Circle;
(800) 634–7711
www.broadmoor.com
Deluxe

Garden of the Gods Motel,
2922 West Colorado Avenue;
(719) 636–5271
www.pikespeak.com
Inexpensive to moderate

Holden House 1902 Bed & Breakfast Inn,
1102 West Pikes Peak;
(719) 471–3980
www.holdenhouse.com
Expensive

Old Town Guesthouse Bed and Breakfast,
115 South Twenty-sixth Street;
(719) 632–9194 or
(800) 375–4210
www.oldtown-guest house.com
Moderate to deluxe

Quality Inn,
555 West Garden of the Gods Road;
(719) 593–9119 or
(800) 828–4347
www.qualityinn.com
Inexpensive to moderate

CRESTED BUTTE

Crested Butte Club,
512 Second Street;
(970) 349–6655
www.crestedbutteclub.com
Moderate to deluxe

SELECTED SOUTHERN COLORADO GENERAL INFORMATION RESOURCES

CAÑON CITY

Cañon City Chamber of Commerce,
403 Royal Gorge Boulevard, 81212;
(719) 275–2331 or (800) 876–7922
www.canoncitychamber.com

COLORADO SPRINGS

Colorado Springs Convention
and Visitors Bureau,
515 South Cascade Avenue, 80903;
(719) 635–7506 or (800) 888–4748
www.coloradosprings-travel.com

CRESTED BUTTE

Crested Butte–Mt. Crested Butte
Chamber of Commerce,
P.O. Box 1288, 81224;
(970) 349–6438 or (800) 545–4505
www.crestedbuttechamber.com

CRIPPLE CREEK

Cripple Creek Welcome Center,
Fifth and Bennett Avenue,
P.O. Box 430, 80813;
(719) 689–3315 or (877) 858–4653
www.cripple-creek.co.us

DURANGO

Durango Area Chamber
Resort Association,
111 South Camino del Rio,
P.O. Box 2587, 81302;
(970) 247–0312 or (888) 414–0835
www.durango.org

GUNNISON

Gunnison Country Chamber
of Commerce,
500 East Tomichi Avenue, 81230;
(970) 641–1501
www.gunnison-co.com

LEADVILLE

Leadville/Lake County
Chamber of Commerce,
809 Harrison Avenue,
P.O. Box 861, 80461;
(719) 486–3900 or (800) 933–3901
www.leadvilleusa.com

Nordic Inn,
14 Treasury Road;
(970) 349–5542 or
(800) 542–7669
www.nordicinn.cb.com
Moderate to expensive

Old Town Inn,
201 North Sixth Avenue;
(970) 349–6184 or
(888) 349–6184
www.oldtowninn.net
Inexpensive to moderate

CRIPPLE CREEK

Cripple Creek Motel,
201 North Bison;
(719) 689–2491
www.cripplecreekmotel.com
Inexpensive

Holiday Inn Express,
601 East Galena Avenue;
(719) 689–2600
www.hiexpress.com
Moderate to expensive

Imperial Casino Hotel
(historic Victorian inn;
authentic Old West
atmosphere),
123 North Third Street;
(719) 689–7777 or
(800) 235–2922
www.imperialcasinohotel.com
Inexpensive to moderate

Independence
Hotel & Casino,
153 Bennett Avenue;
(719) 689–2744
www.independencehotel.com
Inexpensive

MANITOU SPRINGS

Manitou Springs Chamber
of Commerce & Visitors Bureau,
354 Manitou Avenue, 80829;
(800) 642–2567
www.manitousprings.org

MESA VERDE

Mesa Verde Country Visitor
Information Bureau,
(800) 530–2998
www.swcolo.org

Colorado Welcome Center,
928 East Main (Cortez), 81321;
(970) 565–3414

MONTROSE

Montrose Chamber of Commerce,
1519 East Main Street, 81401;
(970) 249–5000 or (800) 923–5515
www.montrosechamber.com

MOSCA

Great Sand Dunes
National Park,
11500 Highway 150, 81146-9798;
(719) 378–2312
www.nps.gov/grsa

PAGOSA SPRINGS

Pagosa Springs Area Chamber
of Commerce,
P.O. Box 787, 81147;
(970) 264–2360 or (800) 252–2204
www.pagosa-springs.com

PUEBLO

Greater Pueblo Chamber
of Commerce,
P.O. Box 697, 81002;
(800) 233–3446
www.pueblo.org

**J.P. McGill's Hotel
and Casino,**
232 Bennett Avenue;
(719) 689–2446 or
(888) 461–7529
Inexpensive to moderate

DURANGO

General Palmer Hotel
(historic bed and breakfast),
567 Main Avenue;
(970) 247–4747 or
(800) 523–3358
www.generalpalmerhotel.com
Moderate to deluxe

Iron Horse Inn,
5800 North Main;
(970) 259–1010, ext. 300
or (800) 748–2990
www.ironhorseinn
durango.com
Moderate

Lightner Creek Inn,
999 CR 207; 3 miles west on
US 160, 1 mile on Lightner
Creek Road;
(970) 259–1226 or
(800) 268–9804
www.lightnercreekinn.com
Expensive

Rochester Hotel
(historic inn; first-class
accommodations; close to
restaurants),
726 East Second Avenue;
(970) 385–1920 or
(800) 664–1920
www.rochesterhotel.com
Expensive to deluxe

Tamarron Resort Durango
(luxurious accommodations),
40292 Highway 550;
(970) 259–2000 or
(800) 678–1000
Deluxe

OTHER ATTRACTIONS WORTH SEEING IN SOUTHERN COLORADO

COLORADO SPRINGS

Flying W Ranch,
(719) 598–4000
www.flyingw.com

Old Colorado City,
(719) 577–4112
www.oldcoloradocity.com

U.S. Olympic Visitor Center,
(888) 659–8687
www.olympic-usa.org/about_us/
visitor_ctr.html

DURANGO

Durango Mountain Resort,
(970) 247–9000 or (800) 982–6103
www.durangomountainresort.com

GUNNISON

The Alpine Tunnel Historic District,
(970) 641–0471
www.narrowgauge.org/alpine-tunnel/
html/

Schofield Pass,
(970) 641–1501
(Chamber of Commerce)
www.gunnison-co.com

Tincup Old Mining Town,
(970) 641–1501
(Chamber of Commerce)
www.gunnison-co.com

Western State College of Colorado,
(800) 876–5309
www.western.edu

GREAT SAND DUNES/ ALAMOSA

Cottonwood Inn Bed & Breakfast
(cozy accommodations),
123 San Juan Avenue
(Alamosa);
(719) 589–3882 or
(800) 955–2623
www.cottonwoodinn.com
Inexpensive to expensive

Great Sand Dunes Lodge
(next to park entrance), 900
Highway 150 North (Mosca);
(719) 378–2900
www.gsdlodge.com
Moderate

GUNNISON

Mary Lawrence Inn
(historic bed and breakfast),
601 North Taylor Street;
(970) 641–3343 or
(888) 331–6863
www.commerceteam
.com/mary.html
Moderate to expensive

Super 8
(less expensive
than competition),
411 East Tomichi Avenue;
(970) 641–3068 or
(800) 800–8000
Inexpensive

Water Wheel Inn (motel),
37478 West Highway 50;
(970) 641–1650 or
(800) 642–1650
Inexpensive

LEADVILLE

Apple Blossom Inn,
120 West Fourth Street;
(719) 486–2141 or
(800) 982–9279
Expensive

Ice Palace Inn Bed & Breakfast
(historic bed and breakfast),
813 Spruce Street;
(719) 486–8272
www.icepalaceinn.com
Moderate to expensive

Timberline Motel,
216 Harrison Avenue;
(719) 486–1876 or
(800) 352–1876
www.timberlinemotel.com
Inexpensive

LEADVILLE

Leadville, Colorado &
Southern Railroad Train Tour,
(719) 486–3936
www.leadville-train.com

MANITOU SPRINGS

Cave of the Winds,
(719) 685–5444
www.caveofthewinds.com

MONTROSE

Owl Creek Pass,
(970) 249–5000 or (800) 923–5515
(Chamber of Commerce)
www.montrose-colo.com/attract/
attracts.htm

PAGOSA SPRINGS

Navajo State Park,
(970) 883–2208
parks.state.co.us/

Wolf Creek Pass,
(800) 252–2204
(Chamber of Commerce)
sangres.com/features/wolfcreekpass.htm

PUEBLO

The Greenway and Nature Center
of Pueblo,
(719) 549–2414
www.gncp.org

University of Southern Colorado,
(719) 549–2100
www.colostate-pueblo.edu

MANITOU SPRINGS

Black Bear Inn,
5250 Pikes Peak Highway,
Cascade;
(719) 684–0151 or
(877) 732–5232
www.blackbearinnpikes
peak.com
Moderate to expensive

El Colorado Lodge
(historic cottage),
23 Manitou Avenue;
(719) 685–5485
www.pikes-peak.com/
elcolorado
Inexpensive to moderate

**Red Crags
Bed and Breakfast Inn,**
302 El Paso Boulevard;
(719) 685–1920 or
(800) 721–2248
www.redcrags.com
Moderate to deluxe

Santa Fe Motel (historic),
3 Manitou Avenue;
(719) 475–8185
www.santafepikespeak.com
Inexpensive

Town-N-Country Cottages
(quiet accommodations),
123 Crystal Park Road;
(719) 685–5427
Moderate to expensive

MESA VERDE

Far View Lodge
(motel; gets busy in summer,
reserve far in advance), at
Navajo Hill; in the park, 15
miles from the entrance;
(970) 529–4422 or
(800) 449–2288
Moderate to expensive

MONTROSE

Best Western Red Arrow
(comfortable),
1702 East Main;
(970) 249–9641 or
(800) 468–9323
www.bestwestern.com
Inexpensive to moderate

Black Canyon (clean motel),
1605 East Main;
(970) 249–3495 or
(800) 348–3495
Inexpensive

Country Lodge Motel,
1624 East Main;
(970) 249–4567
www.countryldg.com
Inexpensive to moderate

Western Motel,
1200 East Main;
(970) 249–3481 or
(800) 445–7301
www.westernmotel.com
Inexpensive to moderate

PAGOSA SPRINGS

Fairfield Pagosa Resort
(tennis, golf, restaurant
on premises),
538 Village Drive;
(970) 731–8000
Deluxe

High Country Lodge
(motel),
3821 US 160;
(970) 264–4181 or
(800) 862–3707
www.highcountrylodge.com
Inexpensive to expensive

The Pagosa Lodge
(newly remodeled),
3505 West Highway 160;
(970) 731–4141 or
(800) 523–7704
www.pagosalodge.com
Moderate to expensive

The Spring Inn
(hot springs),
P.O. Box 1797;
(970) 264–4168 or
(800) 225–0934
www.pagosasprings
resort.com
Moderate to expensive

PUEBLO

Abriendo Inn
(bed and breakfast),
300 West Abriendo Avenue;
(719) 544–2703
www.abriendoinn.com
Inexpensive to expensive

**Best Western Town House
Motor Hotel,**
730 North Santa Fe Avenue;
(719) 543–6530
www.bestwestern.com
Inexpensive to moderate

Days Inn (good value),
4201 North Elizabeth;
(719) 543–8031
Inexpensive to moderate

Places to Eat in Southern Colorado

The rating scale for
restaurants is as follows:
Inexpensive:
Most entrees less than $10
Moderate:
Most entrees $10 to $15
Expensive:
Most entrees $15 to $20
Deluxe:
Most entrees more than $20

**CAÑON CITY/
ROYAL GORGE**

Chile Wagon Restaurant
(Mexican),
807 Cyanide Avenue;
(719) 275–4885
Moderate to expensive

Merlino's Belvedere
(Italian, American),
1330 Elm Avenue;
(719) 275–5558
Moderate

Pizza Madness,
509 Main Street;
(719) 276–3088
Inexpensive

COLORADO SPRINGS

**Charles Court at
the Broadmoor**
(true elegance and class;
large menu),
1 Lake Avenue;
(719) 577–5733
Deluxe

Edelweiss
(German; authentically
European),
34 East Ramona Avenue;
(719) 633–2220
www.restauranteur.com/
edelweiss.com
Moderate to expensive

Flying W Ranch
(Western atmosphere;
chuckwagon suppers),
3330 Chuckwagon Road;
(719) 598–4000 or
(800) 232–FLYW
www.flyingw.com
Expensive

Giuseppe's Depot
(Italian, American),
10 South Sierra Madre;
(719) 635–3111
www.giuseppes-depot.com
Inexpensive to moderate

La Casita Patio Cafe
(Mexican),
3504 North Academy
Boulevard;
(719) 574–1499
Inexpensive

La Petit Maison
(French), 1015 West
Colorado Avenue;
(719) 632–4887
Deluxe

Maggie Mae's
(Mexican, American),
2405 East Pikes
Peak Avenue;
(719) 475–1623
Inexpensive to moderate

CRESTED BUTTE

Crested Butte Brewery
(steakhouse),
226 Elk Avenue;
(970) 349–5026
Moderate

Donita's Cantina
(Tex-Mex, Mexican),
332 Elk Avenue;
(970) 349–6674
Inexpensive to moderate

Le Bosquet
(well-established French
restaurant), Sixth & Belleview,
Majestic Plaza;
(970) 349–5808
Expensive

CRIPPLE CREEK

**The Stratton's Grill at
Imperial Casino Hotel**
(historic; American),
123 North Third Street;
(719) 689–7777
www.imperialcasino.com/
strattonmenu.htm
Moderate to expensive

DURANGO

Ariano's (Italian),
150 East College Drive;
(970) 247–8146
Expensive

Lori's Family Dining
(ribs; Mexican),
2653 Main Avenue;
(970) 247–1224
Inexpensive to moderate

**Mahogany Grille at
the Strater**
(historic; regional American),
699 Main Avenue;
(970) 247–4433
www.mahoganygrille.com
Moderate

Ore House (steakhouse),
147 East College Drive;
(970) 247–5707
www.orehouserestaurant.com
Moderate to deluxe

GUNNISON

Garlic Mike's (Italian),
2674 North Highway 135;
(970) 641–2493
Inexpensive to moderate

Quarter Circle Restaurant
(American),
323 East Tomichi Avenue;
(970) 641–0542
Moderate

The Trough
(steak, seafood, game),
2 miles west on US 50;
(970) 641–3724
Moderate

LEADVILLE

Columbine Cafe (American),
612 Harrison Avenue;
(719) 486–3599
Moderate

La Cantina (Mexican),
1942 US Highway 24;
(719) 486–9021

MANITOU SPRINGS

Adam's Mountain Cafe
(vegetarian),
110 Canon Avenue;
(719) 685–1430
www.adamsmountain.com
Moderate

The Briarhurst Manor
(continental),
404 Manitou Avenue;
(719) 685–1864
www.briarhurst.com
Expensive to deluxe

Craftwood Inn
(Colorado cuisine;
seafood, game),
404 El Paso Boulevard;
(719) 685–9000
www.craftwood.com
Expensive to deluxe

Mission Bell Inn
(Mexican),
178 Crystal Park Road;
(719) 685–9089
www.missionbellinn.com
Moderate

Stagecoach Inn
(buffalo, prime rib),
702 Manitou Avenue;
(719) 685–9400
Moderate to expensive

MONTROSE

Glenn Eyrie
(American), 2351 South
Townsend Avenue;
(970) 249–9263
Expensive

Sakura (sushi, Japanese),
411 North Townsend;
(970) 249–8230
Moderate to expensive

The Whole Enchilada
(Mexican),
44 South Grand Avenue;
(970) 249–1881
Inexpensive to moderate

PAGOSA SPRINGS

Branding Iron Bar-B-Que
(western),
3961 East Highway 160;
(970) 264–4268
Inexpensive to moderate

Elkhorn Cafe
(Mexican, American),
438 Pagosa Boulevard;
(970) 264–2146
Moderate to expensive

Ole Miner's Steakhouse,
3825 Highway 160;
(970) 264–5981
Moderate

Riverside
(Southwestern, American),
439 San Juan Street;
(970) 264–2175
Moderate

PUEBLO

Cactus Flower
(Southwestern),
4610 North Elizabeth;
(719) 545–8218
Moderate

Cafe Del Rio (continental),
5200 Nature Center Road;
(719) 549–2009
Moderate

Gaetano's
(Italian; large portions),
910 US 50W;
(719) 546–0949
Moderate to expensive

La Renaissance
(continental),
217 East Routt Avenue;
(719) 543–6367
Moderate to expensive

**Nacho's Fireside
Restaurant**
(Mexican),
3915 Ivywood Lane;
(719) 566–9648
Moderate to expensive

SEDALIA

Gabriel's
(historic; fine dining),
5450 North Highway 67;
(303) 688–2323
Deluxe

Denver and the Plains

Denver Metropolitan Area

There were the Spaniards and the Native American tribes—Utes, Cheyennes, Arapahos, and Cherokees. Then suddenly came the prospectors to that prairie wilderness 10 miles east of the mountain ramparts. The fate of a tranquil Native American village at the junction of Cherry Creek and South Platte River would be changed forever.

That summer day in 1858, the Anglo visitors found gold in these waters.

Word of the find soon spread. "The New Eldorado!" shouted the midwestern papers. That spring an estimated 150,000 people began to trek across the wide plains aboard wagons and even on foot. Only 40,000 made it or stayed; others turned back.

Gold in paying quantities was far from common. Those first months were very hard. Yet, that year a people's court was organized. The first hotel—the Denver House—opened. Publisher William N. Byers reached Denver on April 21, 1859, with a printing outfit. On April 23 he issued the first newspaper printed in Colorado. William McGaa was the first child born in

Denver. Leavenworth and Pikes Peak Express ran the first stage to Denver. The Auraria Post Office was established.

That May, John H. Gregory discovered a vein of gold-bearing quartz near what was to become Central City. This was big news, and, at first, it nearly evacuated Denver. As mines were developed in the mountains, however, Denver grew in its coming role as an important trade center. Indeed, Horace Greeley suggested, "Go West, young man! Go West, young man!" Denver became the logical jumping-off point for the huge gold finds of Central City and Black Hawk.

Exaggerated accounts of the discovery traveled eastward, causing the Gold Rush of 1859. Thousands of fortune hunters hurried across the plains, on foot, on horseback, in wagons, some even pushing handcarts and wheelbarrows. Most of these failed to find the mineral and trudged wearily back home. But they had founded several little habitation clusters variously known as Auraria and Denver City (named after General James W. Denver, territorial governor of Kansas), and these gradually became the capital city of Colorado.

All through the late 1850s and early 1860s, a great mass of people surged back and forth in search of wealth. Conditions were primitive in these Colorado

AUTHOR'S FAVORITES
DENVER AND THE PLAINS

Brown Palace Hotel,
(800) 321–2599
www.brownpalace.com

Butterfly Pavilion and Insect Center,
(303) 469–5441
www.butterflies.org

**Denver Center for the
Performing Arts,**
(303) 893–4000
www.denvercenter.org

**Governors' Mansion
(Executive Residence),**
(303) 866–3681
www.colorado.gov/dpa/doit/
archives/govs/mansion/front1.htm

Horsetooth Reservoir,
(970) 679–4570
www.co.larimer.co.us/parks/
horsetooth.htm

Lakewood Heritage Center,
(303) 987–7850
www.ci.lakewood.co.us

Larimer Square,
(303) 534–2367
www.larimersquare.com

Sloan Lake Park,
(303) 458–4788
www.denvergov.org/northwest_denver
_parks/template21231.asp

Washington Park,
(303) 698–4930
www.denvergov.org/south_denver_
parks/template21232.asp

Wellshire Inn,
(303) 759–3333
www.wellshireinn.com

camps. Tents were eventually replaced by huts, which grew into shacks, log cabins, and finally houses.

Gold brought more fortune hunters from all over North America, but also Irish engineers, Welsh hard-rock miners, and other Europeans, 100,000 more people in all. For a period between the 1870s and 1890s, Colorado had so many Germans that the laws were printed in both German and English.

trivia

In the 1850s, as Denver competed with other mining towns for the status of being Colorado's premier city, Denver was made up of nothing but crude cabins and one saloon—Colorado's first.

Lots of problems and calamities awaited the city.

Early in 1863, a great fire destroyed much of the business district. The following summer the lush plains were scorched by a drought. The winter was cold beyond all previous experience. Then, in the spring of 1864, a flash flood churned along the Cherry Creek sand bed through the city, washing over houses and bridges and killing twenty people. Nearly $1 million worth of property was destroyed.

In the wake of these natural disasters, the Indians attacked. Stage stations were sacked, communication and supply lines to the East severed. Denver was left with only a week's supply of food.

But the city survived, and because of the hardships the local people developed a determination to keep on surviving. When the Union Pacific Railroad bypassed Colorado on its transcontinental route, Denver citizens raised $300,000 and built their own railroad to meet the Union Pacific at Cheyenne, Wyoming.

Soon the Kansas Pacific crossed the plains. According to historian Richard Grant, "The silver barons built elaborate mansions on Capitol Hill. Gamblers,

Notes on Colorado from a Longtime Denverite

I find it remarkable that I can sit at a different outdoor terrace of my house for a summer breakfast, for an al fresco lunch, and for dinner. During each meal, I can enjoy the gleam and glitter of the Rocky Mountains. More: Depending on the weather I can see Pikes Peak, the famous "Fourteener," about 75 miles to the south; I can spot Longs Peak, another Fourteener, and lastly, Mt. Evans. As I open the cereal box and watch the steaming coffee, I feel very lucky. To live in Colorado! Who could ask for more?

I remember how I came to the state. I had been living in Austria, which had gleaming mountains as well—the Alps! I opted for the Rockies instead, never to regret it.

AUTHOR'S FAVORITE EVENTS IN DENVER AND THE PLAINS

National Western Stock Show, Horse Show and Rodeo;
National Western Complex in Denver;
early to mid-January;
(303) 297–1166 ext. 810
www.nationalwestern. com/nwss/home/
index.asp

Buskerfest;
Denver; late June;
(720) 932–7384
www.buskerfest.com

Cherry Blossom Festival;
Sakura Square, Denver; June or July;
(303) 295–1844
www.jadejapandolls.com/calendar.html

Rocky Mountain Stampede and Rodeo;
Greeley; late June through early July;
(800) 982–2855
www.greeleystampede.org

Larimer County Fair and Rodeo;
Loveland; early August;
(970) 669–6760
www.larimer.org/fair/rodeo

Oktoberfest;
Larimer Square in Denver;
mid-September;
(303) 534–2367
www.larimerarts.org

Great American Beer Festival;
Currigan Exhibition Hall in Denver;
early October;
(303) 447–0816 or (888) 822–6273
www.beertown.org/gabf/index.htm

Winterfest;
Larimer Square in Denver;
late November through early January;
(303) 534–2367
www.larimerarts.org/e-winterfest.html

WILDLIGHTS;
Denver Zoo in Denver;
nightly for the month of December;
(303) 376–4800
www.denverzoo.org

Lincoln Center Showstopper Series;
Fort Collins;
various evenings throughout the year;
(970) 221–6735
www.ci.fort-collins.co.us/llctix/
calendar.php

drifters and gunmen flooded the saloons and gaming halls on Larimer and Market streets. Bat Masterson tended bar here, Soapy Smith ran the West's largest gang of thieves, crooks and con artists, and anyone who was anyone in the 'Old West' paid at least a visit to Denver's mud-filled, honky-tonk streets."

On August 1, 1876, Colorado entered the Union and was called the Centennial State in honor of the one hundredth anniversary of the Declaration of Independence.

By 1879 the Mile High City had a population of 35,000 and boasted the first telephone service in the West. Soon there was a second boom. One silver mining camp after another suddenly prospered. When the silver played out,

Denver settled into a comfortable, respectable life—nearly free of gamblers, drifters, and claim jumpers.

Education now became important. In 1887 Governor Ben H. Eaton told the general assembly: "The schools of Denver are today equal to the best in the world—equal to those of Boston, Paris or Berlin. The capital of our state is the Athens of the plains, with the glory of ancient Athens."

By 1910 the city had become the commercial and industrial center of the Rocky Mountain region, with a large cattle market and the largest sheep market in the world. Denver was in the process of becoming the nation's second capital, thanks to a proliferation of government offices. This situation is still true today; Denver is second only to Washington, D.C., in number of employed government workers.

trivia

Denver has 300 days of sunshine annually—more hours of sun each year than Miami Beach!

Many older Denverites still harbor a nostalgic feeling about Colorado Victoriana, and some people are seriously trying to hold on to the city's remaining old mansions. There is public resistance to the wreckers sent by those who prefer the profit of more office buildings and high-rise apartment houses. Many of the noted old edifices, the Tabor Theater and the Windsor Hotel among them, had to give way to the modern glass-and-steel skyscrapers. "Part of Denver died tonight," wrote a Denverite the day another of the historic hotels was razed.

A few of the Victorian homes still exist, complete with the cherrywood dressers, mantelpieces, hat racks, and mirror frames. The historic **Brown Palace Hotel** (321 Seventeenth Street; 303–297–3111 or 800–321–2599; www.brownpalace.com) and the **Oxford Hotel** (1600 Seventeenth Street; 303–628–5400 or 800–228–3858; www.theoxfordhotel.com) are alive and well. While in the city you may wish to visit one of the old mansions, such as the **Molly Brown House Museum,** where history is preserved.

After she became wealthy, the "Unsinkable" Molly Brown lived her flamboyant life in this mansion of native Colorado lava stone. Following Molly's death in 1932, the building served as a rooming house. Then, at the whim of each new owner, it was remodeled or divided. Rescued in 1971 by "Historic Denver," the mansion was decorated as Molly herself had done, using old photographs Molly had taken of her home's interior. The Molly Brown House has been restored to its exaggerated, extreme opulence. It is located at 1340 Pennsylvania Street; (303) 832–4092; www.mollybrown.com. Admission costs $6.50 for adults and teenagers thirteen and older, $5.00 for senior citizens sixty-five and older, and $3.00 for children six to twelve; children five or younger free. Open year-round Tuesday through Saturday from 10:00 A.M. to 4:00 P.M. and Sunday from noon to 4:00 P.M.; closed Monday and major holidays.

Colorado's **Governors' Mansion** (also known as the **Cheesman-Boettcher Mansion** and the Executive Residence), a redbrick Colonial building with white stone trim, was built by one of the state's distinguished pioneer families, the Cheesmans. (Cheesman Park is named for them.) After serving as the home of John Evans, Colorado's second territorial governor, the property passed into the Boettcher family. Then it became part of their Boettcher Foundation, a philanthropic organization that presented it as a gift to the state of Colorado in 1960. The mansion has been the executive residence of the state's governors ever since.

Furnished with luxurious art, antiques, and furniture, the house is available for limited tours. It is located at 400 East Eighth Street in Denver. For information about tours, contact the Colorado Historical Society's Office of Archaeology and Historic Preservation, 1300 Broadway, Denver 80203; (303) 866–3681; www.colorado.gov/dpa/doit/archives/govs/mansion/front1.htm.

If you enjoy visiting stately old Denver mansions, you might consider the **Pearce McAllister Cottage,** located at 1880 Gaylord Street. This 1899 structure also contains the **Denver Museum of Miniatures, Dolls and Toys.** Open Tuesday through Saturday from 10:00 A.M. to 4:00 P.M. and Sunday from 1:00 to 4:00 P.M. Admission costs $5.00 for anyone age seventeen through sixty-one and $4.00 for ages two to sixteen and senior citizens sixty-two and older. Call (303) 322–1053 or log on to www.dmmdt.com

The **Grant-Humphreys Mansion** was built in 1902 and named after former Colorado governor James B. Grant. It has more than forty rooms. The mansion at 770 Pennsylvania Street, can be rented for special events or toured. For more information contact the Grant-Humphreys Mansion at (303) 894–2505; www.coloradohistory.org/shm/.

The **Byers-Evans House,** a mansion at 1310 Bannock Street built in 1883, has been restored to its original grandeur. Admission costs $3.00 for anyone age seventeen through sixty-four, $2.50 for seniors age sixty-five or older, and $1.50 for young people age six through sixteen. Children age five or younger are admitted free. Hours of operation are 11:00 A.M. to 3:00 P.M. Tuesday through Sunday; closed Monday. For more information contact the Byers-Evans House at (303) 620–4933 or visit www.coloradohistory.org.

Stop in for a visit at the adjacent **Denver History Museum** at 1300 Braodway. The museum is open 10:00 A.M. to 4:30 P.M. Monday through Saturday and noon to 4:30 P.M. Sunday. Admission is $5.00 for adults (thirteen to sixty-four),

Black American West Museum & Heritage Center

Did you know that nearly one-third of America's working cowboys in the Old West were African American? *The Black American West Museum* offers a unique and much-needed look at the history of these and other African Americans and the roles they played in our nation's past. The museum is housed in the former home of Denver's first African-American doctor, Dr. Justina Ford, who delivered more than 7,000 babies during her illustrious career. Admission prices are $6.00 for adults, $5.50 for seniors sixty-five and older, and $4.00 for children five to twelve; children under five free. Call for hours. For more information: 3091 California, Denver 80205, (303) 292-2566; www.coax.net/people/lwf/bawmus.htm.

$4.50 for seniors sixty-five and older and for students with ID, and $3.50 for children six to twelve; children under six free. For more information contact the Denver History Museum at (303) 866–3682 or visit www.coloradohistory.org.

The most sumptuous of all the historic buildings in this part of Denver is the castlelike *Capitol Hill Mansion,* an impeccable, deluxe bed-and-breakfast at 1207 Pennsylvania. The mansion, a landmark building listed in the National Register of Historic Places, is not far from the Governor's Mansion and the Molly Brown House. The 1891 furniture is hand-carved oak and maple. The walls are decorated with original Colorado landscape paintings. Some rooms come with four-posters and mountain-viewing balconies. Unlike many B&Bs, this one offers room TVs, fresh flowers, and a small refrigerator with refreshments (complimentary). For more information contact the Capitol Hill Mansion at (303) 839–5221 or (800) 839–9329; www.capitolhillmansion.com.

Considering Colorado's booming economy and amazing environment, it's no wonder that most Denverites refuse to relocate to another city. "Move?" says one executive. "They offered me a promotion on the East Coast. But I refused. Stayed on at a lower salary." If you ask longtime Denver people why they're so partial to their city, you'll get a long string of explanations. "We ski. The mountains are close." "We love the many parks and green lawns of the homes." "Do you know a more cosmopolitan place between Los Angeles and Chicago? Denver is *it!*"

Because the mountains are only thirty minutes away from downtown, Denver attracts a young, energetic population. This dynamic energy is reflected in Denver's nightlife. The city boasts more than 2,500 restaurants, more than 150 art galleries, almost 30 theaters, 100 cinemas, an $80 million performing arts center, a convention center, and dozens of nightclubs, discos, comedy clubs, singles bars, and concert halls.

If there is one thing Denver does well (after 130 years of practice), it is the saloon. The first permanent structure in Denver was a saloon, and today there are sports bars, art bars, fern bars, outdoor cafe bars, English pubs, "Old West" saloons, rock bars, city-overlook bars, country-and-western bars, art deco bars, and even bars that don't serve alcohol. (Denver however, leads the nation in beer brewing.)

In addition to a plethora of saloons, Denver has more sporting-goods stores and ski shops per capita than almost any other population center in the world and a corresponding number of recreation facilities that include free outdoor tennis courts, city golf courses, and the like.

At the same time, filmmakers, artists, and thinkers all gravitate toward Denver, a city that spent $6 million to build the ***Denver Art Museum,*** located at Thirteenth Avenue and Acoma Street in downtown Denver (720–865–5000; www.denverartmuseum.org). Here art aficionados and others can peruse both temporary exhibits and permanent holdings, including the museum's Modern and Contemporary collection with more than 4,500 works, an Asian art collection unmatched in the Rocky Mountain region, and a European collection that includes a number of Renaissance works. The museum is open Tuesday through Saturday from 10:00 A.M. to 5:00 P.M. (Wednesday until 9:00 P.M.) and Sunday from noon until 5:00 P.M. It is closed Mondays, Christmas, Thanksgiving Day, and New Year's Day. Admission is $8.00 for adults; $6.00 for seniors sixty-five and older, students thirteen to eighteen, and college students with identification; and free for children twelve and under. Colorado residents can enjoy the museum for free every Saturday.

Denver Art Museum

In addition to its high-caliber art museum, Denver is home to an impressive library suited to please the most discerning bookworm. The **Denver Public Library,** with its 4.4 million total holdings, happens to be one of the best—and most versatile—in the country. It is at the library desks that you get the feeling of Denver's wide horizons.

Denver's genuine penchant for culture shows up in several other ways. On a given evening, the visitor to the state capital could take in a play by Dylan Thomas at the boldly designed **Denver Center Theatre,** part of the **Denver Center for the Performing Arts** (DCPA). DCPA, at 1245 Champa Street, is home to two production companies—Denver Center Theatre Company and Denver Center Productions (DCP). DCP is responsible for importing touring Broadway shows, among other roles. DCPA also houses the **Wilbur James Gould Voice Center** (WJGVC). This unique voice center, a part of the National Center for Voice and Speech, offers workshops to help prevent speech difficulties and works with speech- and voice-impaired individuals. WJGVC laboratories also conduct research on the human voice. For more information contact the DCPA at (303) 893–4000. For tickets call (303) 893–4100 or (800) 641–1222; www.denvercenter.org.

Next door to DCPA is the nearly 2,700-seat **Boettcher Concert Hall,** where music lovers enjoy the music of the **Colorado Symphony Orchestra,** among other performers. For ticket information call (303) 893–4100 or (800) 641–1222; www.coloradosymphony.org. The season runs from September through May. Boettcher Concert Hall is located at Fourteenth and Curtis Streets in Denver. The city has come of age culturally, what with its little theaters, its art cinemas, its ballets, and its chamber music ensembles.

Local interest is keen in the rest of the world. And Denver's citizens remain helpful and hospitable, especially toward tourists and guests. Just tell a Denverite that you arrived here yesterday from London or Frankfurt or Minneapolis or wherever. Doors will spring wide open.

Denverites will show off their clean city; they may want to take you to their homes, where the inevitable sprinklers deepen the green of the lawns and flower gardens.

Denver arouses special interest because of its ethnic variety. The Hispanic population is fascinating for its rich and proud heritage. In north Denver, you find the classic Italian grocery stores that sell prosciutto, salami, black olives, and *tonno* as do those in Italy. Genuine Italian restaurants serve you home-made pasta and black olives and you drink Chianti, just as you would in Naples, Salerno, or Parma. There is a Polish club in Denver, where the young Polish girls still wear the pretty national costumes for their national folk dances.

A small Denver contingent is German speaking, with a lasting interest in dancing *schuhplattler* and singing all the old songs. The Germans founded an appropriately named Edelweiss Club, a Goethe Club, and the *Turnverein,* where the men do strenuous calisthenics and play soccer on weekends. Denver has its own German/Swiss *Delikatessen* stores, which import marinated herring from Kiel and Hamburg, Westphalian hams, and landjaeger sausages, and which sell their customers Nivea suntan creams, German Odol toothpaste, and *Der Stern* magazines, much as in Manhattan's Yorkville area.

There is a sizable Japanese population, with its own stores and customs and a Buddhist Temple for weddings. Vietnamese immigrants have their own shopping centers, and you will find Korean shops.

There is also Denver's enthusiasm for international dining. Well-traveled, polyglot restaurateurs like Pierre Wolfe often appear on television or radio. It should come as no surprise that the city has a number of authentic (and expensive) French eating places, such as **Tante Louise,** located at 4900 East Colfax Avenue; (303) 355–4488; www.tantelouise.com. Denver's dozens of superb Asian restaurants include the ever-popular and elegant **Imperial Chinese Restaurant,** 431 South Broadway; (303) 698–2800; www.imperialchinese.com. The visitor can also dine on genuine Ethiopian, Afghan, Moroccan, Greek, Armenian, Hungarian, Swiss, German, Italian, and, of course, Mexican fare.

Denver Firefighters Museum

Looking for something a little farther off the beaten path? Check out this hands-on museum that chronicles the history of fire fighting in Denver since the construction of the first fire station in 1909. The museum is located in the well-preserved original Station No. 1 and features a wide array of fire-fighting memorabilia. Open Monday through Friday from 10:00 A.M. to 4:00 P.M. in summer, 10:00 A.M. to 2:00 P.M. in winter; closed on Sunday and major holidays. Admission is $4.00 for adults, $3.00 for seniors, and $2.00 for children. For more information contact the **Denver Firefighters Museum,** 1326 Tremont Place; (303) 892–1436; www.denverfirefightersmuseum.org.

How about the traveler from the British Isles? At the foot of the new downtown skyscrapers, **Duffy's Shamrock Restaurant** holds court with (inexpensive) Irish home cooking, followed by real Irish coffee. This pub serves a filling supper at a reasonable price (1635 Court Place; 303–534–4935).

To be sure, the city's better restaurants, its bistros and more worldly nightspots, and its extra-elegant central hotels are accustomed to and welcome the visitor from abroad.

Denver and environs attract more than ten million visitors a year. "Smile!" goes one of the state's slogans, "You live in Colorado!" And most Denverites smile a lot as they count their blessings.

Of the numerous annual events that take place in Denver, the **National Western Stock Show, Rodeo, and Horse Show** is the biggest, longest, and most original—a yearly happening that radiates authenticity, excitement, and entertainment. Sixty years ago, cowboys' competitions with one another were formalized into rodeos. The stock show was born in a circus tent in 1906; the high speed of the riders, the antics of the rodeo clowns, and the pungent smells of the animals sometimes still remind you of a circus. For approximately two weeks every January, old Buffalo Bill and his Wild West entertainers seem to return to old Denver Town.

The National Western remains an important stock show, too. You can view more than 15,000 live, scrubbed, and brushed Herefords, Angus, Simmentals, Shorthorns, Longhorns, Arabian horses, Morgan horses, draft horses, miniature horses, ewes, and lambs, all in their neat pens. You watch shearing contests, breeding cattle auctions, and the judging of quarterhorse stallions. Some 600,000 visitors flock to the arenas to buy, sell, learn, and socialize. Millions of dollars exchange hands here.

"This is a cowboy convention for real-life cowboys," says one longtime Stock Show regular. "It's big business for the people who grow the stuff that ends up in our refrigerators and stomachs."

In addition to the judging and auctions, there are lectures, sales booths, meetings, and contests for the cattlemen and -women who show up here. Lots of money is in evidence. Thousand-dollar alligator boots. Hundred-dollar Stetsons. Belt buckles with diamonds. Even silver halters for the horses. A big commerce in livestock supplies, raw wool, saddles, cow tags, western art show and sale, lassoes.

In the areas of both feeding and breeding, new techniques are taught while in nearby arenas, horsewomen demonstate their riding skill, galloping at a breakneck pace. At the same time in yet another venue, red-vested auctioneers call out to a crowd of spectators in an effort to convince them to bid a little higher for each llama that comes up for sale.

A children's area delights the young ones with displays of baby rabbits, geese, and piglets. Each weekday some 1,200 schoolchildren are bused here to see the animals. The multifaceted spectacular not only brings aristocratic, pure-bred livestock to Denver; the Stock Show also regularly attracts the best of the rodeo ring, all top contenders for national championships for female barrel racing, calf roping, bull and bronco riding, steer wrestling, and many more events by more than 1,000 professional rodeo cowboys and cowgirls who are courageous and sporty. More than $400,000 in prizes are at stake.

But not all cowboys do well in Denver. A horse may refuse to buck and the rider will get nothing. A horse tosses him off after two seconds and the rider will get nothing. "They're the great American gamblers on horseback," says a western radio announcer.

Nobody gives the competitors an expense account. They pay their own way to ride at the National Western Stock Show and Rodeo. The rodeo cowboy draws no allowance, has no guaranteed annual wage. The only income comes from earnings in a fiercely competitive sport where he must win not only against other men but against the "rank" (mean) animals. And he must pay for this privilege—entry fees that can run into several hundred dollars per event per rodeo.

Most riders hail from small towns and made their first acquaintance with horses as kids. One typical bareback champ comes from Cora, Wyoming. He started as a ranch hand.

Rodeos, such as the National Western in Denver, may have well begun as a prank, a diversion for ranch hands and cowpokes. A few specialists, the "roughstring" riders who busted wild horses for a livelihood at a few bucks apiece, were quick to show their stuff. They were a tough bunch of men. Hardened by the summer heat and winter blizzards, used to riding through long nights, they had to deal with stampeding herds, crippled animals, and cattle rustlers. Their horses were extensions of themselves. They lived in the saddle.

Rodeo must have started during the early cattle drives and on the scattered ranches. A historian of the Denver-based Professional Rodeo Cowboys Association explains: "When their work was done, the cowboys entertained each other with roping and riding contests, showing off the skills they had sharpened during their everyday work on the range."

In the early 1880s, American ranchers began to develop the "ranch show" as a spectator sport. Already in 1888 Colorado spectators paid money to watch cowboys on bucking broncs. Within twenty years these affairs had become known as rodeos and were drawing crowds on tour in the cities of the United States.

In the early days of rodeo, the rider stayed in the saddle "until the horse was rode or the cowboy throwed." Today, the saddle bronc rider must stay aboard eight seconds, while at the same time not disqualifying himself in any number of ways. A man has to zoom out of the chute with both feet in the stirrups.

As a spectator you can see lots of thrilling action. The Stock Show grounds sprawl across 150 acres, which are only about 100 yards south of Interstate 70. Buses get you there all day long; free shuttles run from various downtown hotels. You can also take a cab or drive. In that case, keep in mind that thousands of visiting livestock folks and rodeo fans compete for room to leave their cars, so close-in parking isn't always plentiful.

Rodeo competition takes place both afternoons and evenings. Tickets cost no more than for a movie. But wait! Have you ever been to a motion picture where you could witness a llama auction, an Australian-style sheep-shearing contest, the world's largest bull show (with one animal actually selling at $300,000), a catch-a-calf competition for teenagers? What film lets you talk to a real, true-blue Colorado rancher?

For more information write to the National Western Stock Show, 4655 Humboldt Street, Denver 80216; call (303) 297–1166, ext. 810; or visit www.national western.com.

How would you like to dine in a historic landmark and museum? How about a steaming platter of elk steak at a table under a stuffed elk, or a plate heaped with buffalo meat, with mounted buffalos staring down? The **_Buckhorn Exchange_** is allegedly Colorado's oldest restaurant (it celebrated its centennial in 1993). It is certainly one of the most original. Moreover, it's a saloon, a magnet for celebrities and tourists, and a moneymaker.

Supper here appeals to well-heeled meat eaters: twenty-four-ounce T-bone steaks, fourteen-ounce New York steaks, buffalo meat, baby back ribs, Rocky Mountain oysters, rabbit—all at hefty deluxe rates in a noisy, congenial atmosphere. The saloon is upstairs, complete with a giant oak bar that was shipped here by oxcart. Nearby walls are filled with 1902 photos of hunting parties; even the men's room has historic pictures of stagecoaches.

The downstairs restaurant-museum is cluttered with more than 500 taxidermy pieces, including antelopes, deer, bears, wolverines, mountain goats, moose, weasels, zebras, and birds of all kinds, shapes, and plumage. You can look at more than one hundred rifles, pistols, and other weapons.

Even the restaurant's history has its fascinating aspects. It was begun in 1893 by owner Henry H. Zietz, a cowboy and scout with Buffalo Bill, no less; personal bodyguard of Leadville's silver millionaire H. A. W. Horace Tabor; and hunting guide of President Teddy Roosevelt, who arrived in his private train in front of the Buckhorn. The restaurant's official history relates that Henry Zietz "catered to cattlemen, miners, railroad builders, Indian chiefs, silver barons, roustabouts, gamblers, the great and the near-great." In December 1900 a masked gunman rode up to the restaurant, waved a .45, and demanded all money and valuables to be placed on the bar, "and be quick about it!" The fellow's horse had been tied to the Buckhorn's hitching post, but when the gunman rode away at a gallop, he found himself pursued by Zietz's rifle-raising customers, who "handily dispatched the miscreant to greener pastures."

After the Zietz family's death, the restaurant-museum passed into the capable hands of several historically minded Denver investors, who put large sums into restoring the building and its contents in 1978. They also raised the prices to twentieth-century levels.

The Buckhorn's redbrick building is easy to find at 1000 Osage Street. The location is between Colfax Avenue and Eighth Avenue, 5 blocks west of Santa Fe Boulevard.

The Buckhorn Exchange is open for lunch Monday through Friday from 11:00 A.M. to 2:00 P.M., and dinner is served seven nights a week, starting at 5:30 P.M. Monday to Thursday, 5:00 P.M. Friday, Saturday, and Sunday. For more information or reservations call (303) 534–9505; www.buckhorn.com.

The *Forney Museum of Transportation* is the perfect place to see some old vehicles, including 1915 Cadillacs, 1905 Fords, various old surreys, a locomobile, an ancient electric car, various carriages, bygone cycles, rail coaches, steam engines, and old airplanes. The notable exhibits include Theodore Roosevelt's Tour Car, Aly Khan's Rolls-Royce, and Amelia Earhart's Gold Bug Kissel. The children run to see the ladies' old, old dresses or the officers' military uniforms dating back to 1750 and 1800.

The Forney Museum of Transportation is located at 4303 Brighton Boulevard. Call (303) 297–1113 or log on to www.forneymuseum.com. Admission is $7.00 for adults, $4.50 for youth (eleven to fifteen), and $3.50 for children five to ten. The museum is open Monday through Saturday from 9:00 A.M. to 5:00 P.M.

Larimer Square is a renovated, eighteenth-century downtown oasis with a national reputation; indeed, it is the second most visited landmark in Colorado. (The Air Force Academy is the first.)

In 1858, General William E. Larimer erected Denver's first building here. It was a mere log cabin. More than one hundred years later, a group of Colorado businesspeople founded the Larimer Square Association for the purpose of restoring the old buildings. The excitement that once was historic Larimer Street soon returned in the form of promenades, carriage rides, and quaint shops between Fourteenth and Fifteenth Streets.

In some ways Larimer Square reminds one of Ghirardelli Square in San Francisco. Or, it may make you think of Greenwich Village or New Orleans's French Quarter; others compare it to Chicago's Old Town or Toronto's Yorktown. By the same token, Larimer Square has its own visual personality; it remains an outstanding example of early Denver Victorian architecture, complete with gaslights, handwrought leaded-glass windows, stairways, historic markers, restored cornices, and handsome outdoor benches for resting and watching. In the restaurants (pricey) and shops, you find Tiffany lamps, cherrywood bars, rosewood paneling, old wallpapers, and lead ceilings.

The Square is paved with the legends of the nineteenth century. Larimer Street in Denver was once one of the most famous thoroughfares in the West. The restaurants, hotels, and theaters of its heyday were renowned. Stories of what happened when the greats, near-greats, and desperados of the West met made good newspaper copy. And tales of what went on behind closed doors in the neighborhood shocked a nation. Gambling and boozing were rampant.

Named for Denver's founder, General William E. Larimer, the street played a prominent role in the city's political and commercial history from November 16, 1858. That first day, Denver City consisted only of Larimer Street's 1400 block. As the western town grew around it, the original site became Denver's first commercial and governmental center. Here were the first post office, the first department store, the first drugstore, and the first bank and government buildings of the 1860s, 1870s, and 1880s.

As the years passed, Denver gradually moved uptown, and Larimer Street became a skid row area. Thanks to the gin mills and flophouses, the handsome Victorian buildings were forgotten, although amid the grime and dirt, their architectural beauty remained. Razing was a frequent threat.

Larimer Square is now a Landmark Preservation District. You find this important Denver tourist attraction listed in the National Register of Historic Places. For more information call (303) 534–2367; www.larimersquare.com.

Walk 1 block north of Fifteenth Street. The **Sixteenth Street Mall,** Denver's ultramodern, $76 million pedestrian thoroughfare, is the best people-watching spot in the city—a place where you can be entertained by a juggler or a classic violinist, shop in large bookstores or small exclusive boutiques, or just sit on one of hundreds of benches and watch Denver go by. A dozen fountains, festive banners, two hundred red oak trees, and a lighting system straight out of Star Wars makes this mile-long mall an attractive shopping and entertainment street. For more information contact the Denver Metro Convention and Visitors Bureau at (800) 233–6837; www.denver.org.

From its international debut in 1892 until the present, Denver's **Brown Palace Hotel** has lived up to its motto, "Where the World Registers." Indeed, this historic hotel is a classic. Nearly every U.S. president since Theodore Roosevelt has spent time here.

"The Brown," as Denverites have nicknamed it, is a remarkable example of Victorian architecture. The hotel lobby impresses the most. Upon entering, your eyes look up the six tiers of wrought-iron balconies to the stained-glass cathedral ceiling. The decorative stone on the pillars is Mexican onyx. Changing displays of historical memorabilia decorate the luxurious lobby. Old guest registers, menus, and photographs take you back to relive the role the Brown Palace played in the history of Denver.

Brown Palace Hotel

The hotel is named for its builder, Henry Cordes Brown. As Brown watched nineteenth-century Denver grow, he saw the need for a fine hostelry for visiting easterners who came to do business with Colorado mining companies and railroads. The builder envisioned this hotel to rise from a triangular plot of land he owned near the center of the city. Henry Cordes Brown examined and studied the blueprints of the world's deluxe hostelries before he developed his "palace."

A prominent Denver architect, Frank E. Edbrooke, designed a building in the spirit of the Italian Renaissance. Because of the geometric pattern of Brown's land, the edifice took on an unusual shape. Edbrooke gave the building a tri-frontage and then planned it so that each room faced a street. Without any interior rooms, every guest could have a view, plus morning or afternoon sunshine! The contractors, Geddes and Serrie, constructed this soon-to-be famous landmark from Colorado red granite and warm brown Arizona sandstone. James Whitehouse then carved a lovely series of medallions in the stone.

Completed in 1892, the 10-story building had 400 rooms. Fireplaces were standard for each room, as well as bathroom taps yielding artesian water straight from the hotel's wells (as they still do today). The finest achievements in steam heating and electricity were incorporated into the structure. The Brown was also noted as the second fireproof edifice in the country.

It took four years and $1 million to complete Henry Brown's luxurious dream. Cool water flowed from the taps; steam heat provided warmth. Ice machines kept the wine chilled and the produce fresh. Turkish baths, hairdressing parlors, billiard rooms—even a hotel library!—were available for guest use. Linens, china, glassware, and silver came from the finest craftsmen. Carpets and curtains in each room had special designs. Excellence abounded at every turn.

The Brown Palace opened for a banquet of the Triennial Conclave of Knights Templar and their ladies. A seven-course dinner at $10 a plate was served in the main dining room on the eighth floor. The guests viewed more than 300 miles of Rocky Mountain grandeur from the wide dining-room windows.

Denver society was formally introduced to the Brown Palace a few months later when the Tabors threw a fancy ball. In the years since, the Brown has hosted thousands of such glittering evenings.

Today the Brown Palace Hotel is listed in the National Register of Historic Places. Even in the midst of modern times, it continues to provide guests with historical authenticity, Victorian charm, and good service. The original decor has been preserved, especially in the restaurants—the hallmarks of the hotel.

It pays to make reservations several weeks in advance. The Brown Palace Hotel is at 321 Seventeenth Street; (303) 297–3111 or (800) 321–2599; www .brownpalace.com.

The *Queen Anne Bed & Breakfast Inn* appeals to honeymooners; *Modern Bride, Bride's,* and *Bridal Guide* have mentioned it. Because this bed-and-breakfast is so close to Denver's financial district, quiet-seeking executives also stay here.

This Victorian masterpiece dates back to 1879. Each of the fourteen bed chambers is different, yet all are crammed with genuine Victoriana: brass beds, canopied beds, four-poster beds, love seats, armoires, stained-glass windows, walnut tables, oak rocking chairs, and the like. (A touch of kitsch is occasionally sighted, too.)

The bed-and-breakfast ambience is carefully enhanced: a glass of sherry upon arrival, against a backdrop of piped-in chamber music; continental breakfast served (upon request) in bed on a white wicker tray, or breakfast with other travelers at the inn, or, weather permitting, in the garden.

The location of the three-storied mansion at 2147-57 Tremont Place in the Clements Historic District couldn't be better. For more information about the accommodations, contact Queen Anne Bed & Breakfast Inn at (303) 296–6666, or (800) 432–4667; www.queenannebnb.com.

Would you like to have breakfast, enjoy Sunday brunch, weekday lunch, presupper snack, or, best of all—dinner!—in a Tudor-style castle overlooking the city of Denver and a green golf course? All this has been possible for almost two decades at the *Wellshire Inn* at 3333 South Colorado Boulevard. You can thank a restaurateur named Leo Goto for the locale and the eating pleasures. Goto transformed a run-down clubhouse into the tasteful English chateau with its heavy wooden doors; antique, colored leaded-glass windows; sparkling chandeliers; luxurious carpets; and dramatic fireplaces. The place radiates intimacy and true elegance. Baronial splendor! Four million dollars' worth of remodeling!

Several local critics have called the Wellshire Inn "one of Denver's most beautiful restaurants." The decor is enhanced by the fresh foods—romaine lettuce, spinach, Chinese vegetables, fruit, Mediterranean greens. The entrees— Tournedos Windsor, fresh salmon filets, Italian-style Scampi, Chicken Dijon, Wellshire Chateaubriand, and Leo's famous Rack of Lamb—can only be called memorable. Scenic, pastoral views, country club atmosphere, good food, friendly service—can anyone ask for more?

For more information contact the Wellshire Inn at (303) 759–3333; www .wellshireinn.com. Open daily; call for details and reservations.

Few Colorado visitors—and not many Denverites—know about *Lakewood Heritage Center* at 797 South Wadsworth Boulevard, with its park, several lakes, free guided nature walks, and some interesting historic buildings. Volunteers will show you a one-room schoolhouse, now used by quilters. Cheerful guides will bring to life an ancient farmhouse. You will learn how the former occupants used the butter churns and coffee grinders or heated the woodstoves. Other buildings contain drawings of Indians, a collection of shotguns, beaver pelts, and bows and arrows. This unique museum also displays 150-year-old farm machinery—threshers, combines, tractors—along with Model Ts and even an antique fire truck. The tours take place Tuesday through Friday from 10:00 A.M. to 4:00 P.M. and Saturday and Sunday from noon to 4:00 P.M. Cost is $3.00 for adults and $2.00 for children four to twelve; children three and younger free. Groups larger than five must make advance tour reservations. For more information call (303) 987–7850; www.ci.lakewood.co.us.

The city of Denver has more than one hundred named parks of various sizes and shapes that stretch in every direction. It is said to be America's largest such system. Green areas abound. If you visit the *Denver Civic Center Park,* for instance, you'll at once notice the many well-tended lawns and trees. Civic Center Park is located at Broadway and Colfax in downtown Denver. For more information visit www.denvergov.org/east_denver_parks/template21180.asp or call (303) 331–4113.

The citizens' fondness for their greenways cannot be denied. Each year, Denverites go in for lawn contests (who has the prettiest one?). Every day, the newspapers print advice on lawn care. A wail goes up if a city father hints at the possibility of rationing the water used for sprinklers. Stores keep large stocks of fertilizer, and commerce is brisk in garden tools and boxes of petunias and geraniums that embellish the most humble Denver gardens.

On weekends, Denverites head for their public parks, which must be among the best-kept and varied in the nation. Each of the city's parks has its own charisma, its own subtle characteristics depending on location, size, and activities.

Denver's Little-Known Parks

Cheesman Park, East Eighth Avenue and Franklin Street, is perfect for a restful hour or so; you can peruse mountain views and plan your conquest of Colorado's "Fourteeners."

Eisenhower Park, South Colorado Boulevard and East Dartmouth, offers a swimming pool, indoor tables for championship-type Ping-Pong players, and a hiking trail.

Congress Park, East Ninth Avenue and Elizabeth Street, has an outdoor pool for lap swimming, tennis courts, and playgrounds.

Bear Valley Park weaves and curves along West Dartmouth near South Sheridan. A bike trail follows a small river here.

For more information visit the Web site www.denvergov.org/parks or call (303) 964–2580.

Begin with Denver's largest, 314-acre *City Park* located at Seventeenth Avenue and York Street (303–331–4113; www.denvergov.org/montclair_parks/template2145.asp). You can reach it from downtown in ten minutes' driving time. Keep in mind that you could spend a full summer day and evening here without a moment's boredom. A family may while away many hours, for instance, in the *Denver Zoo,* located in City Park. Hundreds of animals frolic or loaf on some 80 acres of grounds. Take the children to "Monkey Island," where monkeys swing and leap all summer (in spring you'll find these critters in the Primate House). A special glass edifice contains dozens of colorful chirping, singing, talking birds. Other natural habitat areas are for polar bears, llamas, turtles, baby elephants, rhinos, and giraffes, nearly 4,000 animals in all. A special zoo for small children is popular; here you find young ducks, lambs, chickens, and other farm animals.

trivia

The Denver Zoo got its start when an orphaned black bear named Billy Bryan was given to the mayor as a gift in 1896.

The main entrance to City Park and the zoo is on East Twenty-third Avenue between Colorado Boulevard and York Street.

The zoo is open daily. Hours from April 1 through September 30 are 9:00 A.M. to 6:00 P.M., and from October 1 through March 31, 10:00 A.M. to 5:00 P.M. Admission (April 1 through September 30) is $11.00 for adults and teenagers twelve and older, $9.00 for seniors sixty-five and older, and $7.00 for children three to eleven; children two and younger free. Admission (October 1 through March 31) is $9.00 for adults and teenagers twelve and older, $7.00 for seniors sixty-five and older, and $5.00 for children three to eleven; children two and younger free. For more information call (303) 376–4800; www.denverzoo.org.

Also at City Park are a public golf course, tennis courts, flower gardens, and paddleboats that can be rented on the lakes. The **Denver Museum of Nature and Science (DMNS)** (800–925–2250; www.dmnh.org) is located here. DMNS includes both temporary and permanent exhibits, such as "Egyptian Mummies," "North American Wildlife," and "Botswana: Safari to Wild Africa." In addition, the museum is home to the Phipps IMAX Theater, a Discovery Zone with hands-on activities for children, and the Gates Planetarium. DMNS is open daily from 9:00 A.M. to 5:00 P.M. except on Christmas. General admission is $9.00 for adults and $6.00 for children three to eighteen, students with ID, and seniors sixty and older. IMAX tickets are extra. For more information call (303) 322–7009 or (800) 925–2250; www.dmns.org.

Washington Park (located at South Downing Street and East Louisiana Avenue)—my favorite—is the place to be on a late September morning. One of Colorado's poet laureates, at age ninety, was known to walk around one of the lakes here. Actually, it has started to snow. Winter without the benefit of fall. Yesterday the sun still blazed here, and now the flakes tumble thickly. The lake steams.

Normally filled with cyclists, the park is deserted. Denver's miniblizzard air is being washed clean by the moisture. A few hardy joggers, wool caps over their ears, jog along the lake paths. The grass is still too warm for the snow to stick; the wet meadows seem greener than at any other time of the year.

The miniblizzard stops. Clouds drift overhead.

Through the park you can see some of Denver's old homes at Downing, Louisiana, and Franklin Streets. Typically, all the houses come with lawns and gardens. The latter form the visitor's first impressions.

A weekday may be the best day to stroll through Denver's Washington Park. The wide expanse of green is almost unknown to tourists, despite all the delights here. Small creeks are shaded by willows and cottonwoods. Anything and everything happens at Washington Park on weekends: Young lovers from nearby Denver University walk along the paths; elderly gentlemen play a game of boccie in slow motion on a special well-kept lawn; young champions slam tennis balls across one of the many free courts; an entire family feeds ducks and geese. Washington Park has several playgrounds for small-fry and plenty of picnic tables. Washington Park comes with ample flower beds that remind you of English gardens.

The park also boasts a large recreation center where you can swim indoors, work out in a gym with sophisticated machinery, join a basketball game, or, if you stay in town long enough, take various classes that range from

A Quick Walk at Willow Springs Trail

For tourists who're short on time, there beckons the *Willow Springs Trail.* Access? Take Wadsworth Boulevard south to Belleview, then follow the pastoral signs west toward the reddish foothills. Belleview turns into Highway 48 and leads to the peaceful Willow Springs Country Club. Proceed uphill through the club as far as you can go, park, and head for an open gate, which bans motorized vehicles. The trail sets out past a whale-shaped rock and moves uphill through the meadows along an almost forgotten old wagon road. Leafy trees hug the little valley, and the birds sing as you tramp up and down dale. No cars or highways in sight, and Denver's brown cloud and skyscrapers are far, far below you.

For more information contact *Denver and Metro Convention & Visitors Bureau,* 1555 California Street; Denver 80202, (800) 233–6837; www.denver.org.

puppetry to pottery. The modernistic recreation center is ideal for rainy days. For more information visit the Web site www.denvergov.org/south_denver_parks/template21232.asp or call (303) 698–4930.

Happiness for Denverites is *Sloan Lake Park,* located at Sheridan Boulevard and West Seventeenth Avenue. The lakeshore and the grass often fetch an elderly clientele: pensioners, retired railroad people, old Indians—some fishing out of their automobiles, others sitting near the water—as well as young Vietnamese.

No crowds during the week. Then on summer Saturdays a crescendo of people. The climax comes on July Sundays or holidays. From the Fourth of July to Labor Day, the parking lots cannot hold all the automobiles with picnickers and their baskets; with more anglers hoping for a ten-pound carp; with teenagers ready to toss footballs, baseballs, plastic platters; with ladies and their grandchildren; with three-year-olds waving bags of bread. Orange-beaked ducks waddle eagerly ashore; wild Canada geese float with nonchalance toward the toss of popcorn.

You see father-and-son teams playing—surprise!—a game of croquet; you see water-skiers in black wet suits. Windy days produce sailboats—thirty of them? fifty?—a regatta! Sailors ply the blue Sloan Lake surface in their dinghies, Snipes, or Sunfish vessels. The joggers are always in evidence, too, and in any weather a few old, sometimes overweight couples walk around the lake—doctor's orders. On sunny days, the Rockies wink in the background.

You can enter the park from West Seventeenth Avenue or from Sheridan Boulevard and from several other points, all west of Federal Boulevard.

Actually, Denver's more than 300 municipal parks stimulate plenty of outdoor life on more than 3,000 acres; to these you may add another city-owned 14,000 acres in the foothills. Wildflowers! Spruce trees! Pines! Meadows!

Small wonder that Denver is called "The City of Green."

For more information about Denver's parks, contact the Denver Parks and Recreation Department's Parks Division, 2300 Fifteenth Street, Denver 80202; (303) 964–2580; www.denvergov.org/parks.

If you really want to see Denver, take a hike.

The Beaver Brook Trail, on Lookout Mountain, can be accessed from Denver by car via I–70 (take Lookout Mountain exit). Drive past Buffalo Bill's grave until you see the sign on your left, BEAVER BROOK TRAIL. You will be delighted by the varied flora and fauna and the varied terrain. One Caveat: The trail can be icy in winter. For more information contact Jefferson County Open Space, 700 Jefferson County Parkway, Suite 100, Golden 80401; (303) 271–5925; www.co.jefferson.co.us/ext/dpt/comm_res/openspac/windy.htm.

Belmar Park, at 801 South Wadsworth Boulevard in Lakewood, provides an hour's worth of foot trails through undulating wildflower and sedge meadows. Canada geese occupy an attractive lake; Lakewood Heritage Center, with its old farm machinery adds a pastoral note to the landscape. Barns and sheds round out the picture. Recommended for runners and in winter for cross-country skiers.

For more information call (303) 987–7850; www.ci.lakewood.co.us.

Finally, before you leave the Denver Metro area entirely, delight your children (or the child inside you) with a stop at the *Butterfly Pavilion and Insect Center,* located in Westminster—a short jaunt up U.S. Highway 36 off I–25 heading north from Denver. This attraction, which opened in 1995, is one of only a dozen or so similar institutions in the United States. Borne of a need for people to gain greater understanding of arthropods, this fun "zoo" houses more than 1,200 free-flying butterflies from more than fifty species. In addition, numerous other insect species and tropical plants round out the pavilion's holdings.

trivia

The nonprofit Butterfly Pavilion and Insect Center in Westminster is the only such stand-alone institution in the United States.

Open daily from 9:00 A.M. until 5:00 P.M. year-round, the Butterfly Pavilion offers an escape from wintry weather with its climate-controlled, 7,200-square-foot tropical conservatory. Admission is $7.95 for adults, $5.95 for senior citizens sixty-five and older, and $4.95 for children four to twelve. Two children three and under free if accompanied by adults. The pavilion is located at 6252 West 104th Avenue, Westminster. Take the Church

Ranch Boulevard/104th Avenue exit off US 36 and head east on 104th. For more information call (303) 469–5441; www.butterflies.org.

The Great Plains

"Colorado? Ah, high peaks! Mountain towns! Skiing!" This is how many easterners, southerners, and midwesterners describe their idea of a state that has mountains on its license plates. Even Europeans know about the Rockies. The plains—especially Colorado's eastern plains, the farmer's domain—come as a surprise.

Yet, much of the land belongs to agriculture. As you drive east from Denver, Colorado Springs, Pueblo, or Trinidad, the country takes on the flat character of Kansas and Nebraska, with which Colorado shares its eastern border. The names turn rural: Punkin Center, Wild Horse, Deer Trail.

Communities like Wray, Holyoke, and Yuma all got their start through homesteading. About 94 percent of Colorado's land consists of dry or irrigated farmlands, rangeland, and forests.

Eastern Colorado was first settled during the middle and late 1880s. Little agricultural communities like Haxtun, Kiowa, and Eads sprang up. Oats, barley, wheat, and corn were planted; harvesting was done with primitive machinery. Some of the farms were the result of the early railroads selling cheap tracts of land to immigrants.

The homesteaders fought hard financial battles when the droughts hit in 1890. But the Homestead Act, which presented volunteer farmers with 160 free acres, was a big incentive in Colorado. Many of the settlers demanded few luxuries from their homesteads. They tilled, planted, harvested, and faced blizzards and hailstorms, grasshoppers, and more droughts. The worst ones hit during the 1920s.

Still, through the years, eastern Colorado produced not just corn and wheat but also dry beans, alfalfa, potatoes, onions, rye, sorghum, and commercial vegetables. In Rocky Ford, year after year, the citizens grew watermelons and cantaloupes.

The farmers endured the summer heat and dust storms. World War II was good to the Colorado farm economy. New well-drilling techniques and irrigation improved the situation. During the 1960s wheat sales hit record figures. The 1970s brought prosperity. The export trade flourished. Land prices soared. Farmers splurged on newfangled $100,000 machinery.

When exports shrank, as everywhere in the Midwest and West, the Colorado farmers suffered. The 1980s were harsh to the eastern part of the state. Prices dropped for crops, while everything else cost more.

Yet some farmers survived. A few lucky ones—close to cities like Denver, Fort Morgan, and Sterling—switched to sod farming.

Sod creates instant lawns for suburbia, as an adjunct to the housing explosion. Near Parker you see miles and miles of green carpets, well watered, neatly rolled up, ready for shipment. New homes still go up in Englewood, Littleton, Aurora, Thornton, and Castle Rock, and each new house clamors for its swath of green, often supplied by sod farmers.

Others stay on and grow "Hard Red" winter wheat and specialty items like asparagus, flowers, peas, and sunflower seeds. A small number build greenhouses or mushroom cellars. Dry beans and millet bring profits.

Others sell out to giants, go bankrupt, or look for jobs in the city. Third-generation farmers sometimes give up; regretfully, their children move to town. Some are lucky enough to sell their land to developers of condos and shopping centers. One well-known dairy farmer plans to develop the land himself. Farmers turn into land managers for absentee agribusiness owners.

The scenery packs little excitement. Abandoned houses, an occasional silo, and fields in all directions. A grain elevator. A weighing station. Plows holding court. Small communities where one automatically slows down for the sights of feed stores or an old twelve-unit motel or the cafe with home cooking.

Many of the little hamlets in eastern Colorado seem alike. Small houses with porches. Shop windows with tools placed helter-skelter. After nine at night almost everything is closed. Main Street is so silent that you can hear the crickets in the field.

Try a Yurt Vacation!

Within the **Colorado State Forest State Park,** 75 miles west of Fort Collins, the **Never Summer Nordic Yurt System** offers highly unique opportunities to cyclists.

Consider, first of all, staying in a "yurt" here. Yurts are portable, round dwellings that were first used by nomadic Mongols in Central Asia; they sleep six comfortably and are well situated as push-off sites for some great rides.

One such bike trip is the **Grass Creek Loop.** It's a tough 16 miles round-trip. Along the way you will pass the North Michigan Reservoir and the 10,000-foot Gould Mountain.

For more information about Never Summer Nordic, Inc., log on to www.never summernordic.com/yurts.htm or call (970) 723–8366.

For information about Colorado State Forest State Park, log on to parks.state.co.us.

Each little town has several churches, which get busy on Sunday. Sermons crackle on your car radio. A quick glance through a picture window shows a farmer watching a television evangelist.

The inhabitants of eastern Colorado are reserved, not too friendly, perhaps distrustful, certainly preoccupied. But they have time. "Oh, sure," says one of them to an inquirer from the city. "Sure, we have problems. But there's more space to have them in."

Most visitors—and even new immigrants to Colorado—think the state consists mostly of Denver and suburbs and perhaps a few mountain towns like Vail and Aspen. They often forget northern and eastern Colorado. When Mark Twain visited in 1862, however, he reveled in the prairie and the horses. "It was a noble sport galloping over the plain in the dewy freshness of the morning," Twain wrote.

The dewy freshness is still there, along with the star-filled sky, some farms with their tilled fields, the big cottonwoods. Despite the giant interstates, the air is still pure. Unlike in Denver, where the car-caused pollution backs up against the mountains, the breezes from the northwest do a fine purification job. The cities of Fort Collins, Greeley, and Longmont have expanded; luckily, however, there is very little smokestack industry. You see new shopping malls and Holiday Inns and Kentucky Fried Chicken outposts. The tourists flock to communities such as Loveland, with its lakes and access to Rocky Mountain National Park.

In the same region, **Fort Collins** may well be the most sophisticated community in northern Colorado. With 115,000 inhabitants, it is the largest. Hordes of eager, serious **Colorado State University** students are here, and the visitor quickly becomes aware of wider interests. Fort Collins has several bookstores, numerous foreign-car dealers, and shops catering to the young. The distance to Denver is a manageable 66 miles.

River Adventures in Northern Colorado

A Wanderlust Adventure in Fort Collins will give you the opportunity to see the Poudre River up close and personnel. Since 1982, 60,000 people have enjoyed trips run by this Fort Collins–based outfitter. From three-hour trips for the whole family to daylong and multiday paddling affairs guaranteed to give anyone a workout, Wanderlust will have a trip to fit everyone (who's old enough, that is—minimum age of seven for easiest trip). Trips run from May through August and range in price from $39 to $91 per person. For more information contact A Wanderlust Adventure (800) 745–7238 or (970) 484–1219; www.awanderlustadventure.com.

Much of Colorado's famous corn-fed beef comes from Fort Collins. The dry climate is ideal for the Hereford and Angus cattle, and northern Colorado cattle feeders have worked out precise feeding systems. From this region the aged beef is shipped all over the world.

In recent years, the area's ranchers have adapted themselves to the times. They now raise calves that are leaner and less cholesterol-laden. Low-fat feeding methods are in. Marbled meat is out. Moreover, some of these contemporary cattlemen shun growth stimulants and avoid antibiotics.

The Fort Collins–based Colorado State University is strong on agriculture and also trains forestry students, whose tree nurseries you can visit. For more information contact Colorado State University at (970) 491–1101; www.colo state.edu.

The city has its own symphony orchestra and a theater. "We're often underestimated," says one Fort Collins official. "We shouldn't be. We're a microcosm of Denver, but without the air pollution and crime."

The Fort Collins region is known for its nearby fly-fishing possibilities. Among others, you might head up the drama-filled *Poudre Canyon* and the *Poudre River,* which is uniformly praised by serious anglers in search of trout. For more information contact Canyon Lakes Ranger District, Arapaho & Roosevelt National Forests, 1311 South College Avenue, Fort Collins 80524; (970) 498–1375; www.fs.fed.us/r2/arnf/.

For camping and boating, there is the *Horsetooth Reservoir* west of town. Horsetooth has 1,900 acres of water and attracts huge summer crowds with camping, boating, biking, and climbing.

trivia

Horsetooth Reservoir, elevation 5,430 feet, holds 1,900 acres of water.

To reach Horsetooth Reservoir, drive west on County Road 38E (Harmony Road) from its intersection with Taft Hill Road in Fort Collins. Park permits are available from stations throughout the park; cost is $6.00 per vehicle. For more information contact Larimer County Parks and Open Lands, 1800 South County Road 31, Loveland 80537; (970) 679–4570; www .co.larimer.co.us/parks/horsetooth.htm.

While in Fort Collins, mountain bikers will not want to be without a free map of the city's bikeway system. This pocket guide illustrates the 56 miles of local bike trails, lanes, and routes. You can pick it up at any Fort Collins bicycle shop or download it online at fcgov.com/bicycling/bike-maps.php.

Lory State Park offers great single tracks for more advanced riders. This former ranch is now a 2,400-acre park that tempts bikers with challenging mountain biking almost year-round; snow is frequent in winter, but abundant sunshine keeps the trails relatively clear.

Just beyond the park entrance at the Timber Recreation Area is the Timber Trail. This single-track route is not very technical, except loose gravel adds a challenge. Take U.S. Highway 287 north from Fort Collins through LaPorte. Turn left at the Bellvue exit onto County Road 23N. Turn left again (23N turns). Go 1⁹⁄₁₀ miles and take a right on County Road 25G. The park entrance is another 1⁵⁄₁₀ miles away. The park is open daily and hours vary according to the season. Cost is $5.00 per vehicle.

Just south is **Loveland,** about half the size of Fort Collins, yet it has carved a national name for itself. Loveland calls itself "Colorado's Sweetheart City."

Each year many sacks of valentines are being remailed here; the sentimental souls who send these love messages are backed by the town's civic leaders, who volunteer their time. Cupid has worked here for some four decades. Loveland's postmasters themselves often create the corny poems that appear in cachet form next to the Loveland stamp. A typical verse:

> *The day is full of gladness*
> *And eyes with stardust shine*
> *When Cupid works his magic*
> *In this lovely valentine.*

The Loveland Post Office patiently copes with the extra work of some 300,000 valentines with the blessing of the town officials. Local high schools paint heart signs. On the Chamber of Commerce maps, Loveland appears in the shape of a heart, and the yearly "Miss Valentine" wears hearts on her apron. The local business community has no objections; there are now even Sweetheart shops and a Sweetheart Lane. Ironically, Loveland was named after a railroad robber baron.

trivia

Loveland is also known as the "Gateway to the Rockies," due to its location on Highway 34, which brings travelers from I-25 to Rocky Mountain National Park.

Actually, agriculture and tourism go on strongly here, too: you spot cornfields and sugar beets, ride horses at local stables, use local campgrounds, and visit the numerous Loveland recreation areas. And the thousands of valentines via "Cupid's Hometown" or "The Valentine Capital of the World" are a business by themselves. For more information contact the Loveland Chamber of Commerce at (970) 667–6311; www.loveland.org.

The city of **Greeley** (founded by Horace Greeley, the newspaper publisher) is a few miles to the east of Loveland. Greeley was meant to become an agricultural colony, too, and succeeded. All around the town's perimeter you see sugar-beet fields, barley, and other crops.

Much of the local sightseeing harks back to agriculture. At the **Centennial Village,** the curators have erected a sod house, a homesteader's wagon house, and a one-room rural school. In addition, Centennial Village has graceful Victorian homes. In all, some thirty structures take the visitor through the history of the High Plains, spanning the years 1860 to 1930. Open mid-April through mid-October; call for hours. Admission is $5.00 for adults and teenagers twelve and older, $4.00 for senior citizens sixty and older, and $3.00 for children six to eleven; children five and younger free. Centennial Village is open free to the public on the first Saturday of each month. For more information call (970) 350–9220; www.greeleycvb.com/historical.

Visit the **Meeker Home Museum,** formerly the home of Nathan Meeker. It contains many of his furnishings and the plow that turned the first sod in the Union Colony. It's listed in the National Register of Historic Places. Open from May through September; walk-in visitors are free. Call for hours, (970) 350–9220, or visit www.ci.greeley.co.us.

Another point of interest in the area is the **University of Northern Colorado** (501 Twentieth Street, Greeley 80639; 970–351–1890; www.univnorthco.edu). This institution has grown to some 11,000 full-time students, plus 6,000 part-timers who take continuing education courses.

trivia

Horace Greeley's original concept for his namesake town was a utopian agricultural colony modeled after the Oneida, New York, experimental settlement.

The late James Michener was one of UNC's famous alumni. To be sure, he was inspired to write his bestselling novel *Centennial* through his familiarity and on-location research in Greeley and surroundings.

Those Western Doings in the Greeley Area

The *Rocky Mountain Stampede* is held the first week of July, with nine rodeos, parades, and fireworks, as well as events on all downtown plazas. The rodeos are at Island Grove Park, Fourteenth Avenue and "A" Street. For more information call (970) 356–2855 or (800) 982–2855; www.greeleystampede.org. The **Weld County Fair** takes place in late July at the same location, with horse shows and livestock displays, plus various contests. For more information call (970) 356–4000 ext. 4465; www.weldcounty fair.com.

Michener's ficticious pioneers built their town of Centennial on the Platte River. The story is one of struggle, success, failure, and, above all, endurance. Perhaps the closest thing to his invented Centennial is the near–ghost town of **Keota,** Colorado, 40 miles northeast of Greeley. Michener returned to Keota more than a dozen times to absorb its atmosphere and talk with postmaster Clyde Stanley.

Stanley had lived in Keota most of his seventy years. He had seen the eager farmers come, only to be displaced by drought and dust storms. He watched the town dwindle from 129 people in 1929 to 6 in 1970. Michener dedicated the book to Stanley, "who introduced me to the prairie."

To visit Keota today, take exit 269 off I–25 (near Fort Collins). Head east on Highway 14 approximately 50 miles past the town of Briggsdale to County Road 103. Go north 5 miles to Keota. See www.ghosttowns.com/states/co/keota for details.

Not many people—or even Michener's readers—realize that the famous author had good reasons to turn to Greeley and northwestern Colorado for his research. In 1936, at the age of twenty-nine and not yet a writer, Michener taught in Greeley at what was to become the University of Northern Colorado.

He never regretted his decision. "In Greeley, I grew up spiritually, emotionally, intellectually," he later noted in John P. Hayes's *James A. Michener: A Biography.*

While there, Michener became friends with Floyd Merrill, Greeley's newspaper editor. The pair set out on almost weekly ventures into the surrounding country. At least three times a month, Merrill and the future best-selling author took off for exploration of the intricate irrigation systems that produced Colorado's vegetables and fruit, sometimes to the mountains. "We would look down into valleys crowded with blue spruce and aspen, and quite often out onto the prairie east of town where majestic buttes rose starkly from the barren waste," Michener relates in Hayes's biography.

Merrill also taught the young professor to use a camera. Michener credits the photos he took in Colorado with keeping his images of the West alive and vital long enough for *Centennial* to be conceived.

Already well known in 1970, the author returned to Colorado, determined to write an exhaustive story of the western experience. He explored the natural and social history of the region.

And he made northeastern Colorado famous.

One of the landmarks in his book *Centennial* is the fictitious "Rattlesnake Buttes." "They were extraordinary, these two sentinels of the plains. Visible for miles in each direction, they guarded a bleak and sad empire," Michener wrote.

These promontories exist and are known as the ***Pawnee Buttes,*** part of the Pawnee National Grassland. Administered by the Forest Service, the grasslands encompass nearly 200,000 acres.

The wind here is nearly constant. The terrain made history in the 1930s when drifts of wind-driven topsoil piled up like snow over fences, closing roads and killing crops. This Pawnee grassland was born from tragedy.

A gravel road goes to the Buttes trailhead. From there, a 1½-mile path takes you on foot or by mountain bike to the first butte, the western one. The eastern butte lies ¼ mile east. From a plateau the trail drops to the prairie floor, crossing open pastureland, then dropping again into a deep ravine. Cream-colored chalk cliffs form the promontories. Call it a short-grass prairie here, somewhat like a tundra. The steadily moving air masses keep growths low to the ground. Prickly pear cactus, blue gramma grass, sagebrush, and buffalo grass grow no higher then 6 inches.

Lack of water and trees do not prevent many species of birds from flourishing in this country. Lark buntings—the Colorado state bird, with its distinctive white wing patches against a black body—thrive here. So do horned larks, meadowlarks, kestrels, mountain plovers, common nighthawks, and long-billed curlews—some of the 200 species recorded here. A 36-mile self-guided birding tour is a great ride over the prairie in a high-clearance car or on a mountain bike. Cattle share this area with pronghorn antelope and windmill-powered water tanks for stock. For information contact Pawnee National Grassland, 660 O Street, Greeley 80631; (970) 353–5000; www.fs.fed.us/arnf/about/organization/png/index.shtml.

The eastern plains of Colorado saw much travel activity and bloodshed in the early days of this country. Indians, trappers, traders, settlers, Mexicans, and the Spanish used what was called the Santa Fe Trail, which followed along the Arkansas River for many miles.

The Bent, St. Vrain and Company, a frontier trading and retailing business, built and owned ***Bent's Old Fort*** near what is now La Junta. The fort was a trading place for Mexicans, Indians, and trappers. Mexico got quality manufactured goods from the United States. The Indians got cookware, metal, rifles, and other goods. Trappers obtained supplies, a market for their furs, and the company of other people following lonely months of hunting. The Bent, St. Vrain and Company traded with all these folks and among themselves. Furs and buffalo robes were sold back east.

In the mid-1800s, Bent's Old Fort was caught between resentful Indians and the whites who were moving in on them. The Indian wars began and the trade faded away. Charles Bent was killed in a revolt in Taos, New Mexico, and

St. Vrain left to do business further south. Cholera spread through the Indian tribes. William Bent, the remaining partner, left a disillusioned and disappointed man. For a time, Bent's Old Fort fell into ruins.

Designated by the National Park Service as a National Historic Site, Bent's Old Fort has been rebuilt almost exactly as it was constructed originally. Authentic materials and tools were used in the reconstruction. Today, the adobe structure remains a monument to past and present-day craftspeople whose skill and patience built and rebuilt it again.

Just outside La Junta, Bent's Old Fort stands as it did almost one hundred years ago. To preserve the authentic atmosphere of this trade center, visitor parking is ¼ mile from the building. The long paved walk toward the fort, with its backdrop of cottonwood trees by the Arkansas River, takes you into history.

In deference to realism, there are no concessions for food, drink, or curios. In fact, you begin to believe the only bathroom may be the one rebuilt as part of the fort. But not to worry. Tucked into a corner are modern toilets and water fountains. A small bookstore exhibits numerous historical volumes.

The building is truly a fort. Four high walls surround a central courtyard. Entrance is through an archway with huge wooden doors. The two levels in the fort contain mostly community rooms, including the well room, trade room, dining area and kitchen, wash house, warehouses, and blacksmith's and laborer's modest quarters. Other accommodations are on the second level, providing more privacy and ventilation. Corrals at the back were for military horses and some cattle.

Uniformed park employees are often on hand to answer questions. But to get into the spirit of the place, join one of the $3.00-per-person ($2.00 for children six to twelve) guided tours conducted by an individual dressed in period clothes. These "interpreters" stay in character, thanks to the authentic costumes. Their tour will be informative and will make you feel like you lived here in the 1880s. Scheduled special events go on all year, such as the Fur Trade Encampment, a mountain-man type of rendezvous in July.

For more information contact Bent's Old Fort, National Historic Site, 35110 Highway 194 East, La Junta 81050; (719) 383–5010; www.nps.gov/beol. Open every day except Thanksgiving, Christmas, and New Year's Day. Open June 1 through August 31 from 8:00 A.M. to 5:30 P.M.; September 1 through May 31 from 9:00 A.M. to 4:00 P.M. From U.S. Highway 50 in La Junta take Highway 109 north 1 mile to Highway 194. Go east on Highway 194 for 6 miles to the fort.

For a trip even further back into history—150 million years further back—visit **Picket Wire Canyonlands** in **Comanche National Grasslands,** about 25 miles south of La Junta. Picket Wire opened to the public in 1991. The attractions? The clear footprints of dinosaurs on a solidified limestone shelf just a few feet over the Purgatory River, as well as rock art and pioneer ruins.

Though the area is considered extremely fragile, mountain biking and hiking are allowed in Picket Wire. From a parking area near a cattle pen, an 8-mile ranch road takes the biker/hiker across a high mesa, then drops suddenly into the canyon. As you follow along, the relics of abandoned adobe houses, a church, a graveyard, and ranch buildings hold up against the dry climate.

This area gets very hot in summer, and rattlesnakes are a real hazard. This is, however, an ideal trip on a mountain bike. Would-be hikers should consider this 17-mile round-trip. Using a bike you can zip along the dusty road and catch glimpses of the current inhabitants: a coyote, kestrels, orioles. Snakes are supposed to nap in the tall grass. The dinosaur tracks are marked by small signs pointing the way. Right next to the river, you come to a shelf of limestone that looks like someone mucked around in it while it was wet. On further examination you discover that these muddlings are dinosaur tracks. You may have to clean the dirt and sand out to truly determine that these are dinosaur tracks. The brontosaurus left big holes like you'd expect from an elephant, yet much bigger. The meat-eating allosaurus left distinctive three-toed, wicked-looking footprints.

It's hot in this Colorado country. Take plenty of water and a hat to put on after you take off your bike helmet. Expect to spend about three hours for the round-trip. But also expect to be alone. There are no human inhabitants of this area now. Overnight camping is prohibited.

Petroglyphs dot the rock canyon walls. These rock etchings aren't identified by signs; you just have to find them on your own. If time is important, do this trip for the dinosaur tracks. Try to walk in their footprints, left more than 150 million years ago. Contact the Comanche National Grassland, 1420 East Third Street, La Junta 81050; (719) 384–2181; www.fs.fed.us/r2/psicc.

Places to Stay in Denver and the Plains

The rating scale for hotels is based on double occupancy and is as follows:
Inexpensive:
Less than $75 per night
Moderate:
$75 to $100 per night
Expensive:
$100 to $150 per night
Deluxe:
More than $150 per night

DENVER

Brown Palace Hotel
(excellent downtown location),
321 Seventeenth Street;
(303) 297–3111 or
(800) 321–2599
www.brownpalace.com
Deluxe

Capitol Hill Mansion
(good for business people;
you can reach downtown
with ease),
1207 Pennsylvania Street;
(303) 839–5221 or
(800) 839–9329
www.capitolhillmansion.com
Expensive to deluxe

**Castle Marne Bed
& Breakfast,**
1572 Race Street;
(303) 331–0621 or
(800) 926–2763
www.castlemarne.com
Moderate to deluxe

Doubletree Hotel Denver
(newly renovated; onsite
fitness center),
3203 Quebec Street;
(303) 321–3333
www.doubletree.com
Moderate to expensive

Oxford Hotel
(close to Union Station),
1600 Seventeenth Street;
(303) 628–5400 or
(800) 228–5838
Expensive to deluxe

**Queen Anne Bed
& Breakfast Inn,**
2147 Tremont Place;
(303) 296–6666 or
(800) 432–4667
www.queenannebnb.com
Moderate to deluxe

FORT COLLINS

**Best Western
University Inn,**
914 South College Avenue;
(970) 484–1984
www.bestwestern.com
Inexpensive to moderate

SELECTED DENVER GENERAL INFORMATION RESOURCES

DENVER

**Denver Metro Convention
& Visitors Bureau,**
1555 California Street,
Suite 300, 80202;
(800) 233–6837
www.denver.org

FORT COLLINS

**Fort Collins Area Chamber
of Commerce,**
225 South Meldrum, 80521;
(970) 482–3746
www.fcchamber.org

GREELEY

**Greeley Convention &
Visitors Bureau,**
902 Seventh Avenue, 80631;
(970) 352–3567 or (800) 449–3866
www.greeleycvb.com

LOVELAND

Loveland Chamber of Commerce,
5400 Stone Creek Circle,
Suite 200, 80538;
(970) 667–6311
www.loveland.org

Edwards House
(historic bed-and-breakfast),
402 West Mountain Avenue;
(970) 493–9191
www.edwardshouse.com
Expensive

Helmshire Inn,
1204 South College Avenue;
(970) 493–4683
Moderate to expensive

Holiday Inn,
425 West Prospect Road;
(970) 482–2626
www.holiday-inn.com
Moderate to expensive

GREELEY

Best Western Inn,
701 Eighth Street;
(970) 353–8444
www.bestwestern.com
Inexpensive to moderate

**Country Inn and Suites
by Carlson,**
2501 West Twenty-ninth
Street;
(970) 330–3404
Moderate to expensive

**Sod Buster Bed and
Breakfast Inn**
(historic inn),
1221 Ninth Avenue;
(888) 300–1221 or
(970) 392–1221
www.colorado-bnb.com/
sodbuster
Moderate to expensive

LOVELAND

Best Western Coach House
(across the street from Loveland Visitor Center),
5542 East Highway 34;
(970) 667–7810
www.bestwestern.com
Moderate

Budget Host Exit 254 Inn,
2716 Southeast
Frontage Road;
(970) 667–5202
Inexpensive

**Cattail Creek Bed
& Breakfast Inn,**
2665 Abarr Drive;
(970) 667–7600 or
(800) 572–2466
www.cattailcreekinn.com
Expensive to deluxe

Places to Eat
in Denver and
the Plains

The rating scale for
restaurants is as follows:
Inexpensive:
Most entrees less than $10
Moderate:
Most entrees $10 to $15
Expensive:
Most entrees $15 to $20
Deluxe:
Most entrees more than $20

DENVER

Buckhorn Exchange
(steak, game, wildfowl),
1000 Osage Street;
(303) 534–9505
www.buckhorn.com
Deluxe

**Duffy's Shamrock
Restaurant** (Irish home-style),
1635 Court Place;
(303) 534–4935
Inexpensive to moderate

**Imperial Chinese
Restaurant** (seafood),
431 South Broadway;
(303) 698–2800
www.imperialchinese.com
Expensive

Old Spaghetti Factory
(Italian; good value),
1215 Eighteenth Street;
(303) 295–1864
Inexpensive

Tante Louise
(French; elegant),
4900 East Colfax Avenue;
(303) 355–4488
www.tantelouise.com
Deluxe

Wellshire Inn
(steak, seafood; adjacent to
a well-kept golf course),
3333 South Colorado
Boulevard;
(303) 759–3333
www.wellshireinn.com
Deluxe

Zaidy's Deli (kosher deli),
121 Adams Street;
(303) 333–5336
Inexpensive to moderate

FORT COLLINS

BeauJo's (American, pizza),
100 North College Avenue;
(970) 498–8898
Moderate

**Coopersmith's Pub and
Brewing Company,**
5 Old Town Square;
(970) 498–0483
www.coppersmithspub.com
Moderate

**Rio Grande Mexican
Restaurant,**
143 West Mountain;
(970) 224–5428
www.riograndemexican.com
Moderate

GREELEY

Blackjack Pizza,
820 Sixteenth Street;
(970) 356–2500
Inexpensive

The Egg & I
(American),
3830 West Tenth Street;
(970) 353–7737
Inexpensive

LOVELAND

Cactus Grille North
(American),
281-A East Twenty-ninth
Street;
(970) 663–1550
Inexpensive to moderate

Cactus Grille South
(American),
1329 Eagle Drive;
(970) 663–4500
Inexpensive to moderate

Parsonage Restaurant
(continental; historic),
405 East Fifth Street;
(970) 962–9700
Moderate to expensive

The Savoy
(French),
535 Third Street, Berthoud;
(970) 532–4095
Expensive

OTHER ATTRACTIONS WORTH SEEING IN DENVER AND THE PLAINS

DENVER

Denver Art Museum,
(720) 865–5000
www.denverartmuseum.org

Six Flags Elitch Gardens,
(303) 595–4386
www.sixflags.com/parks/elitchgardens/
home.asp

Ocean Journey,
(888) 561–4450
www.oceanjourney.org

University of Denver,
(303) 871–2000
www.du.edu

FORT COLLINS

Lincoln Center,
(970) 221–6735
www.ci.fort-collins.co.us/lctix/

GREELEY

Fort Vasquez,
(970) 785–2832
www.greeleycvb.com/dayvasquez.shtml

Index

About the Author

A Denver resident, the late Curtis Casewit wrote more than forty books, eight of them travel guides. He wrote travel columns regularly for newspapers nationwide and lectured at several writing workshops during the summer. He taught creative writing at the University of Colorado for thirty years.

About the Editor

Alli Rainey lived in Boulder, Colorado, from December 1997 until August 2001. An avid rock climber, she became a permanent traveler in September 2001. She now travels around the country visiting climbing areas (and other offbeat destinations) with her husband, Matt Wendling, and her cat, Sassy. When she's not climbing or traveling to the next climbing area on her list, Alli finds time to pursue her freelance writing career. For more information, visit www.allirainey.com.